Real-Time Microprocessor Systems

Real-Time Microprocessor Systems

Stephen R. Savitzky

Zilog, Inc.

VNR VAN NOSTRAND REINHOLD COMPANY
———————— New York ————————

Library of Congress Catalog Card Number: 84-15209
ISBN: 0-442-28048-3

Manufactured in the United States of America

Published by Van Nostrand Reinhold Company Inc.
135 West 50th Street
New York, New York 10020

Van Nostrand Reinhold Company Limited
Molly Millars Lane
Wokingham, Berkshire RG11 2PY, England

Van Nostrand Reinhold
480 Latrobe Street
Melbourne, Victoria 3000, Australia

Macmillan of Canada
Division of Gage Publishing Limited
164 Commander Boulevard
Agincourt, Ontario M1S 3C7, Canada

15 14 13 12 11 10 9 8 7 6 5 4 3 2 1

Library of Congress Cataloging in Publication Data

Savitzky, Stephen.
    Real-time microprocessor systems.

    Includes bibliographies and index.
    1. Real-time data processing.   2. Microprocessors.
I. Title.
QA76.54.S28   1985   001.64′404   84-15209
ISBN 0-442-28048-3

This book is dedicated to my wife, Karen,
and to my parents.

Trademark Acknowledgments

Preface

Purpose

This book is intended to teach design and implementation principles and techniques for microprocessor-based real-time systems. Both hardware and software will be covered, but with a strong concentration on software. Topics covered include the general concepts of real-time systems, design and implementation techniques, and specific examples. The accent will be on practical advice, not theory (which indeed is in short supply in this field).

Audience

The book is intended primarily for working engineers and programmers, who may be familiar with microprocessors or computers, but not specifically with real-time systems. The book will also be useful to advanced hobbyists, or could serve as a text for a college-level course.

I picture my reader as a programmer or engineer, alone or part of a small team, newly assigned to a project involving a microprocessor in a real-time application, and somewhat unsure of where to start.

Structure

The book is divided into three parts. The first introduces the general concepts of real-time systems, and of microprocessor hardware and software. This part serves both as an introduction to the terminology of the field, and as a "crash course" in the basics of microprocessor hardware (for programmers) and software (for engineers). The second part describes the design and implementation process, with emphasis on the techniques useful for real-time applications. The third part is a detailed examination of specific system organizations and their appropriate implementation techniques.

Another, and perhaps useful, way of looking at this book is as a survey of microprocessor design techniques, organized and motivated by the general theme of "real-time applications," and its more specific corollary of speed.

Prerequisites

The reader should be familiar with at least one programming language, and preferably both a high-level language such as Pascal and at least one assembly language. Some knowledge of digital electronics is also helpful, but not essential.

Sample program fragments will be given in the "C" language, which is described in Appendix C. Readers familiar with only some other language should not despair—a rule of thumb suggests that after having mastered one programming language, it takes only five percent as long to learn another.

Welcome to the "real" world!

S.R.S.

Contents

Appendices

Real-Time Microprocessor Systems

I
Basic Concepts and Components

1

Real-Time Microprocessor Systems

INTRODUCTION

Subject Matter

This book is about real-time microprocessor systems. This chapter introduces the basic terms and concepts, starting with "systems," "microprocessor," and "real-time." Later chapters will cover the components and design techniques used in microprocessor systems (in a rather general way, but with an emphasis on real-time aspects), and finally specific techniques of use in real-time systems.

Emphasis

In any system involving a computer, most of the complexity will be found in the software. Indeed, the computer's presence is usually justified by its ability to simplify designs by using a relatively simple machine to run what amounts to a simulation of a complex hardware controller. As a result, the same computer hardware can be found in many different applications, distinguished only by software.

For example, a computer with a CRT terminal, memory, and two analog-to-digital converters could be an oscilloscope, an audio-frequency spectrum analyzer, a pulse and heartbeat monitor, a music transcriber, an automobile engine analyzer, or any of hundreds of other devices.

Partly as a result of this fact, this book will focus almost entirely on the software aspects of real-time systems.

DEFINITIONS

Here, as in the rest of the book, words used in a technical sense will be *italicized* when they first appear. "Jargon" words or phrases, with less well-defined meanings, will appear in quotation marks. The jargon category also includes obsolete terms, neologisms, misapplied terms, approximations, and words that displease the ear of the author. Words will also be quoted when the words themselves are being discussed, rather than the things they refer to. All italicized and some quoted words and phrases will appear in the glossary (Appendix A). Acronyms and trademarks will also appear in Appendix A.

Systems

A system is any collection of related parts which performs some complex function. In this book, the word *system* will usually refer to a *computer* system, i.e., a system in which at least one of the parts is a computer. Indeed, the words "computer" and "system" are often used interchangeably.

Real-Time

The term *real-time* covers a wide range of computer (and other) systems, but all share the common feature that results of some kind are demanded by deadlines imposed by the "real" world outside the system. The range of time scales is immense, from microseconds (as in a digital signal processor) to years (in an airline reservation system, or a seismic data logger).

This book attempts to cover a middle range of time scales. Events occurring more than a million times a second are too fast for present-day microprocessors without auxiliary hardware (which can batch the events, so the computer may only have to respond every millisecond or so). Events at the other end of the time scale either pose no problems, or pose problems relating to reliable long-term storage rather than timely computation.

Two Kinds of Real Time.   "Real-time" is used to describe two very different kinds of system. The older usage, now fading, applied to such things as airline reservation systems and message-switching centers. These systems were considered "real-time" because there was an operator sitting at a terminal waiting for a response. These systems are now more commonly called *interactive*. Another older term for them was *on-line*.

The other kind of real-time system was once, before the advent of the minicomputer and the microprocessor, less common; the situation is now reversed. This is the *process-control* system, in which the computer is directing or monitoring some ongoing physical process.

The distinction is fuzzy, of course. A person typing at a terminal can be considered as a process which demands response within a definite time (before the next key is struck), and indeed the terminal (and sometimes even the keyboard!) probably has a microprocessor in it, making it a legitimate real-time system.

Kinds of Real Times.   There are at least three measures of time which apply to real-time systems: *response time*, *survival time*, and *throughput* or *bandwidth*.

Response Time.   Response time is the time the computer takes to recognize and respond to an external event. This is the most important measure in control applications; if events are not handled in a timely fashion, the process may literally go "out of control."

Survival Time.   Survival time is the time during which data will "stick around" waiting to be noticed. This is not the same as response time: the data may be valid for a brief time without requiring rapid response, or may remain valid long after any response would be futile.

Throughput.   Throughput is the total number of events which the system can handle in a given time period. For example, a communication controller may have a throughput expressed in characters per second. Throughput may be the reciprocal of the average response time, but is often less, since it could be necessary to "clean up" after giving a response. This "clean-up" time is called *recovery time.*

Bandwidth.   When throughput is measured in bits per second, as it is in signal-processing applications, it can be equated with, or related to, the analog notion of *bandwidth.* If sampling is involved (as in digital filtering or other applications involving digital-to-analog conversion or vice versa), it is important to distinguish the bandwidth of the analog signal from that of its digital counterpart, which is the product of the sampling rate and the sample width in bits, and is usually considerably greater.

Microprocessors And Microcomputers.

A *microprocessor* is a computer implemented on an integrated circuit "chip," or at least on several chips. A *microcomputer* is a computer whose central processing unit (CPU) is a microprocessor. There are even single-chip microcomputers, complete with CPU, memory, and input-output devices (I/O). These are probably the most numerous and least obvious members of the computer family: they can be found hiding in everything from toys to laboratory instruments, and most of their applications involve real-time control.

The differences between micro-, mini-, and maxicomputers (also called *mainframes*) are more or less imaginary. A single-chip computer of today may have more memory and a faster CPU than a roomful of vacuum tubes such as ENIAC, and microcomputers are routinely used in applications for which a minicomputer was used only a few years before. Indeed, with such minicomputers as DEC's PDP-8 and PDP-11, and Data General's Nova already reduced to single chips, and with IBM's System 370 not far behind, the distinction has essentially vanished.

The primary practical distinction between a microcomputer and its "larger" cousins is that a handful of chips is likely to be used in places a room or rack filled with computer equipment could not possibly be employed. We will look at a few of those applications.

TYPICAL APPLICATIONS

Even excluding the older on-line or time-sharing systems, real-time applications for microcomputers cover a wide range. Most applications for real-time systems are *embedded*, in that the computer is built into a larger system, and is not seen by the user as a computer. There are, however, a few general-purpose applications, in which the computer can be used for program development, data reduction, and other data-processing applications while it controls a real-time process.

Embedded Applications

Process Control.   Most microcomputer real-time applications fall into the loose category of "process control." This simply means that the computer is controlling some ongoing process in the outside world. In most cases, the computer is "embedded" in some other product, and does not appear to the user as a general-purpose computer, or indeed as a computer at all. The computer is simply performing a function which a few years ago might have been performed by a collection of cams, levers, and switches driven by a timing motor. The microcomputer is not apparent to the user of a washing machine, blender, or automobile, but it is likely to be there.

More elaborate process control applications are found in laboratory and industrial equipment. The processes being controlled include chemical reactions, assembly lines, and numerically controlled machine tools.

Telecommunications.   Applications in the field of telecommunications are many and varied. Large systems include store-and-forward message-switching systems, telephone exchanges, and inter-computer networks. Smaller applications include terminal concentrators (multiplexors), and intelligent modems.

Intelligent Instruments.   An increasing number of laboratory instruments and related devices are incorporating microcomputers. This has several advantages: computers can add functions without increasing cost (a good example is a hand-held digital multimeter that includes a calculator); they can perform functions that are simply impractical by other means (for example, digital oscilloscopes, which include disk storage for signals, signal averaging, and Fourier transform analysis); and they can provide an improved user interface.

Once an instrument includes a computer, many things become possible, including the increasing use of buses such as the IEEE 488 bus to interconnect instruments into larger systems. Another trend is the appearance of a new kind of instrument which is simply a peripheral to a personal computer. Because the computer is separate from the instrument, the instrument itself can be very inexpensive; it can be a simple plug-in board, with no cabinet, power supply, or front panel.

Consumer (and Other) Products.   In many consumer products, the micro-computer is primarily a cost-reduction tool, replacing the electro-mechanical controller in microwave ovens, washing machines, and so on. In addition, toys and games are using microcomputers to do entirely new things; the computer's ability to simulate almost anything is what makes video games and robot toys possible. One remarkable toy truck not only includes a computer, but even has peripherals!

In automobiles, computer-controlled engines permit more accurate control over the combustion process to meet increasingly tight emission standards. From this application they have expanded into the areas of built-in trouble-shooting aids and improved instrument panels.

One can hardly class airplanes and copying machines as consumer products, but these and many other products are including microcomputers for the same reasons as automobiles and washing machines. The Boeing 767 airliner contains several hundred microprocessors. One major improvement possible on air-planes (and other large systems) is the reduction of wiring. Instead of huge bundles of wires leading from the cockpit to each individual sensor or actuator, a single high-speed bus connects everything on the plane.

Robots.   A *robot* is a computer-controlled device capable of manipulating or maneuvering through its environment in a flexible, programmable way. This rather loose definition is intended to include both industrial robot arms and programmable toy trucks, while excluding milling machines and line-following automatic mail-trucks.

Robotic applications are essentially a form of process control: the robot's motion makes it a process to be controlled, and it is also a part of some larger manufacturing process. Since industrial robots have to move quickly and accurately through complex trajectories, they present a rather demanding application.

Computer Peripherals.   An increasing number of computer peripherals are incorporating microcomputers, either to improve performance or, more often, to reduce cost. Obvious examples include terminals, printers, and disk drives. Disk drives, especially, face tight time constraints; a double-density floppy disk provides a byte of data every 13 microseconds.

General-Purpose Applications

Laboratory Computers.   Computers are finding an increasing role in laboratories, and in other places complex measurements have to be made. In contrast to intelligent instruments, which are dedicated to a single set of functions, a laboratory computer is usually found controlling a large system, often including several instruments as peripherals. One of the first microcomputers to find wide use in the laboratory was the Commodore PET, not because of any great merit as a computer but because it was the only low-cost personal computer to use the IEEE 488 bus as an I/O interface.

Interactive Systems.   Interactive systems include home, engineering, and office computers and workstations. They include both operating system software (controlling the various peripherals), and applications such as text editors (word processors), interactive spreadsheets, computer-aided design and drafting systems, and games (which usually take the form of some kind of real-time simulation: "Spacewar," invented at MIT in 1962 by Steve Russell, is a classic example).

Interactive systems by their very nature require real-time response. The response time required may vary, but programs that interact with a user via a keyboard and CRT must not keep the user waiting too long. (Response times in the range from a tenth to half a second are usually acceptable, with half a second being a noticeable delay.)

The lower-level I/O routines that handle the keyboard, screen, joy-sticks, and other means of interaction are of course indistinguishable from other event-driven real-time applications.

TAXONOMY

Real-time systems can be classified in two basic ways: according to their speed (response time or throughput), and according to the structure of their software.

Speed Taxonomy

Low Speed.   Low-speed applications are essentially those in which the computer does not need to hurry in order to meet its deadlines (the computer field is rife with anthropomorphism). Clumsy but simple programming techniques can be used; functions usually performed by hardware can be pushed off onto the software to save money. Low-speed applications are characterized by a response time in seconds or minutes.

Low-speed applications include security systems (the door has to be opened within about a second of inserting the key or punching the combination), low-speed data recording (counting cars going through an intersection), and the control of slow processes (such as environment control for energy saving: turning lights on in the evening and off when everyone is asleep, and controlling the heater to minimize energy use).

Medium Speed.   In medium-speed applications, the computer is being kept busy. Some assembly-language programming may be required in the more critical response paths, events may have priorities, data may have to be buffered. Things get complicated. Medium-speed applications require a response time in milliseconds or seconds; the important thing is that the response time required is only slightly more than the time the computer takes to perform the necessary actions.

High Speed.   In high-speed applications, the required response time is approximately equal to the computer's capacity. Microseconds count, and all the tricky coding techniques and hardware shortcuts come crawling out of the woodwork. High-speed systems are often remarkably simple—there isn't *time* to do anything complicated. Response time is from tens of microseconds to tens of milliseconds.

High-speed applications include digital filtering and other signal processing, fast process control, computer-controlled servo loops, and so on. Many computer peripherals, such as disks and printers, have high-speed processing requirements, and are often controlled by a dedicated microprocessor. A double-density floppy disk drive supplies a byte every 13 microseconds.

The use of special-purpose hardware, such as DMA controllers, can often turn a high-speed system into a medium-speed one.

Structure Taxonomy

Polling Loop.   The simplest kind of software structure for a real-time system is a *polling loop*: the program examines (polls) each of its inputs in turn to determine whether an event has occurred which requires a response. If it has, the program takes the required action before proceeding to the next input.

Interestingly enough, this structure is encountered at both the low- and high-speed ends of the speed spectrum. Its simplicity makes it desirable at the low end, and necessary at the high end.

Event-Driven Systems.   A system which responds directly to external events is called *event-driven*. This rather imprecise designation covers three main types of system: foreground/background, multitasking, and multi-processor.

Foreground/Background.   Probably the most generally useful software struc-ture is the *foreground/background*, or *interrupt-driven*, system. A polling loop runs in the "background," while "foreground" events cause processor inter-rupts. Control is temporarily transferred to a routine which handles the event, and then returned to the background process.

In one limiting case, the "background" is simply a loop which does nothing at all, and all the event processing is done in the interrupt routines. More often, the interrupts handle only those events which require fast response, moving data between I/O devices and "buffers" in memory. The background process is then signaled when a buffer has been filled or emptied.

Most I/O in "traditional" computer systems is handled using foreground/background techniques.

Multitasking.   When several more-or-less independent processes are going on at once, it is convenient to handle each one with an independent program (espe-cially when each program is fairly complex). When all of the programs are running on the same computer (processor), the result is called *multitasking*, *multiprogramming*, *multiprocessing*, or *timesharing* (the latter especially when the system supports several users).

Multitasking is done via a piece of software called an *operating system*, whose job is to make each program, called a *task* or *process*, seem to be run-ning on its own separate computer. This trick is accomplished by saving the processor "state" (registers, flags, and program counter) for one task, and load-ing the state of another task. There is a vast range of different kinds of oper-ating systems, distinguished by the facilities they provide for scheduling tasks, synchronizing their actions, and passing data between them. Operating systems intended for real-time applications tend to provide a wide range of such facilities.

(In this book we will use the term "task" for a process running under the control of a multitasking system, and use the more general term "process" to include computations taking place inside of interrupt handlers, and physical processes in the real world.)

There are two major ways of organizing a set of tasks for multitasking: either all tasks are identical programs operating on different data, or else each task does a single operation on a set of data, and passes it on to the next task after the fashion of an assembly line.

The two tasking structures are related to the structure of the external sys-tem: when an item is operated on by a sequence of processing stations, an *item-oriented* system assigns a task to each item, which follows it through the pro-cess, while a *station-oriented* system assigns a task to each station, and infor-mation on each item is passed from task to task.[1]

Station-oriented systems are most appropriate to processes involving continuous flow, while item-oriented systems are appropriate to situations in which discrete items with different processing requirements are moving between workstations (as in an automobile assembly line).

Multi-Processor. When there is too much work for a single computer to do, add another computer. The result is a *multi-processor* system. (The words "multiprocessing" and "multiprogramming" are easily confused. "Multitasking" and "multi-processor," at least, are unambiguous.) As microprocessors become smaller and less expensive, multiprocessor systems become more common.

As with multitasking, there are the same two ways of assigning tasks to processors: either all processors perform the same operations on different data, or they specialize. The latter is more common in real-time applications: there is often a cluster of small, specialized processors under the control of a larger central one (which may itself be multitasking). A good example is the controller for a plotter, with separate processors for controlling the X-axis and Y-axis motors, and a central processor to translate line-drawing commands into X and Y motions. Robots and other machines are often multiprocessor systems.

It is becoming increasingly possible to buy single-chip or single-board microcomputers dedicated to particular tasks, such as motor control or signal generation. This makes the design of multi-processor systems especially easy, since the tasks that run in the specialized processors are already written and (even better!) tested.

REFERENCES

1. Huenning, Goeffrey H. Designing Real-Time Software Systems. *Sigsmall Newsletter* 7(2): 34-39 (Oct. 1981).

2

Hardware for Real-Time Systems

There is little to distinguish real-time microcomputer hardware from that in other microcomputer systems. A microcomputer used in a real-time application has a CPU, memory, peripheral chips, and so on. There are, however, reasons for choosing one kind of CPU, peripheral chip, or whatever over another, and these sometimes have to do with the use to which the system will be put (although other considerations, such as cost and familiarity, are usually more important).

There are also some hardware items rarely found in other than real-time systems: analog-to-digital and digital-to-analog converters, relays, solenoids, stepping motors, and so on. These items are part of the interface between the computer and the "real" world, and it is not surprising that they bring "real"-time along with them.

This chapter is basically an list of the hardware elements of a computer system, with notes on the things to look for when choosing them for real-time applications. The "traditional" system diagram (Fig. 2.1) will be the road map for this chapter. After discussing the various families of digital IC's, we will begin in the middle, with the Central Processing Unit. A computer consists of a Central Processing Unit (CPU), which executes instructions to perform operations on data, some Memory, to hold the data, and some Input and Output devices (I/O) which enables the computer to communicate with the "real" world. All of these are held together by a "bus," along which data travel between the various parts.

The reader familiar with computer hardware may want to skim or skip this chapter.

LOGIC FAMILIES

The *integrated circuits* (usually called *chips*) out of which microcomputers and other digital devices are made fall into two broad families, Metal Oxide Semiconductor (MOS) and bipolar. The former are built out of MOS field-effect transistors, the latter out of *bipolar* (ordinary) transistors. MOS devices are small and use little power, so most microprocessors, memories, and complex peripheral chips (LSI, for Large-Scale Integration) use them. Bipolar transis-

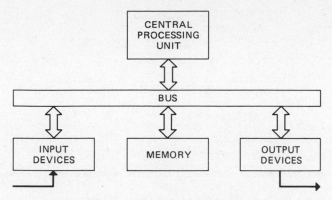

Figure 2.1. A single-processor computer system

tors are somewhat larger and use more power, but are faster and more robust. They are found in the SSI (Small-Scale Integration) and MSI (Medium-Scale Integration) "glue" chips, and in devices that have to run at high speed, or interface with the "real" world.

The MOS family is further divided into PMOS (P-channel MOS), NMOS (N-channel MOS), and CMOS (Complimentary MOS). PMOS is now nearly extinct—it is slow and uses unusual voltages. NMOS is the most common family in microprocessors. CMOS, which uses both N- and P-channel transistors, uses very little power (when not switching), and is ideal for battery-powered applications. CMOS is also very tolerant of variations in supply voltage and clock speed. It takes more chip area and more processing steps than NMOS, however, which makes it more expensive, and its power advantage disappears at high switching speeds.

Bipolar logic comes in two major families: TTL (Transistor-Transistor Logic) and ECL (Emitter-Coupled Logic), with a few more arcane types in fringe applications. ECL is power-hungry, and is used only when raw speed is required. TTL is the workhorse of the digital world. It runs on the nearly universal 5-volt power supply, and can be connected directly to NMOS and CMOS microprocessors and memories. TTL comes in several sub-families. The "LS" series (Low-power Shottky transistors) is the current favorite—it is both fast and fairly low in power consumption.

CPU'S

As you can see from Fig. 2.2, the *central processing unit* (CPU) of a computer system is itself a computer system in miniature (and by using *microcode* to control it, can even be implemented as such). It has input and output (the

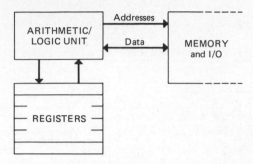

Figure 2.2. The Central Processing Unit, considered as a computer system.

interfaces to main memory and I/O devices), memory (called *registers*), and control. The control is further divided into the *Arithmetic and Logic Unit* (ALU), which performs computations, and the *instruction decoder*. The specific details of the CPU's structure, or of a computer system's structure, are called its *architecture*.

Since this is not a book on computer architecture we will do no more than indicate the range of structures, operations, data types, and addressing modes common on microprocessors. The interested reader is referred to Bell and Newell[1] , and the programming manuals for particular microcomputers. Also, many of the trade magazines, such as *EDN* and *Electronic Design*, publish annual reference issues with short descriptions of all current microcomputers.

Registers

The registers on the CPU can be divided into an arithmetic group, which hold data to be operated on, and a control group, which hold control information. The arithmetic group includes *accumulators*, which take the results of arithmetic operations, and *index registers*, which can be used to hold addresses (see the discussion of Addressing Modes below). Sometimes arithmetic registers are general-purpose, and can be used for both arithmetic and addressing.

The control registers invariably include a *program counter*, which holds the address of the next instruction to be executed, and a *flag register* (also called flag-control word or program-status word), which holds single-bit indicators such as the carry from the last arithmetic operation. Almost all microprocessors include a *stack pointer* (which may be more or less general-purpose), which holds subroutine return addresses, parameters, and local variables.

The Instruction Set

The *instruction set* of a computer is the set of operations that it can perform on data. An instruction in general has three components: the *operation* it performs, the *data types* that it operates on, and the *addressing modes* by which the operands are indicated. The bits that distinguish the operation, and the assembly-language mnemonic that represents it, are usually called the *opcode*.

The boundaries between operation, data type, and addressing mode are often fuzzy, and different manufacturers draw the boundaries differently (occasionally changing their philosophy from one machine to another). Sometimes, for example, the register being operated on is considered as part of the operation (as in LDA: "load accumulator") while other manufacturers call "register" an addressing mode (LD A: "load register A"). Data type, also, is sometimes part of the operation (as in LDW: "load word" and LDB: "load byte"), and sometimes implicit in the addressing mode. Even the underlying operation can be disputed: Are "load" and "store" different operations, or simply variations of a "move" operation?

This kind of quibble can make it hard to switch from one CPU or assembly language to another, and is the sort of philosophical question that is impossible to resolve rationally. An attempt is being made by the IEEE to develop a standard for assembly language notation, but its success is by no means assured. Unlike users, who naturally favor portability, manufacturers *want* their chips to be different.

Operations.   Operations in an instruction set can be broken down into a few broad categories: data transfer (load, store, and so on), arithmetic, logical operations (and, or, and so on), shifting operations, tests and comparisons, control transfer (conditional and unconditional jumps, subroutine calls and returns), I/O, and control (a miscellaneous category that includes instructions to halt the processor, load control registers, enable and disable interrupts, and the like). Almost all CPU's have representatives of all of these categories, and the details are too many to list.

Data Types.   Most microprocessors can operate on eight-bit bytes—the only exceptions are some four-bit, single-chip microcomputers found in small controller applications and mercifully becoming extinct. Most also have a few operations on 16-bit words, since this is the usual size for an address. Some can operate on 32-bit and even 64-bit quantities. Such quantities are generally treated as signed integers in two's complement notation.

Apart from integers and addresses, there are two other data types of interest: floating-point numbers and strings (arrays of bytes). There are still no single-chip CPU's in common use that handle floating-point, but many manufacturers have "co-processor" chips that do. These can either be accessed as I/O devices, or by means of "hooks" in the instruction set (Intel's 8086 and 8087 interact in this way, as do Zilog's Z8000 and Z8070).

Some microprocessors *do* support strings, usually by means of "block move," "block I/O," and "string compare" instructions, which repeat an operation such as load or compare while incrementing one or two pointer registers and decrementing a counter register. Zilog's Z80 and Z8000 have the largest repertoire of such instructions. This kind of instruction is especially useful in applications involving text or large blocks of data, such as terminals and disk controllers.

Addressing Modes.   The *address* of a piece of data is its location in a computer: it might be in main memory, a register, or in I/O space. The *addressing modes* of an instruction specify how the addresses of its operands are to be determined. The simplest way is directly, by storing their addresses as part of the instruction. Operands in registers are almost invariably specified this way, and most microcomputers allow data in main memory to be directly addressed as well.

Another common addressing mode is *indirect*, usually through a register: the instruction indicates a register, which in turn contains the address of the data (the *effective address*). MOS Technology's 6500 family is the only common microprocessor family which allows indirection through a word in memory; this is a common addressing mode on mainframes and minicomputers.

Indirection can also involve incrementing or decrementing the register that holds the address. Most microprocessors support such "auto-increment" and "auto-decrement" modes only on indirect loads and stores involving the stack pointer register, in other words "pop" and "push" operations. They are also found in string or block operations, and subroutine calls and returns (which push and pop the program counter register).

Finally there are *indexed* and *based* addressing modes, in which an address and an *offset* are added to produce the effective address. If the address and the offset are the same length, there is no distinction between the two modes. If the offset is shorter than the address, however, there is a difference: the address might be in the instruction and the offset in a register (indexed addressing), or the address might be in a register and the offset in the instruction (based addressing). Indexed addressing is used to access an element of an array located at a fixed address in memory; based addressing to access a field of a data structure given a pointer to it. Most microprocessors support one or the other, and call it indexed addressing regardless; Zilog's Z8000 is currently the only chip on which the distinction is made (because it supports both).

Regularity. If any combination of operation, data type, and addressing mode is a possible instruction, the instruction set is said to be *regular*, or *orthogonal* (in the mathematical sense of orthogonal co-ordinate axes). Regular instruction sets are important both to the assembly-language programmer (who has to remember what combinations are possible), and to the compiler-writer (who has to write a *program* to decide which combinations to use).

Regularity is also important to the designer of the computer, since regular designs tend to be simple ones. In spite of this fact, no microprocessor instruction sets are completely regular, and most are extremely irregular (the term "baroque" is often used). Manufacturers are, however, slowly coming to recognize the benefits of regularity, and the situation is improving.

The Memory Bus

The interface between the CPU and its memory is called the *memory bus* (because the data rides back and forth on it). If there is a separate interface to I/O devices it is called an *I/O bus*, but most microprocessors have only a single bus which serves both purposes. A bus consists of address and data signals, which are sometimes *multiplexed* on the same set of pins.

Control signals related to the bus include some way of distinguishing between read and write transactions, between I/O and memory transactions, and (on multiplexed buses) between addresses and data. Most microprocessors also have a *wait* line which is used by slow memory to inform the CPU that the transaction is not yet complete, and *bus request* and *bus acknowledge* lines which are used by other processors or DMA devices to gain access to the bus.

I/O and Memory. Many microprocessors distinguish between I/O and memory transactions on their bus and in their instruction sets. However, as far as devices connected to the bus are concerned, the I/O-memory line can be regarded as just another address bit. Carrying this a bit further, I/O devices can be located in part of the memory space and operated on with ordinary load and store instructions. This is called *memory-mapped* I/O. The concept was used on the PDP-11 minicomputer, and is now used on many microcomputers, including the 6800, 68000, 6500, and Z8 families.

Memory-mapped I/O can be used even on processors with a separate I/O space and specialized I/O instructions. It is especially useful for devices with lots of buffer memory, such as CRT controllers.

(Some computers actually have separate buses for I/O and memory. This structure is rare in the microcomputer world.)

Other Control Signals

Other control signals include a *reset* signal, to force the CPU into a known state, and *interrupts* (which we will examine in more detail later on). Interrupts are particularly important in a real-time environment.

SOME POPULAR MICROPROCESSORS

Comparing Microprocessors

It is difficult to compare computer architectures, and almost impossible to rank them in any consistent way. For any two architectures it is usually possible to find some measurement on which either is better than the other. Most comparisons, then, tend to be either subjective, or biased toward particular applications. Our bias here will naturally be toward those features that affect real-time performance.

Manufacturers often attempt to rank processors either by clock speed or by performance on "benchmark" programs. Clock speed is useless as a measure, since processors vary widely in the number of clock cycles required for memory accesses and instruction executions. Benchmarks are more useful, but still tend to reflect the skill of the programmer almost as much as the capabilities of the processor. The best benchmark is *your* application, or at least the most performance-sensitive part of it.

New microprocessors are being developed all the time, and existing families are being extended with improved models. The brief comparisons given here should therefore be treated more as a guide to what to look for when selecting a processor, rather than as actual ratings. Even at the time of writing, the processors mentioned are only a fraction of the number available, and selected less for their good qualities than for their popularity or historical importance. This section is no substitute for a good, up-to-date survey.

Single-Chip Microcomputers

A *single-chip microcomputer* is a complete system on a single piece of silicon. All such chips have RAM for data, ROM or PROM for program, and parallel I/O. (Manufacturers may confuse the issue by calling the on-chip RAM "registers.") Many have memory bus connections, for expanding the on-chip memory; these can usually be used as additional parallel I/O ports if external memory is not required. Many have serial I/O, counters, and timers. Some even have analog I/O.

By simplifying the computer part of an application to a single component, single-chip microcomputers significantly reduce the cost of manufacturing a system. This is especially true because the cost of putting a chip into a system is only partly determined by the cost of the chip. There is a relatively constant overhead for socket or soldering, PC-board area, testing, and so on, which depends more on the number of pins than on anything else.

This reduction in manufacturing cost is counterbalanced by an increase in engineering cost and, in the case of chips with on-chip ROM, one-time mask programming (tooling) charges. The single-chip system has limited memory and limited power, and these are usually just barely sufficient for the application at hand. (This makes a devilish kind of sense: since single-chip processors are available with a wide range of capabilities, you chose the smallest one that will do the job.) As a result, writing the program to handle the application is usually far overshadowed by the task of making it fit on the chip. (I vividly remember a microwave oven controller that took two weeks to write, and two months to trim down to half its original size. There was one byte left over out of a kilobyte of ROM.)

The programming effort is then matched (at least) by the effort of testing the program; a mistake on a 10,000-part ROM order is expensive! Mask charges for new ROMS are typically several thousand dollars, and the minimum order is several thousand chips. A minor bug could easily cost your company tens of thousands of dollars, so careful simulation and testing are essential. Fortunately, most single-chip microcomputers can be emulated by PROM- or RAM-based relatives. The Intel 8048, Motorola 6801, Mostek 3870, and Zilog Z8 all have PROM-based emulator chips which fit into the same socket as the ROM versions. The first two do this by incorporating PROM on the CPU chip itself; the others by "piggybacking" a standard PROM chip on top of a special ROM-less emulator.

It is usually a good idea to ship the first few hundred systems with PROM-based emulators. This gives you (the vendor) a chance to get the bugs out, and also avoids the delay associated with manufacturing the ROM versions.

Popular Families By far the overwhelming majority of computers (of any kind!) in the world are single-chip microcomputers with four-bit data paths. They are difficult to program, with strange architectures, but they are cheap. Examples are TI's TMS 1000 family, National's COP-400, and AMI's S2000. All come in many variations, with different size ROM's, NMOS and CMOS versions, and different kinds of I/O devices. Most are capable of driving displays and reading keyboards; they are commonly found in small appliances.

Eight-bit microcomputers include Mostek's 3870, Intel's 8048 and 8051, Zilog's Z8, Motorola's 6801, and Rockwell's 6500/1. The latter two are single-chip versions of the 6800 and 6502 microprocessors; the 3870 is a single-chip version of Fairchild's F8, and has by far the oddest architecture of the lot.

Eight-bit microcomputers are usually available with some kind of serial I/

O as well as the usual parallel ports. Sometimes this is a "bit-banger"—a single bit which must be controlled in software. However the Z8, 3870, 6500/1, 6801, and 8051 have built-in UART's, as well as counter-timers to provide the bit rate. All have at least some interrupts and counter-timers. Most are available in CMOS as well as NMOS, and with varying amounts of ROM including none at all, for development.

Pre-Programmed Single-Chip Microcomputers

Several manufacturers produce single-chip microcomputers whose ROM's contain an interpreter for some programming language, usually a "tiny" Basic, although Forth is also starting to appear. These include the Zilog 8671 and National 8073. The result is a CPU which, as far as the user is concerned, directly executes a high-level language. All that is needed is some memory, a terminal, and a power supply—it is possible to build a complete system with as few as five chips! Moreover, there is no need for a development system—the chip includes a simpleminded text editor.

Since the application is programmed in a high-level language, it is simpler and quicker to develop. As usual, there is a price. The interpreters are usually dismally slow, so inner loops, interrupt handlers, and so on, must be written in assembly language (or even absolute hexadecimal—no development system, remember?). Still, it is a good way to get started, and the chips make excellent educational tools. There is yet another advantage if you can use it: the Basic interpreter can be made available to the end user.

Another form of pre-programmed microcomputer is the special-purpose controller. This is not programmable at all in the usual sense, although like many ordinary I/O chips they tend to have many options. These chips include interfaces to keyboards, displays, and motors.

Eight-Bit Microprocessors

The overwhelming majority of microprocessors (as opposed to single-chip microcomputers) in the world today use so-called "eight-bit" CPU's, mostly the Intel 8080 and its descendent, the Zilog Z80. So-called, because word length is a difficult concept to pin down. Most eight-bitters have 16-bit addresses, and at least a few 16-bit registers. Some have a fairly complete set of instructions for 16-bit arithmetic. Some (including the 8080 and Z80) have 4-bit internal data paths. The most reliable measure is the number of data lines in the memory bus, although many newer CPU families (such as the 8086 and 68000 families) include low-cost members with 8-bit buses. These are often described by their manufacturers as 16-bit CPU's. To make matters worse, at the time of writing Zilog is working on its Z800, a Z80 with a 16-bit ALU and memory bus. Will it be called an 8-bit or 16-bit processor? Only their advertising agency knows.

Popular Families.   The most popular 8-bit CPU families are the Intel 8080 family (8080 and 8085), the Zilog Z80 (an 8080 derivative) , the Motorola 6800 family (6800 and 6809) and the MOS Technology 6500 family (6502 and variations, closely related to the 6800). The Intel 8088 and Motorola 68008 are 8-bit versions of 16-bit processors. RCA's 1802, though less popular due to an unusual architecture, is still in use because it was the first 8-bit microprocessor to be implemented in CMOS, making it suitable for battery-powered applications. (CMOS versions of the other 8-bit families are now available.)

Comparisons.   From a programming point of view, the cleanest 8-bit microprocessor architectures are the 6809, and the 16-bit derivatives, the 8088 and 68008. They have regular instruction sets and a good set of addressing modes and 16-bit arithmetic instructions. This makes them both easy to program in assembly language, and easy to write efficient compilers for. All have multiply and divide instructions, which makes them good for signal-processing applications.

In terms of support, the Z80, 8080, and 8085 have the largest amount of software, both operating systems and programming languages. The 8088, however, is rapidly developing a large software base as well, due mainly to its use in IBM's personal computer.

From a performance point of view, the Z80, 6500 series, and the 8-bit derivatives of 16-bit processors are probably the best. The Z80 benefits in some applications (especially those involving text processing) by having block move and block I/O instructions. The 6500 and 8088 have a good collection of addressing modes. The Z80 has a rather irregular architecture, and the 6500 totally lacks 16-bit registers (except for the program counter); both require tricky coding to achieve good performance.

The 6800 family has an advantage for interrupt processing and multitasking: the registers are automatically saved on the stack when an interrupt occurs. There is also a "software interrupt" instruction which can be used as an operating system interface. The Z80 also has an advantage: a vectored interrupt mechanism, and I/O chips that take advantage of it. It also has a set of "alternate" registers that can be used by interrupt routines (although not in a very general way).

The 16-bit derivatives have the added advantage of larger addressing range. Although this is not a factor in most embedded applications, it is important in general-purpose systems and in applications such as color graphics, for which large memories are required. The Z800, a new member of the Z80 family, has on-chip memory mapping and I/O devices. Intel's 80188, an 8-bit version of the 80186, also has on-chip I/O.

Sixteen-Bit Microprocessors

Sometimes an application needs more speed or memory than an 8-bit processor can provide. In the real-time field, the limiting factor is usually speed. In both cases, the answer is to process more bits at a time.

Popular Families. The leading 16-bit microprocessor families are the Intel 8086, the Motorola 68000, and the Zilog Z8000, with National's 16000 and Texas Instruments' 9900 bringing up the rear in popularity, the 16000 because it is new, and the 9900 because it is old. (By the time this book is published there will undoubtedly be several additions to the field.)

In addition, several minicomputers exist in microprocessor form: the Digital Equipment PDP-11 and the Data General Nova (and probably more by the time this book is published). Just to confuse matters, Motorola advertises the 68000 as a 32-bit machine (it has 32-bit registers, but only a 16-bit data path), and both the 8086 and 68000 come in versions with an 8-bit data bus.

Comparisons. The National 16000 has the cleanest architecture, by far, and the 8086 the most irregular. The Z8000 is also very clean if you stick to its "non-segmented" mode, which uses 16-bit addresses. In its "segmented" mode, with 24-bit addresses, the addressing modes become rather irregular. In the 8086, many instructions and addressing modes only apply to specific registers.

The 9900 has a feature which seems to make it attractive for real-time work: it keeps its working registers in main memory, referring to them only by means of a single pointer register. This means that context-switching for interrupts or multitasking is very fast—only the pointer needs to be changed. Unfortunately, keeping the registers in main memory also makes the chip slower, which wipes out most of the advantage.

All of the 16-bit machines have good interrupt-handling mechanisms: interrupts have several priority levels and a clean interface. All but the 9900 have one disadvantage in terms of interrupt handling: there are more registers that have to be saved.

All of the popular 16-bit microprocessors except the TI 9900 have more than 16 bits of addressing capability. All have optional memory-management chips available except for the 8086 family, which has memory management built onto the CPU (very simply on the 8086, and a more elaborate form on the 80286). Another member of the 8086 family, the 80186, has I/O devices built onto the chip.

SPECIAL-PURPOSE MICROPROCESSORS

There are a number of special cases in the microprocessor world: processors designed not as general-purpose computers, but specialized toward particular applications.

Bit-Slice Processors

There is an ambiguity in the word "microprocessor." Before the days of integrated circuits, it meant a computer which was *microprogrammed*; a small internal ROM containing *microcode* controlled the internal workings of the computer, emulating the "macro" instruction set seen by the programmer. This took advantage of the fact, already mentioned, that the CPU looks very much like a computer itself.

Microprogrammed processors still exist, and in fact many of the newer microprocessor CPU's are implemented using microcode. However, when special instruction sets or word lengths are needed, there are now available IC's designed specifically for executing microcode. These are called *bit-slice* computers, because the chips, usually containing an ALU (Arithmetic-Logic Unit) and some registers, come in two- or four-bit-wide "slices" which are put together to make up the target word length. (See Fig. 2.3.) Most of these bit-slices use bipolar logic for speed.

Bit-slice processors are most often found emulating minicomputers, but are occasionally used in real-time controllers (in which case the application may be implemented directly in microcode, without attempting to emulate an instruction set). Tailoring the word length and instruction set to the application makes possible extremely high performance, at the usual price of increased design and implementation cost.

Popular bit-slice families include the AMD 2900 series and Motorola's 10800 series. The 2900 is implemented in low-power Shottky TTL, and the 10800 in ECL (making it faster and more expensive).

High-Speed Controllers

A few bipolar microprocessors, notably the Signetics 8x300 family and AMD 29116 are intended specifically for high-speed control applications.

The 8x305 has 15 8-bit registers, a 16-bit instruction word, and an instruction set specializing in bit manipulation and shifting; its predecessor the 8x300 had 8 registers and a 12-bit instruction word. There is no addressable data memory; the memory bus, if there is one, is treated as an I/O device. Signetics has recently announced a peripheral chip, the 8x330, for use in disk controller

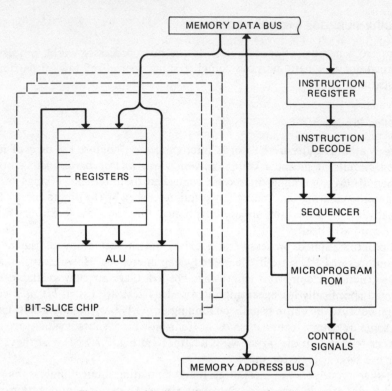

Figure 2.3. A bit-slice, microprogrammed computer.

applications, for which the 8x305 is also well suited. The family also includes the 8x305 CPU (a lower-power version of the original 8x300), the 8x310 interrupt controller, the 8x320 bus interface, and the 8x360 memory interface.

The AMD 29116 is similar to a bit slice, but 16 bits wide. Like a bit slice it has no program counter; this is provided by an external sequencer chip such as the AMD 2910. It has 32 16-bit working registers.

Signal-Processing Processors

The Intel 2920, TI TMS320, and AMI S28211 are examples of another breed of special-purpose chip: the signal processor. These have high-speed multipliers, and are usually pipelined, making them suitable for digital filtering and other formerly analog functions. The Intel chip, in fact, has no conditional branches, a measure designed to ensure that the program always processes each sample in the same amount of time.

The Intel chip has a purely analog interface, with A/D and D/A converters built in. The AMI chip is designed to function as a peripheral to a more traditional microprocessor. The TI chip has a more-or-less standard computer architecture. All have separate buses for instructions and data, so that instruction and data fetches can proceed simultaneously for higher throughput. Some are available with pre-programmed ROMS for standardized functions such as fast Fourier transforms or digital filtering.

It is also possible to build signal processors directly out of multiplier, adder, and register chips. These are fast, but of course are completely dedicated to a single task, and programmable only in the sense that their coefficients can be changed: the function they compute is completely fixed.

MEMORY

If all computer systems are very much alike, all memory systems are almost identical. A given bit pattern (a *word* or *byte*) is written into memory at a given location (*address*), and later that address is given again and the bit pattern read out, presumably unchanged.

Memory systems are characterized by four basic parameters: size, speed, volatility, and price.

Size

Memory size is two-dimensional: the number of words, or distinct addresses (usually a power of two), and the number of bits per word. Thus, a typical memory chip might be "1024×4," meaning 1024 words of four bits each. 1024 (2^{10}) is usually abbreviated 1K, so the memory above would be called "1K-by-4" or, going by total bit count, a "4K" memory.

The maximum available size of memory chips tends to go up by a factor of four every two to four years (the trend is slowing down). The price per bit tends to go down by about the same factor, so that the price per *chip* remains approximately constant (which is reasonable). The numbers in this book are, therefore, subject to inevitable change.

Notice that a memory with 65536 words (2^{16}, the total memory size of a typical 8-bit microprocessor) is called a 64K memory, since 1K = 1024. This is convenient, since 64 is a power of two, but confusing, since a 1K resistor (or anything else) is 1000 ohms (or whatever). Where confusion can result (not likely), use "k" for 1000 (small k), and "K" for 1024 (big K).

A word of data in memory is not necessarily the same size as a word in the CPU chip. In particular, when reliability is needed, extra bits can be added on for error detection and correction. To detect errors, a *parity check* bit is added to make the total number of "1" bits in the word either odd or even (usually an arbitrary choice). Then if a bit gets accidentally changed by the memory, the word will have the wrong parity.

Error correction is more complicated, and requires more bits. A word of 2^N bits has $N+1$ check bits added to it, according to an encoding technique called a *Hamming code*. Essentially, each check bit is a parity bit for half of the data bits. When an error appears, the pattern of incorrect check bits can be used to identify the incorrect data (or check) bit. There are now IC's which generate and check Hamming codes, and their use in systems which have to be reliable is highly recommended.

Speed

There is little to say about speed, except that it costs money, so it makes no sense to use memory faster than you need for your application. It is possible to make a fast processor slow down for slow memory (by pulling on its "wait" input, if it has one). This is necessary in systems with more than one speed of memory (usually the slow memory is PROM, which is expensive or even non-existent in high speeds).

Speed depends on how the memory is constructed: it is usually possible to get higher speeds at the expense of chip area, and hence price. Speed is also costly in terms of power; higher switching speeds mean higher currents. Higher power consumption has indirect costs in power supplies and cooling.

Volatility

A memory is *volatile* if its data are lost when power is removed, and *non-volatile* otherwise. The term also applies to the data. There is a wide spectrum of volatility, depending on just what has to be done to change the data, or keep it in place.

ROM. Read Only Memory (ROM) is actually written once, when the chip is manufactured. Thereafter the data are in for good—they can't be changed. This is both good and bad: ROM is very cheap in large quantities, because it is simple. On the other hand, you have to make a large quantity of the same pattern, because of the tooling charges (typically a few thousand dollars). The data are safe, because they are "cast in silicon." On the other hand, if there is a bug in your program it will be very expensive to fix. ROM's are available in sizes from 32×4 to $128K \times 8$ bits (so far).

PROM. Programmable Read Only Memory (PROM) is also written once, but after the chip reaches the user. Data are written by using high voltages to selectively blow fuses corresponding to the bits that have to be "programmed." PROM's are fairly inexpensive, very reliable, and cost-effective in small quantities.

PROM's are usually made with a bipolar process, and are therefore quite fast. They can often be used in place of large blocks of random logic in a circuit. PROM's are available in sizes from 32×4 to $16K \times 8$ bits.

EPROM.   Erasable Programmable Read Only Memory can be written many times, after being erased with a dose of ultraviolet light through a little quartz window on top of the chip. This takes several minutes to half an hour, and the time required to test the process makes EPROM's quite expensive. They are well worth their price, however, in prototypes and short production runs.

The most common EPROM's are those in the line of 27xx parts originated by Intel and second-sourced or copied by almost everyone. They come in 24-pin packages and sizes from 4K bits (the 512×8 2704 chip, now nearly extinct) to 64K bits (the $8K \times 8$ 2764, still rare). The more recent parts (2716 and up) run on a convenient 5-volt supply, while the older ones require several voltages.

EEPROM.   Electrically Erasable Programmable Read Only Memory works like EPROM, but can be erased by applying a voltage to a pin instead of UV-light to a window. This means that they can be used to store information while a piece of equipment is turned off. EEPROM is sometimes called "Read Mostly Memory"—it usually takes much longer to write memory than to read it, so writing is done very infrequently compared with reading.

RAM.   Finally we get to so-called Random Access Memory, which ought to be called "Read/Write Memory," but isn't. All memory chips are "random access" in the more technical sense of being able to directly address their contents in any order. But we seem to be stuck with the term. (A few people are suggesting "Randomly Alterable Memory" as a new reading of the acronym. Some of us still call the main read/write memory of a computer system "core.") RAM is available in an immense range of sizes, organizations, and speeds, and several different levels of volatility as well.

Static RAM.   Static RAM holds data in flip-flops, which stay in one state until they are explicitly re-written. Dynamic RAM, on the other hand, stores data in tiny capacitors, which must be periodically "refreshed," usually by reading (since the data are destroyed when they are read, the chip automatically writes them back, good as new).

There are, as usual, trade-offs. Flip-flops take four or six transistors to build, while a dynamic RAM cell only takes one. Thus, dynamic RAM chips tend to be smaller and hence cheaper. They also consume less power when running. (CMOS static RAM's consume almost no power when not being accessed; when running their power requirement rises. Bipolar static RAM is power-hungry all the time.)

Dynamic RAM.   Dynamic RAM is a good choice for large memories, where the refreshing circuitry becomes insignificant, or for things like CRT-controller refresh buffers, in which the data are constantly being read out anyway. (Some CPU's, such as the Z80, provide automatic refresh ciruitry.) Older dynamic RAM's require unusual voltages; the 64K and newer 16K parts run on 5 volts, and some include automatic refresh circuitry.

Width.   RAM also comes in varying widths: one, four, and eight bits are the usual choices. Dynamic RAM is usually one bit wide—having only a single data pin results in a smaller package (and a simpler chip). Four- and eight-bit-wide chips come in larger packages, so they are useful for small memory configurations, typically of fewer than eight chips (otherwise, you could use eight smaller and cheaper 1-bit-wide chips).

Recently, eight-bit-wide RAM's (also called byte-wide) have been appearing that have nearly the same pin configurations as the common eight-bit-wide EPROM's. Most of these are static, but there are a few "quasi-static" chips—dynamic RAM's with on-chip refresh circuitry. These chips are especially convenient because they let you design a board which will take any combination of RAM or EPROM, depending on current requirements. You can, for example, develop an application in RAM and sell production units with the software in EPROM.

So far, no one has come out with a RAM chip with built-in error correction.

Memory Mapping

Sometimes (not very often in real-time systems, which tend to be small) the amount of memory that a CPU can address directly is not enough. The technique of *memory mapping* alleviates this difficulty.

The idea is to "map" the addresses generated by the CPU (called *logical* addresses) onto a subset of a larger *physical* address space. There are three basic techniques: *bank switching, paging,* and *base-bounds registers* (segmentation).

Memory Mapping Techniques.   *Bank switching* involves using the high-order bits of a logical address to select a "bank" of physical memory, and enabling one of several blocks of physical memory that respond to that address (Fig.

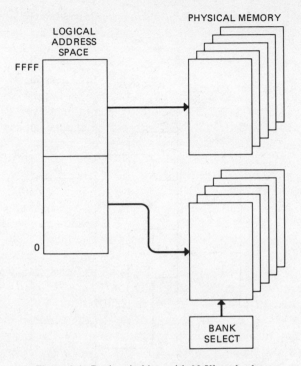

Figure 2.4. Bank switching, with 32-Kbyte banks.

2.4). Banks are usually fairly large: 4K bytes or more, and sometimes as large as 32K. Bank switching is particularly simple to implement in random logic, and to add to a system not originally designed for memory mapping.

Paging is done by taking the high-order bits of the logical address and using them to look up the high-order bits of the physical address in a small, fast RAM (Fig. 2.5). The high-order logical address bits are called a page number; the corresponding location of the page in physical memory is called a page frame.

Paging is also relatively simple to implement. Page sizes range from about 64 bytes to about 4K, with 512 bytes being a common size. It is no coincidence that 512 bytes is the sector size of most hard disks.

Base-bound registers are used to define a starting physical address (base) which is added to the logical address, and a limit (bound) to which it is compared. Sometimes the high-order bits of a logical address are used to select one of several base-bound pairs, in which case they define a *segment*.

One recent implementation of base-bound memory management is Zilog's Z8010 MMU (Memory Management Unit) for the Z8000 microprocessor. The Z8010 can hold the bases and bounds for up to 64 memory segments.

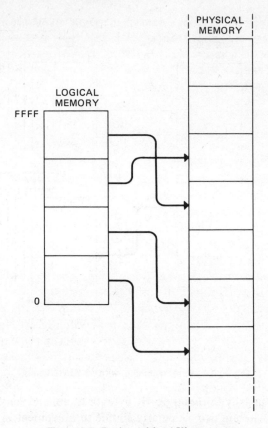

Figure 2.5. Paging, with 16-Kbyte pages.

Memory Attributes.   If memory is being divided into pieces (banks, pages, or segments), it is possible to attach *attributes* to each piece, specifying how it is intended to be used. For example, common attributes are read-only and exe-cute-only. This can be used for protection.

Virtual Memory.   It is also possible to mark a piece of memory as "non-exis-tent." If a reference is made to such a piece, one of two things can happen: either an error can be signaled, or an appropriate piece of memory can be brought in from mass storage. This latter technique is called *demand paging* or *demand segmentation*, and implements something called a *virtual memory*, a logical memory not all of which resides on main physical memory. Since bringing in a desired page takes time, this technique is more common in time-sharing systems than in real-time systems.

Memory Management Chips.   Memory mapping techniques are supported by memory-management chips from several manufacturers, mainly for specific 16-bit processors. There is usually a rather intimate relationship between the architecture of a processor and the kind of memory management that is best for it. Newer members of the various 16-bit CPU families support virtual memory.

PERIPHERAL INTERFACE CHIPS

Most microprocessors come with families of compatible *peripheral* chips: chips designed to interface between that CPU and the outside world, or more recently to extend the CPU's basic instruction set by adding memory management or floating point functions. (The latter are sometimes called *co-processors*.) In addition to providing advanced functions in a conveniently packaged and easy-to-interface form, these chips each represent several man-years of someone else's design expertise.

It is important to remember that although most peripheral chip families are sold with one microprocessor (or a family of related ones from the same manufacturer), it is usually possible to mate a CPU from one family with a peripheral chip from another. A common example is Motorola's M6845 CRT controller chip—it has an excellent set of functions, and can easily be made to work with almost any microprocessor. Some companies, such as Western Digital, explicitly design their peripheral chips for general use. Co-processor chips such as Intel's 8087 floating-point co-processor are usually an exception, being rather tightly coupled to their CPU.

Peripheral chips can get almost arbitrarily complex—their designers try to anticipate every possible variation on some theme, and to provide enough control bits to yield all of them. Several dozen 8-bit registers are not uncommon. Good documentation is *very* uncommon, especially for programmers. There is usually very little information about what should be done before or after what, or about what interacts with what.

Interfacing To I/O

Peripheral chips and other kinds of input-output devices can be connected to the CPU in one of three ways: memory mapping, I/O instructions, or shared memory.

Memory mapping is the simplest: the I/O devices are controlled by writing into special memory locations, and data are transferred by ordinary load and store instructions. This technique was pioneered by DEC's PDP-11, and Motorola has continued the tradition with its 6800 and 68000 families.

Having separate I/O instructions (usually called IN and OUT) to move data between the processor and the I/O device dates back to the days when I/O and memory communicated with the CPU along separate buses. In almost all microprocessors, however, the memory data and address lines of the chip are also used for I/O transfers, and a special signal (effectively an address bit) distinguishes I/O from memory. An I/O address is usually called a *port address*.

The third method is to have the I/O device and the computer communicate by leaving messages in some memory that they both can access. This assumes that the I/O device has some intelligence.

Parallel Interfaces

Probably the simplest peripheral interface chips are the parallel interfaces. These are basically just a set of addressable latches and buffers, and indeed the earliest were just that. Most modern parallel interface chips, however, include at least direction control (input vs. output, sometimes on a bit-by-bit basis), "handshake" lines (data-available and acknowledge), and interrupt generation.

Counters, Timers, and Interrupt Controllers

Counter-Timers.   Almost every microprocessor system (especially the real-time ones) needs at least one counter or timer. Most counter-timer chips come with several *channels*, each of which can be configured to count or time external events, generate clock pulses of a given frequency, or provide interrupts at given intervals.

Counter-timers are most often used as bit-rate generators for serial I/O chips and as "real-time" clocks (that is, clocks that support timing and delay functions in real-time control systems). Since counter-timers include interrupt generators suitable for their CPU family, it is not uncommon to see a counter programmed to interrupt after a single event.

An interesting variation on the counter-timer is Zilog's CIO (Counter Input/Output) chip, which includes not only four counter-timer channels but two 8-bit parallel ports and some handshake lines. They can all interact in strange and wonderful ways—the kind of all-things-to-all-people versatility that makes hardware designers rub their hands together with glee, and makes programmers tear their hair out. For example, a timer can be connected to generate a timed pulse whenever a byte is written to an output port.

Clocks.   Many real-time systems need to know not only the interval between external events, but the actual date and time of day that they happen. There are a number of clock chips, usually derived from digital watch chips, that are designed to connect to microprocessor systems. They are usually CMOS, so that they can run on a battery when the system is turned off, and have a binary-coded decimal interface in place of the direct display interface usual for watches and clocks.

Interrupt Controllers.   Although counter-timer chips are often used to generate interrupts from external events (by setting them to interrupt after counting a single event), there are also chips designed specifically as interrupt generators. Most of these are for families which do not directly support vectored interrupts: they combine a priority encoder and a latch, and after generating an interrupt from one of several (usually eight) inputs, can be polled to determine which input caused the interrupt. Examples are the Intel 8259 and Motorola 6828 for the 8080 and 6800 families respectively.

Serial Interfaces

Perhaps the most common peripheral interface chips are the serial interfaces—common because most computers talk to a terminal or other serial device. The earliest form was the so-called UART, for Universal Asynchronous Receiver and Transmitter. These were clumsy beasts, since all of their many options (such as word length, parity, number of start and stop bits, and so on) were programmed from individual input pins.

The UART's were soon superceded for most purposes by chips designed as microprocessor peripherals. Zilog's SCC (Serial Communications Controller) is perhaps the most elaborate of these at the moment; it includes two complete bidirectional channels supporting a wide variety of synchronous and asynchronous protocols, clock generators for both channels, CRC (Cyclic Redundancy Check) code checking, and a digital phase-locked loop for FM demodulation. This may be over-elaborate for most purposes, especially if all you need to do is talk to a simple terminal, but it's very convenient.

In a higher-speed range, interface chips have started to appear for the Ethernet and other network interfaces. These are all high-speed synchronous interfaces. The chips may implement more or less of the software protocol.

Floppy Disk Interfaces

A variant on the serial interface is the floppy disk controller. These useful chips do serial-to-parallel and parallel-to-serial conversion, and perform most timing and formatting chores. Most require an external clock/data separator, although newer chips may incorporate one.

Recently, faster versions of these chips have appeared for interfacing to Winchester-technology hard disks, which supply data about ten times faster.

Intelligent Interfaces

A few "peripheral controller" chips are actually specially programmed single-chip microcomputers in their own right. This approach is usually slower than providing the same function in custom hardware, but is inexpensive, versatile, and very quick to implement. For example, the first data-encryption chips to appear following the adoption of the Data Encryption Standard (DES) were microcomputers. The special-purpose chips that followed were about ten times faster, but by that time their slower ancestors had been in the field for a year.

Intelligent peripherals are good for controlling slower devices, such as keyboards, printers, and LED or LCD displays.

DIRECT MEMORY ACCESS

Most of the peripheral chips described above are designed to be accessed via "programmed" I/O. In other words, the input and output instructions of the CPU (or the memory load and store instructions, if the I/O device is memory-mapped) are used to transfer data to and from the device under program control. There are two problems with this: the device has to get the CPU's attention, and the CPU can't be doing anything else while it is transferring data.

The solution to this problem is to let the device get at the computer's memory directly. This is called Direct Memory Access (DMA) (See Fig. 2.6). It costs a certain amount of hardware, but gains a lot in performance. Indeed, DMA is often performed at transfer rates no CPU can match. (This can be illustrated very simply. In order to transfer a byte from an input device to memory, the

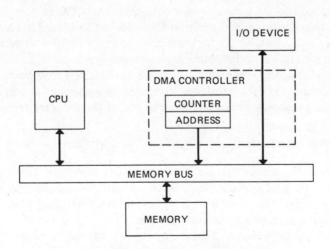

Figure 2.6. Computer system with DMA I/O.

CPU has to read from the device, then write to memory, taking two bus transactions. With DMA, a device can write to memory with a single bus transaction.)

Simple DMA

Often, a DMA controller can be implemented using a handful of TTL counter chips. This is especially true if the starting address of the data, and the number of bytes to be transferred, can be fixed at a power of two. In this case it is not even necessary to provide for loading the counters. The existence of general-purpose LSI chips should not blind us to the virtues of simplicity.

A random-logic DMA controller becomes complicated if the starting address or count has to be programmable, or if interrupts have to be generated. In this case, it is usually better to use one of the LSI chips.

DMA Controller Chips

Most DMA controller chips include one or more programmable "channels," each consisting of an address register and a count register, a "request" line which says that the device wants to transfer some data, and an "acknowledge" line which tells the device that the data have been transferred. When all of the data have been transferred, an interrupt can be generated.

In DMA chips with two such channels, the channels can be coupled in several interesting ways. First of all, one channel can be used to read data, and the other to write the same data. The address register in one or both channels can be kept from incrementing, so as to address the same I/O port, or both can increment to transfer data from one part of memory to another. This mode of operation is sometimes called "flow-through," in contrast to the more usual mode of operation, called "fly-by."

A second kind of coupling, called *chaining*, occurs when one DMA channel is used to fetch new control parameters (address, count, etc.) for another after each transfer is completed. This makes the DMA controller an "I/O Channel" in the old, IBM sense of a more-or-less independent processor executing its own "channel program." Intel's 8089 I/O processor takes this to its obvious conclusion—it is actually a microcomputer, with an instruction set specialized for doing I/O transfers.

CRT Controller Chips

A special case in the DMA world is the CRT controller (Fig. 2.7), which performs the specialized task of transferring data from memory to a raster-scanned display screen. The task can be partitioned in several ways. Some chips

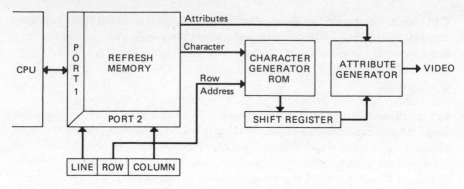

Figure 2.7. CRT controller block diagram.

include everything except the refresh memory (for example the Motorola 6847, which is intended for personal computers with low-resolution TV screens). Most (such as the popular Motorola 6845) include the timing and address generation, but leave out the character generator, shift register, and attribute generator (which can be provided rather simply in TTL, or all together on a chip like the CRT8002 by SMC).

Alternatives

As useful as DMA is, it has a limitation: the bandwidth of the memory bus. Since the memory bus is shared by the CPU and any DMA devices, the CPU has to wait while a DMA transfer is being done. A CRT controller transfers about a million bytes per second, comparable to the memory transfer rate of most CPU's. This means that either the CPU is slowed down intolerably, or the memory has to be twice as fast to handle the doubled traffic.

Dual-Port Memory.   One answer to this problem of disparate speeds is to provide two memory buses: one for the I/O and one for the CPU (Fig. 2.8). If memory can be organized into banks, the CPU can be accessing one bank while the DMA device is accessing the other. You have to worry about what happens when both want to access the same bank, and there are three possibilities: the

Figure 2.8. Dual-ported memory.

CPU waits for the DMA device, the DMA device waits for the CPU (usually undesirable), or the DMA device gets garbage while the CPU gets data. That last choice may seem ludicrous, but is quite common when the device is a CRT controller. The result is that little flickers appear on the screen while the CPU is accessing it.

If the memory is twice as fast as the DMA device or the CPU requires, you can let them take turns. This works especially well with the 68xx and 65xx families, which use a two-phase clock and only access the memory on one phase.

Something like a dual-ported memory is often used for refreshing dynamic RAM, with the refresh generator being the DMA device on the other port.

FIFO Buffers. Another alternative to DMA is to put the data into a FIFO (First-In, First-Out) buffer (Fig. 2.9). Data can be put into such a buffer at one rate, and taken out at another, at the same time. This works best when the CPU has a block transfer instruction which can move data faster than the I/

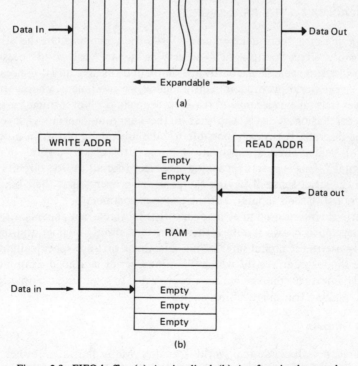

Figure 2.9. FIFO buffer. (a) As visualized. (b) As oftem implemented.

O device. The CPU can transfer a block of data to or from the FIFO, then proceed without having to wait for the I/O device. Usually an interrupt is generated when the FIFO "pipe" is empty or full.

A FIFO is really just a small, specialized dual-port memory, and indeed a chip is available which turns any RAM into a FIFO. A "full-featured" FIFO is available from Zilog (the FIO), which can be configured with different kinds of bus-control or handshake signals on its two ports. Small, fast TTL FIFO's are also available.

Wait-Synchronized I/O.   A very simple technique can sometimes be used to speed up programmed I/O: make the I/O device look like slow memory, and make the CPU wait until the device is ready to transfer data. This works if there is time for the CPU to do the data transfer, but not enough to also test for whether the device is ready. This can be slightly dangerous: if the device never responds, the system hangs up, and if there is dynamic memory in the system, the stretched cycles have to be taken into account when computing the refresh rate. This method is, however, simple, cheap, versatile, and fast, especially if the CPU has block I/O instructions (like the Z80).

INTERFACING TO THE REAL WORLD

On one side of a "peripheral interface" sits the computer. On the other side, presumably, sits a "peripheral"—something in the "real world" outside. We will now look at some of the hardware that can be used to affect the real world.

The "real world" is predominantly analog, or continuous, characterized by variables that take on a range of real-number values. (Never mind for now that this is an illusion of scale, and that at the quantum-mechanical level things become discrete. It is rarely possible to take advantage of this in a computer system.) Analog circuits, especially IC's, are often called "linear," in contrast to "digital." This is strictly speaking incorrect (not all analog circuits are linear, in the strict sense of having the pleasant property that their outputs are proportional to their inputs), but the usage is common.

Interface circuits used to be made mostly of discrete components. Later, IC's were developed in two families: those that are strictly analog, and only incidentally useful for digital interfacing, and those that are specifically designed for the digital interface, of which TI's 75xx series is a good example. More recently, interface components have been added to some single-chip microcomputers, making true single-chip systems.

Digital Outputs

Of course, not all of the real world is analog. Many things are either "on" or "off"—motors, house lights, automobile spark plugs, and so on. These are controlled via various kinds of digital switches.

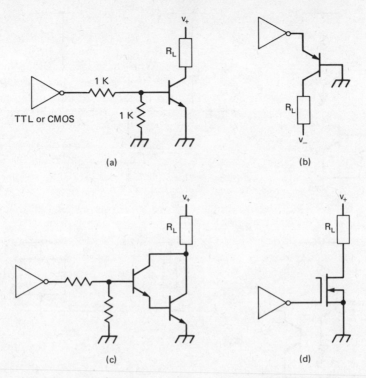

Figure 2.10. Transistor output switching. (a) Basic inverting switch. (b) Load connected to negative voltage. (c) Darlington connection for higher current. (d) Power FET for high current.

Transistors. Switching inside the computer is done using transistors; most outside switching is also done that way. If you don't want to build discrete circuitry, interface chips are available with transistor outputs designed for switching considerable voltages and currents, and with a wide variety of logic inputs. The 7545x series from TI is a good example: it includes both AND and OR inputs, and several output configurations. (Fig. 2.10 shows some typical transistor switching arrangements.)

The output transistors of ordinary logic gates should not be ignored: a standard TTL gate will sink 16 mA (that is, supply a current to ground through a load connected to a positive supply). Unfortunately, it will not source (supply current from a positive supply through a grounded load) nearly as much. This means that the device being controlled must be connected between the gate and the positive supply, and is turned on by a low output, or logic zero. This is invariably confusing to programmers. It helps if the hardware designer can make the gate in question an inverter, so that a "1" bit turns on the device. (Fig. 2.11 shows typical TTL output circuits, and ways of connecting loads to them.)

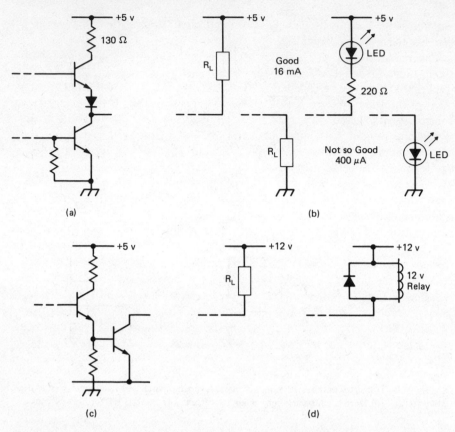

Figure 2.11. Direct connections to TTL outputs. (a) TTL output. (b) Load connections. (c) Open-collector TTL output. (d) Configuration that permits higher-output voltage.

For heftier currents, transistors are available which will switch up to several hundred amps, or several hundred volts.

Field-effect transistors designed for high-power switching are now becoming available: they are faster, and much easier to use. The ease of use is largely due to the fact that they are controlled by a voltage and not by a current. This makes them almost ideal for logic interfacing.

Thyristors.   The *thyristor* family is composed of the Silicon Controlled Rectifiers (SCR's), for switching DC, and Triacs, for switching AC. SCR's are basically two transistors back-to-back, merged into a single four-layer structure and operating as a switch with positive feedback. A very small current is required to turn the SCR on; once on, current continues to flow until the voltage across the outputs drops below a critical value. In other words, something *else* has to turn the current off.

This makes SCR's very good for switching AC, since the voltage of an AC signal drops to zero every half-cycle. Unfortunately, SCR's are, as the name implies, rectifiers: current only flows in one direction. This led to the development of the *triac:* effectively two SCR's back to back, but arranged so that a control signal of either polarity controls an output current in either direction.

When switching AC signals, it is usually best if the switching is done at certain points in the waveform: zero voltage for resistive loads, maximum voltage for inductive loads such as motors. This is done to reduce surge current, which keeps the device being controlled happy, and radio-frequency interference, which keeps the neighbors happy. The "signal" being switched with triacs is almost always 110 volts at 60Hz. A half-cycle of 60Hz is 8.33 ms, which is plenty of time for a computer to figure out when to turn the signal on or off.

Optical Isolators. When it is necessary to switch a signal at a high voltage relative to the computer, some kind of isolation is necessary. These days, the isolation is usually optical: the computer turns on an LED (light-emitting diode), which is coupled to a photo-transistor or photo-diode, which in turn switches the load. The light source and detector are usually packaged together in a single IC; they are available in considerable variety. There are even optically-controlled SCR's.

Relays. The first electrically-controlled switches were the relays, and they still have their uses. A relay is essentially a switch actuated by an electromagnet. Their advantages are large current-handling capacity, low contact resistance, high isolation between controlling and controlled circuits, and ruggedness. Their disadvantages are slow operation (in the millisecond range), and the fact that they present an inductive load, which is hard on the transistor that, ultimately, switches the current activating this mechanical device.

With the advent of computers, and especially TTL logic, small relays have appeared which can be driven from logic voltages. Most of these are reed types, with limited current-carrying capacity (under 1 amp). These are most useful for isolation, when switching high voltages or very noisy signals. They are also useful when low contact resistance is needed, as for very low-level signals.

The so-called "solid-state relays" are not relays, but thyristors or transistors, usually optically-isolated.

Digital Inputs

Note that a switch can be either an input or an output: although one usually thinks of the computer as turning some external device on or off, it is also possible for some external voltage or event to control an input to the computer. The most obvious example is a simple mechanical switch, but electrically-controlled switches can also be used, to detect events that appear as voltages outside the range of the computer's zero-to-five-volt signals.

Optical isolators are very good as inputs, since they tend to protect the computer against real-world voltages. Even comparatively small spikes can damage logic IC's. MOS and CMOS are especially prone to damage by static electricity: *always* protect your LSI by buffering any signals that go off a board. Even a TTL gate or interface chip helps—at least if it gets zapped, it's cheaper than your CPU.

Optical detectors are also common for detecting non-electrical events; many kinds of physical object can be put in the way of a light beam. Examples include the old "electric eye" people-detector, and the optical tachometer, consisting of a toothed wheel rotating between a LED and a photo-detector.

Signal Switching

All of the above switching methods can be used to route signals, rather than just power. IC's for switching signals come in three flavors: simple switches (AND gates, usually several to a package), multiplexers, and decoders. The difference between a multiplexer and a decoder is direction; a multiplexer selects one of several inputs and directs it to a single output, while a decoder sends a single input to one of several outputs.

IC's designed for switching analog signals usually use FET switches, and will pass signals in both directions. Thus, they will serve as either multiplexers or decoders. They are usually called multiplexers.

Digital-to-Analog Conversion

To get an analog effect from a digital signal, a Digital-to-Analog Converter (DAC) is required. The primary parameter of a DAC is *precision*: the number of bits in the word being converted. This determines the maximum number of distinct values that can be output. The other main parameter is of course speed, the time it takes to perform a conversion. The fidelity of the conversion can be specified in any of several ways.

DAC Parameters.   The *accuracy* of a DAC is a measure of the difference between an actual output value and the intended one. Accuracy can be specified in several ways, the most common being as a fraction of the full-scale value or as a fraction of the value of the least-significant bit (typical accuracy being $\frac{1}{2}$ LSB). Values closely related to accuracy are *linearity*, the deviation of the DAC's output curve from a straight line, and *monotonicity*. A DAC is monotonic if increasing input values always produce increasing output values; some DAC designs inherently have this property.

The primary way of specifying a DAC's speed is *settling time*, the time it takes for the DAC's output to reach a stable value after a change in the input.

Types of DAC's.   The most common form is a set of digitally-controlled switches, each controlling an analog signal proportional to the weight of the corresponding bit (Fig. 2.12).

The output of a DAC can be either voltage or current (we ignore for the moment a few bizarre cases in which the output is mechanical). Some DAC's also have an analog reference input; the output voltage or current is a digitally-controlled fraction of the input. These are called *multiplying* DAC's (MDAC's), since the output is the product of the (analog) reference times a (digital) fraction. MDAC's are useful for digitally controlling the amplitude of an analog signal (which might well be a waveform generated with another DAC). An MDAC with current input and current output is effectively a digitally-variable resistor.

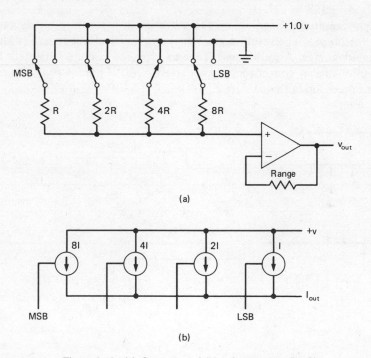

Figure 2.12. (a) Current- and (b) voltage-output DAC's.

A slower and cheaper form of digital-to-analog conversion is pulse-width modulation. This is actually a time-output DAC: a series of pulses is generated with duty cycle (on-to-off ratio) proportional to the digital quantity. It is usually done by counting. The pulses can then be integrated to give a proportional voltage. This method is inherently monotonic. Accuracy is limited by how fast the circuit can count, or by how much time is available for the task, and by the accuracy of the integrator.

DAC's are available in IC form up to 16 bits wide, in a considerable range of accuracy, speed, and price.

Encodings for DAC's.   Two forms of encoding are common on DAC's: binary and binary-coded decimal (BCD). (BCD is more often seen on analog-to-digital converters that were originally intended as digital voltmeters rather than computer input devices.) A third form, a modified binary called Gray code, is used mainly on mechanical position encoders (see below).

There are also two ways of encoding signed numbers: offset-binary and sign-magnitude (Fig. 2.13). Offset-binary is the simplest to implement; half of the full-scale value is subtracted from the output of an ordinary positive-output DAC. The result is that input values from 0 to 255 (say) represent output values from -128 to 127.

In sign-magnitude encoding, on the other hand, a separate bit selects the sign of the output. The result is inherently symmetrical about zero, which is often an advantage. Also, because the sign inversion is done separately from the digital-to-analog conversion, you get an extra bit of precision without needing extra precision in the converter.

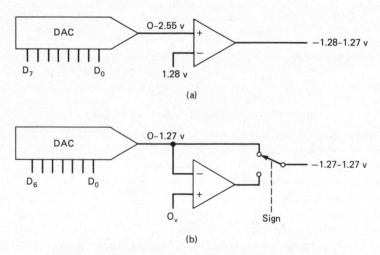

Figure 2.13. (a) Offset binary and (b) sign-magnitude DAC's.

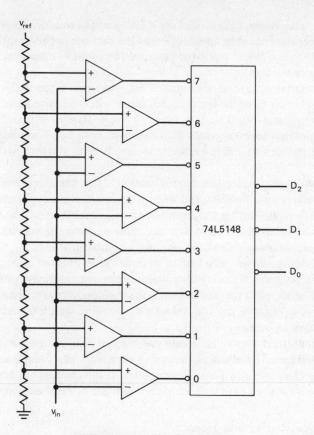

Figure 2.14. 3-bit flash ADC.

Analog-to-Digital Conversion

Converting an analog signal to a proportional digital number is done by an Analog-to-Digital Converter (ADC), of course. This is generally slower than going the other way. The fastest and most expensive ADC is called a "flash" converter; it consists of 2^n comparators, each comparing the input signal with a different voltage (Fig. 2.14). Digital circuitry then converts the resulting number from base one (i comparators high and 2^{n-i} low) to base two. Flash converters are becoming more common as IC technology improves.

A special case is the simple comparator, a 1-bit ADC. Sometimes this is enough, as when a voltage is being compared against a pre-set limit.

The most common form of ADC consists of a DAC and a comparator, comparing the output of the DAC with the input signal. The logic driving the DAC can be a simple counter, counting up if the DAC's output is too low, and down if too high. This is a so-called *tracking* ADC, and is good for following slowly-changing signals. It has the advantage that the number in the counter is always equal to the value of the input (or close, of the input is changing faster than the counter can follow).

The alternative is to start with all bits off, and turn on the high-order bit. If the result is higher than the input signal, turn it off; otherwise leave it on. Then proceed to the next bit. This is a *successive-approximation* converter, and is the most common form of ADC. It is comparatively fast (one clock per bit), and the output can be made available in serial form, starting with the high-order bit.

A disadvantage of successive approximation is that the computer has to wait until the conversion is finished, and so does the input. If the input changes more than one bit's worth during the conversion time, the output will be inaccurate.

It is worth noting that a computer can easily perform the successive approximation function using a DAC output and a comparator input.

Corresponding to the pulse-width modulation method of digital-to-analog conversion are several analog-to-digital conversion methods which rely on counting. The simplest method is voltage-to-frequency conversion. A variable-frequency signal can be transmitted on a single wire, which is useful, and frequency is easy to measure digitally.

More accurate and more elaborate counting techniques are commonly used in digital voltmeters, and occasionally find their way into computer-controlled equipment. They are slow ($\frac{1}{10}$ to $\frac{1}{2}$ second for a conversion), but accurate, and inexpensive compared to other techniques with the same precision.

Non-Electrical Analog Interfaces

Direct Digital Input.   Not everything in the world is a voltage or current. (In the electronics field we sometimes lose sight of this fact.) Many analog quantities are easiest to measure by direct digital methods.

Foremost of the easy things to measure are time and its inverse, frequency. The time between two events is measured by counting the number of pulses of a high-frequency clock that occur between the events (Fig. 2.15a). Frequency is measured by counting the number of cycles of the input signal that occur in a specified interval (Fig. 2.15b). Nothing in the universe can be measured more accurately than time. Chips are available which implement counters and timers with varying degrees of speed and precision.

Rotation and position can also be measured digitally, via devices called *shaft* and *position encoders*. These can be either "absolute," giving a number corresponding to position, or "incremental," giving a pulse when position changes by a specified interval (Fig. 2.16). An incremental encoder is simply a slotted wheel or strip with an optical detector (sometimes two, 90 degrees out of phase,

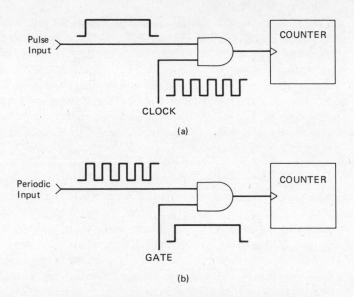

Figure 2.15. (a) Timer. (b) Frequency counter.

to give direction). It can also be used as a tachometer. An absolute encoder is more complex, since it needs a separate strip for each bit.

For a really accurate incremental position encoder, it is possible to use a laser interferometer. In this case, the "slots" in the encoder are interference fringes between two beams of light.

Absolute position encoders sometimes produce a modified binary code called *Gray Code* (see Table 2.1), which has the advantage that adjacent codes differ

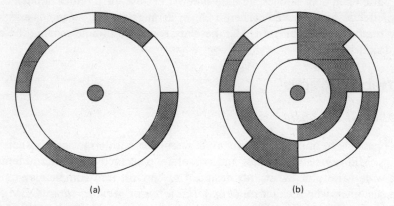

Figure 2.16. (a) Absolute and (b) incremental shaft encoders (3 bits).

Table 2.1. Binary and Gray Codes

DECIMAL	BINARY	GRAY
0	0000	0000
1	0001	0001
2	0010	0011
3	0011	0010
4	0100	0110
5	0101	0111
6	0110	0101
7	0111	0100
8	1000	1100
9	1001	1101
10	1010	1111
11	1011	1110
12	1100	1010
13	1101	1011
14	1110	1001
15	1111	1000

by a change in a single bit. This avoids the glitches that occur in a normal encoder when several bits are supposed to change simultaneously.

Direct Digital Output.   It is possible to *control* rotation and position digitally, too. A digital rotator is called a *stepping motor* or "stepper:" pulses, applied in the proper sequence, cause it to rotate in discrete steps. There are also *linear* steppers as well, although these are less common.

Another direct digital (albeit single-bit) output device is the *solenoid*: an electromagnet that, when turned on, attracts an iron pole piece and so produces an incremental movement. Solenoids are often found controlling valves; they can also open door latches, actuate typewriter keys, or produce other mechanical effects. As suggested earlier, a clever arrangement of solenoids and levers can produce a mechanical DAC; these are sometimes found moving the heads in disk drives.

INTERCONNECTIONS

CPU Buses and Boards

It is possible to build a computer system starting with larger components than chips. Midway between chips and complete, packaged computer systems are the wide variety of PC boards designed to be built into complete systems by the customer, who is called an *Original Equipment Manufacturer* (OEM). The OEM then sells the resulting system to *its* customers, the end users. Most of these "OEM boards" are designed to plug into one of several widely-used backplane buses, although some boards are designed for buses unique to their manufacturer.

Some peripheral boards are designed to plug into the backplane of some popular mini- or microcomputer (DEC's PDP-11 Unibus and LSI-11 Q-bus, and the bus of the Apple personal computer, are popular.) These are well worth considering, if you are planning to buy a complete computer and supplement it with some specialized I/O. Here we will simply mention some of the most popular OEM buses, those supported by boards from many manufacturers (although in all cases except the IEEE 896 bus, which does not yet exist, they have originated as proprietary buses from a single manufacturer).

Multibus.   The Multibus originated at Intel, and is mainly oriented toward the 8080 and 8086 CPU's, but all major 8- and 16-bit CPU's are available on it. It supports both 8- and 16-bit data paths, and up to 20 bits of address. The card is 6.75 in. by 12 in., with two connectors, one for the memory bus and the other for I/O and expansion. An additional 4 bits of address can be carried on the expansion connector.

The Multibus is supported with the largest selection of I/O and other boards of any bus at the moment, and is an excellent choice.

STD Bus.   The STD Bus originated at Pro-Log, and is mainly an 8-bit bus. It uses a small (4.5 in. by 6.5 in.) card and a single 55-pin connector. The small form factor makes it good for small systems with specialized I/O—the card will just hold an LSI I/O chip and its associated support. This means that each board performs a single function, and a system needs to contain only those functions it uses. The price, of course, is the overhead—many boards, connectors, and bus interfaces. The STD bus is an excellent choice for small real-time systems.

S100 Bus.   The S100 bus originated at MITS, and was the bus of the very first hobbyist-oriented microcomputer. It was not originally designed as a general-purpose bus, but so many boards have been designed for it that most of its reliability and compatibility problems have perforce been solved, and it is one of the best-supported buses in terms of available hardware. Unfortunately there are *still* some compatibility problems: some manufacturers, especially the small ones, have not followed the standard exactly. The S100 bus should be considered only for small, one-of-a-kind systems.

Eurocard Buses.   A few newer buses are worth watching. In particular, boards are becoming available in the European standard Eurocard formats. These are smaller than Multibus boards, but have a very reliable two-piece connector instead of the card-edge connectors of the buses mentioned above. (The connectors are usually the least reliable parts of a system; it is not uncommon to fix intermittent problems by pulling all the boards in the system, cleaning their contacts with a rubber eraser, and plugging them in again.) Motorola and others have devised the VME bus, derived from Motorola's Versa-Bus, and a Eurocard variant of the STD bus is also available. The IEEE P896 committee is producing a specification for a high-performance "Futurebus" which will also use Eurocard formats. Intel and a large number of manufacturers are working on a "Multibus II" which is likely to be very popular.

Eurocard buses are becoming more popular as people discover the advantages of their two-piece connectors, (and the size of the European market!) and we can expect many more products to become available on them soon.

Parallel I/O Interconnections

Moving up the scale from boards to systems, we find some standardized interfaces for connecting computers with I/O devices. Most are supported not only with computers and peripheral devices that use them, but with OEM boards and even chips that implement the interface.

I/O interfaces can use either serial (one bit at a time) or parallel data transmission; we will consider the parallel interfaces first.

IEEE 488 Bus.   The most common parallel I/O bus (not counting minicomputer and mainframe I/O buses) is the IEEE 488 bus, which was designed by Hewlett-Packard to connect smart laboratory instruments into complex measurement systems. This is a 16-line bus with 8 address/data lines and 8 handshake and control lines. This bus is also used by some computer manufacturers to communicate with intelligent peripherals—this feature has made Commodore's PET personal computer very popular in laboratories. Chips are available which implement this interface.

SCSI Bus.   The Small Computer System Interface (SCSI), based on the Shugart Associates System Interface (SASI), was originally developed as an interface for hard disk drives, and is now being standardized by ANSI as a generalized interface for intelligent, high-bandwidth peripherals. It interconnects up to eight host computers and peripherals at rates of up to 1.5 Mbytes per second. Chips are becoming available to support this interface.

Centronics Printer Interface.   One common one-way interface deserves mention: the Centronics printer interface. This is now used for a wide variety of printers and other parallel output devices (including voice synthesizers and plotters). The Centronics interface is simple, and can be implemented with any parallel I/O chip.

Serial I/O Interconnections

For transmission of data over long distances, the cost of wires and the interface circuitry required to drive them starts to become significant, and serial transmission becomes attractive. Serial transmission is also *necessary* for transmission via the telephone network, radio, and other media. Now that serial interface chips have become common and cheap, parallel interfaces have no price advantages even for short distances—the latter's advantage lies solely in bandwidth.

Terminal Interfaces. A large family of serial interfaces has developed out of the use of serial teletypewriters (originally developed for telegraphy) as computer terminals. Since many computer systems have terminals (including almost all general-purpose microcomputer systems), computer-terminal interfaces have become very widespread, and are now used for computer-computer communication and for communication with an immense variety of peripherals.

RS-232C. The most widely-used standard for serial data transmission is the RS-232C standard, which uses a voltage of 5 to 12 volts to indicate a zero, and −5 to −12 for a one. The thresholds for the receiver are 3 and −3 volts, giving reasonable noise margins. RS-232C is usable for cable lengths up to 50 feet, and speeds up to 20 Kbits/second, and is often pushed beyond these limits (with lower but sometimes acceptable reliability).

The standard also specifies a connector (the ubiquitous 25-pin "D" connector) and pinouts for the data signals, and a set of control signals which are variously implemented, abused, or ignored. An RS-232C serial link is often the only way of getting information from one computer to another—it is the only interface most computers have in common. The RS-232C signals and pin numbers are shown in Table 2.2.

RS-232C is intended to link a computer or terminal (Data Terminal Equipment or DTE) to a modem (Data Communication Equipment or DCE). The RS-232C connectors on computers are often configured as if they were modems, to allow terminals to connect to them directly. This is non-standard, but very common. A cable or other connection that links two DTE's or DCE's (by crossing the Transmit and Receive signals and crossing or feeding back the various pairs of modem control signals) is called a *null modem*.

Table 2.2. RS-232C Signals and Connector Pinouts

PIN	SIGNAL	DCE-DCE	FUNCTION
1	PG	—	Protective Ground
2	TD	←	Transmitted Data
3	RD	→	Received Data
4	RTS	←	Request To Send
5	CTS	→	Clear To Send
6	DSR	→	Data Set Ready
7	SG	—	Signal Ground
8	DCD	→	Data Carrier Detect
9			
10			
11			
12	SDCD	→	Secondary DCD
13	SCTS	→	Secondary CTS
14	STD	←	Secondary TD
15	TC	→	Transmitter Clock
16	SRD	→	Secondary RD
17	RC	→	Receiver Clock
18			
19	SRTS	←	Secondary RTS
20	DTR	←	Data Terminal Ready
21	SQ	→	Signal Quality Detect
22	RI	→	Ring Indicator
23			
24			
25			

RS-423 and RS-422.   Recently, two new standards have been proposed to alleviate some of the limitations of RS-232C. These are RS-423, which uses voltages of ±5, and RS-422, which uses two differentially-driven wires and 5-volt signals. The differential scheme has much better noise immunity than a single-ended signal, because only the *difference* in voltage between the two wires matters—a noise signal appearing equally on both (the most common case) is canceled out. Despite their advantages, RS-422 and RS-423 are going to be slow to gain acceptance, because of the extreme popularity of RS-232C.

Current Loops.   Another way of dealing with noise is to use a so-called *current loop*. In this scheme, a current (the most common value being 20 milliamps, although 60 mA is also used) is switched on and off in a wire. The voltage applied is whatever it takes to produce the required current, so the resistance of the wire is compensated for. The old Teletype terminals used this scheme, and many newer ones have followed suit, providing current loops as an alternative to RS-232C. This is becoming less common.

Current loops are also used to send analog values in industrial situations. Usually values of 4-20 mA are used. This scheme has the added advantage that, since current is always flowing through the circuit, the sensor can take its power from the signaling loop.

Modems. Finally, for transmission over longer distances, an AC signal is required. An interface between a digital system and an analog, AC transmission medium is called a *modem*, for "modulator-demodulator." The most common modulation systems are those used over telephone lines. The restricted bandwidth of the telephone system (about 3 KHz) limits its use to low- speed transmissions, with 300 and 1200 bits/second being the most common. (Higher speeds are possible over leased lines, but the modems required are quite expensive.)

For higher bandwidths, comparatively inexpensive cable television technology is being used, employing digital signals to modulate carrier frequencies in the commercial television broadcast band. These are called *broadband* systems, in contrast to *baseband* systems in which the digital signal is put on the cable directly.

Other Media. With the recent advent of local networks linked by coaxial cable, communication bandwidths have increased to about 10 Mbits/second. The Ethernet standard, developed by Xerox and now being standardized by the IEEE (as part of the IEEE-802 standard) in a slightly different but largely compatible form, is the most popular, and chips are now available which implement it.

Coaxial cables can be driven either in the baseband or broadband modes. Broadband transmission is better for long distances, and gives greater bandwidth in any case, but is more expensive. Ethernet is a baseband scheme.

Optical Fibers. Optical fibers are another new and sometimes useful transmission medium. Their main advantage is noise immunity—a glass fiber is completely immune to electrical interference. Fibers also have good bandwidth (limited mainly by the transmitters and receivers). Expect the price of fiber optics to drop as this medium becomes more common.

Wireless Transmission. Signals can also be broadcast or beamed, using either radio or light. (And sometimes ultrasonic sound, which tends to be much less reliable due to reflections.) Consider radio or light-beams when wires are inconvenient. Infra-red broadcasting is useful in a confined space such as a single room: a single LED, or a cluster of them, can transmit to an infra-red photosensor anywhere in the room. Because of reflections from the walls, the LED and the sensor do not have to be pointed directly at each other. Interference is minimal, since there are few sources of near infra-red in the normal environment.

Infra-red broadcasting is commonly found in TV remote-control units, and is starting to find its way into the business and industrial environments as well. It is replacing ultrasonics in these applications because of its greater reliability and lower cost.

Carrier Current.   Another "wireless" method is to put a high-frequency signal on a building's main AC power lines. This is not practical in an industrial environment, but entirely possible in a home. BSR makes a line of appliance- and light-control modules that use a 40 KHz signal on the house wiring, and there are several interfaces available for home computers.

Philips and other companies are working on proposals for standardizing household process-control signaling; we can soon expect to find inexpensive interface chips for these applications.

Serial Data Transmission

Asynchronous Transmission.   The most common way of transmitting serial data is asynchronous. The line is normally idle, in the "mark" (1) state. Each character (Fig. 2.17) is preceded by a "start" bit (a "space," or zero), followed by the actual data bits, usually with the low-order bit first. The character is followed by one or more "stop" bits ("mark" again), to return the line to an idle state so that the next character's start bit can be recognized. Since an eight-bit character takes at least ten bit-times by this method, you can see that its advantage is not in speed.

The advantage of asynchronous transmission is, of course, that characters can be sent at random intervals. A secondary advantage is that if a bit is scrambled due to noise, only the character that contains the scrambled bit is affected. Finally, since the start of each character is explicitly marked, small differences in clock speed between transmitter and receiver can be compensated for.

Synchronous Transmission.   It is also possible to send characters synchronously, one after another, without intervening start or stop bits. (This has a significant effect on performance: with 8-bit data the two extra bits take up 20% of the bandwidth.) To do this, it is necessary for sender and receiver to agree on when a character starts, and on exactly when each bit starts. Either a bit clock has to be sent along with the data, or a modulation method has to

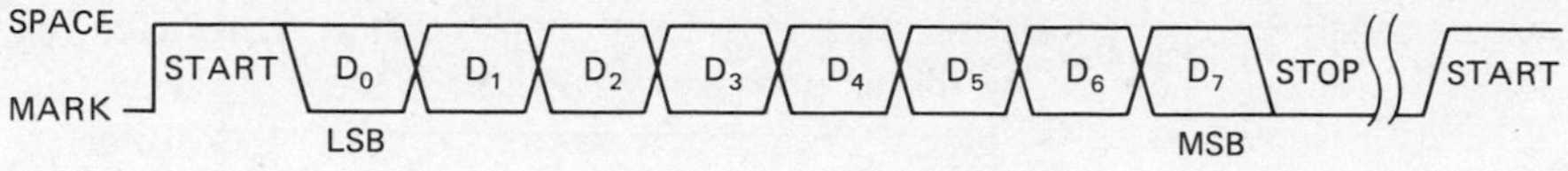

SPACE

MARK

START D_0 D_1 D_2 D_3 D_4 D_5 D_6 D_7 STOP START

LSB

MSB

Figure 2.17. Serial character frame.

be used that allows the clock to be separated out. A number of such modulation techniques exist, including Frequency Modulation (FM), "Modified FM," and Manchester encoding. The simplest modulation technique, in which a high level represents a one and a low level represents a zero, is called Non-Return to Zero (NRZ). We will not discuss them here beyond presenting their waveforms for comparison (Fig. 2.18).

Some modulation techniques define a zero as a level transition, and a one as the lack of a transition, at a given time. In order to guarantee a minimum density of transitions (for example, to allow clock-extraction circuitry to work), an extra zero bit is inserted after a string of five ones. Most synchronous serial interface chips are capable of doing the required insertion and extraction.

Because it is difficult (if not impossible) to maintain complete synchronization forever (and because you have to *start* somehow), data are usually sent in blocks, preceded by a bit pattern that is used by the receiver to synchronize its clock. Data blocks are usually preceded by a header containing housekeeping information such as block numbers, and followed by a checksum or CRC

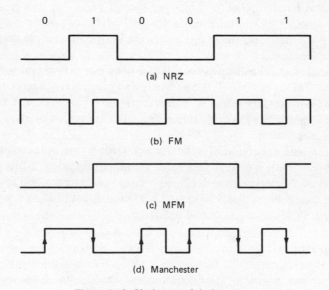

Figure 2.18. Various modulation types.

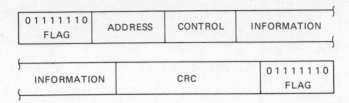

Figure 2.19. SDLC data format.

(cyclic redundancy check) word. CRC can be used for correcting, as well as detecting, errors, although the computation required to do this is considerable. At least one chip (the AMD/Zilog 8065 Block Error Processor) exists for doing these computations.

Several synchronous data formats are in use. The SDLC (Synchronous Data Link Control) standard (Fig. 2.19) is one, and being a standard, most recent serial interface chips that handle synchronous transmission support it in all its glory. The SDLC packet includes a destination address and a checksum, and is transmitted with zero insertion.

Transmission Speed.   The problem with serial interfaces is simply that sending information one bit at a time takes longer than sending it all at once. Unless DMA is used, though, this is not much of a problem—serial I/O chips run at up to several hundred thousand bits per second. (And the new generation of network interface chips run even faster—10 MHz, or over a megabyte per second.) With interrupts, most processors are in trouble at more than 40 Kbits (5 Kbytes) per second.

The speed of serial transmission is the *data rate* or *bit rate* measured in bits per second. The term "baud" is commonly and incorrectly used instead of bits per second—it actually refers to *flux transitions* (zero-crossings) per second, and there are several ways of getting a single flux transition to carry more than one bit of information.

With the lone exception of 110 bits per second (the speed of a Teletype model 33 terminal), standard data rates are all multiples of 75 bits per second (the speed of a Teletype model 15). The most common are 300 and 1200 for telephone connections, and 9600 and 19,200 for direct links. Very few terminals handle 38,400 bits per second or higher.

REFERENCES

1. Bell, C. G. and Newell, A. *Computer Structures: Readings and Examples*. New York: McGraw-Hill, 1971.

3
Software for Real-Time Systems

This chapter does for software what the preceding chapter did for hardware; it provides an introduction for the uninitiated, and will give the more experienced programmer some insight into the author's prejudices.

It is difficult to overstress the importance of software. Without software a computer is a few pieces of exceptionally pure silicon embedded in a heap of metal and plastic. Power goes in, heat comes out, and nothing happens. With software, the computer becomes whatever the programmer tells it to be.

The software field divides naturally into three parts: the user's (your) application programs, the languages and other tools used to write them, and the operating systems and other programs that make up the environment in which they run.

LANGUAGES

Probably the most obvious tool used in the development of an application program is the language (or languages) it is written in. It is so obvious that it is sometimes overlooked, but nothing more directly affects the program's structure, nor its readability and modifiability. Choice of language also strongly affects a programmer's productivity. Its effect on the resulting program's performance, though often cited (mainly as an excuse for using a "more efficient" language), is often less important.

In programming languages, as in most things, there is a hierarchy (Fig. 3.1). In this case, languages on the "bottom" of the hierarchy are closest to the machine they run on; languages toward the "top" are farther from the machine and contain constructs that are closer (one hopes!) to the constructs one would choose in describing the actual application.

Machine Language

There is actually a company which still (1984) insists that "engineers" should treat microcomputers as "just another component," and that the way to do this is to write programs in hexadecimal, with absolute addresses. It is also possible to build computers by soldering together discrete transistors and resistors, just

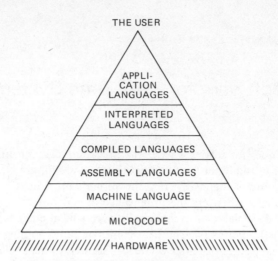

Figure 3.1. The language pyramid.

as it is possible to balance one's checkbook using Roman numerals. Most of us have better things to do with our time.

Machine language, the actual bit patterns that the computer understands, is in fact one of those things which is is usually better not to know. Regrettably, in debugging a piece of hardware, you may find yourself looking at some bits on a logic analyzer or oscilloscope, and having to figure out which instruction they represent. You may even find yourself having to hand-assemble an instruction or two (my limit, given even a bad assembler, is about three instructions). This is usually not a skill worth getting good at (if you *can* do it, people may expect you to).

Assembly Language

Since the earliest days of digital computers, people have made use of the machine's great capacity for drudgery to make programming easier by converting alphabetic names for instructions (*mnemonics*) into binary operation codes, converting numbers from decimal, hexadecimal, or octal into binary, and assigning alphabetic *labels* to addresses in the program. The program that does all this is called an *assembler*.

Assembly language has for years been the workhorse of the real-time field. Since it is mapped very directly into machine language, it lets the programmer make use of every trick that the machine allows. This is often a bad thing— tricky code is difficult to understand, fix, or modify. On the other hand, when time or space is at a premium in the target machine, and when the *programmer's* time is not, it's time to haul out the assembler and get tricky.

Assemblers have some hidden merits. Most good assemblers have a conditional assembly feature, and a macro facility. These are often misunderstood, and are becoming hard to find. They are almost never present in compilers, which is a pity (C is a notable exception). Assemblers are also unequaled for building tables and other data structures, especially those with variable-length entries.

Conditional Assembly.   Conditional assembly is the ability of an assembler to perform tests *at assembly time*, to determine whether or not a block of code is going to be assembled or ignored.

Conditional assembly is good for two things. First, it lets you put debugging and testing constructs into a program, and then make them "go away" for the final production version. Second, and most important, it lets you keep several versions of a program, to run in slightly different environments, together in the same place by conditionally assembling the differences.

Macros.   A *macro* (from the archaic "macro-instruction") is the assembly-time version of a subroutine: a named block of instructions that is assembled whenever its name is used as an opcode. Macros, like subroutines, may have parameters; the parameters are usually substituted into the body of the macro as strings. (A very few assemblers substitute the *values* of the parameters into the macro body.)

The "traditional" use of macros is to provide a more efficient form of subroutine, by expanding the body of the routine "in-line." This is indeed useful, especially when the subroutine is only a few instructions, so that it takes less time to execute than it does to call and return! But there is another important use of macros which is often forgotten (even by implementors, who thereby make it difficult for those of us who remember). This is the use of macros to define a new programming language.

This form of macro-processing can be taken to two extremes. In one, the target machine's operations are buried completely, and macros are provided for a complete set of application-oriented operations. This is often a quick and easy way of implementing a language, especially when compiler-compilers and other such tools are unavailable. The resulting language tends to be slightly clumsy, with odd constructs and funny restrictions, but it works.

In the other extreme form, macros are used to implement the opcodes of the target machine's assembly language, rather than having them built into the assembler. This is called a "meta-assembler." Meta-assemblers seem to have died out, but the technique is still useful: sometimes you have an assembler for machine A, and you need to write a short program for machine B (whose manufacturer wants $20,000 for a developmental system). Write some macros. The macro processor's syntax and name conflicts with existing (machine A) opcodes will force some compromises, but once again it's quick and relatively painless.

Between the two extremes, macros are most useful for building complex tables and other data structures in a comprehensible way. This is where an assembler can outshine most compilers, especially, as noted, when the tables have variable-length entries. (Most compilers have a hard time with structures containing variable-length parts, such as strings of characters.)

When To Use An Assembler: When execution time is more important than programmer time; for small projects; in the inner loops and other bottlenecks of big programs (a program spends 90% of its time in 10% of its code); for building tables; when a compiler isn't available; for quickly implementing a special-purpose language using macros.

When Not To Use An Assembler: For small projects when a compiler is available; for very big projects (it's *not worth it*); when programmer productivity is important.

It often pays to write a program twice: once using a high-level language as a prototype, then again in assembler if (and *only* if) extra performance or smaller size is needed. (To give a hardware analogy, build a breadboard before laying out the PC board.)

Compilers

The next step in the language progression is the compiler, a program that takes as its input a program written in a "high-level language" and converts it into machine language (or sometimes into assembly language). The languages implemented using compilers are usually "algebraic" in notation:

$$\text{LOAD} \quad \text{register, B}$$
$$\text{ADD} \quad \text{register, C}$$
$$\text{STORE} \quad \text{register, A}$$

vs.

$$A = B + C$$

Although the difference between an assembler and a compiler is usually obvious at a glance, it is sometimes difficult to define. This leads to some hybrid languages which often combine the worst features of both types, sometimes going under the title of "structured assemblers." My own version of the difference is this: a compiler is a language for *specifying algorithms* (operations to be performed on data) and data structures. An assembler is a language for *initializing data structures*. The fact that some of those data structures happen to be instructions which, when interpreted by a computer, perform a computation is really incidental. Thus assemblers are still useful for initializing complicated tables.

Regrettably, most compilers for microprocessors are not very good. The code they produce is bulky and slow, the compilers themselves are bulky and slow, and the languages they implement are usually subsets of the "big machine" languages. Most single-chip microcomputers will never have compilers. This situation will improve, but gradually.

Fortran.   The first compiler-based language to gain any real popularity was Fortran (which stood for *For*mula *Tran*slation). One of the goals for the Fortran project was to produce code that was better than the best hand-optimized assembly language. The project was successful, and Fortran is still extremely popular (and is still one of the few languages whose compilers produce good code). On the other hand, despite attempts to modernize it, Fortran is still a difficult language in which to write good (well-structured) programs. Although long the mainstay of real-time work on minicomputers, it is fortunately rather rare on microprocessors.

Algol.   Algol was developed in the late 1950's as an "International Algorithmic Language;" the best-known version is that published in 1960 (Algol 60). Its document, "Report on the Algorithmic Language Algol 60,"[1] is a small gem of clarity and elegance—it should be required reading for anyone attempting to write a programming language manual.

Algol is much more common in Europe than in the U.S., and is virtually unknown on microprocessors. It is important mainly because of its derivatives, especially Pascal.

Pascal.   Pascal[2] is a derivative of Algol 60; it was originally developed by Niklaus Wirth as a teaching language, that is, one which embodied the principles of "structured programming." Due to the proselytizing efforts of professors and students familiar with it, it has been put forward as a good language in which to write real applications. Unfortunately, it remains best suited for short, student programs.

Pascal's main weakness is also its strength: strict type-checking. Every variable has a "type"—for example, you can declare a variable to be of type "Day," and refer to its values as "Sunday," "Monday," . . . "Saturday." Type-checking is usually good for you: it reduces errors, and makes things run more efficiently—if you know something is of type "Day," you *know* that its values are between 1 and 7. On the other hand, it can get in the way: the size of an array is part of its type, so you can't write a program to, say, invert a matrix of any dimension. Since character strings (e.g. messages) are variable-length arrays, this means that Pascal is very bad at handling them.

Many "real" implementations of Pascal extend the language by various means to get around some of the problems of type-checking. Unfortunately, they all do it differently.

Most microcomputer implementations of Pascal leave out some of the more complex features, and add extensions (especially character strings and disk-file I/O) which make it more useful as a "real" programming language. The most common version is UCSD Pascal, originally developed at the University of California at San Diego by Ken Bowles and his students. It is not well-suited for real-time applications because rather than compiling into machine language, it compiles into an intermediate form (P-code) which is then interpreted. This gives very compact programs, and makes the system very portable (since only the small interpreter has to be rewritten for different machines). But it's not fast.

A version of Pascal called "Concurrent Pascal" also exists: it is Pascal augmented with some operating system constructs, including tasks, semaphores, and messages. It is described in Brinch-Hansen's book *Operating System Principles* [3], which also contains examples in the language.

Modula-2. Modula-2 [4] is Pascal inventor Wirth's most recent language design: it fixes most of the problems in Pascal. It permits separate compilation of modules, variable-length arrays and character strings, and type-conversions. It also allows such low-level operations as direct access to memory, pointer arithmetic, and bit manipulation.

Modula-2, like C, is a good language for real-time projects. It has many of the advantages of both C and Pascal, and few of the disadvantages. It is hampered at the moment by the scarcity of compilers for it, and by the overwhelming popularity of C. Look for its popularity to increase in the future.

PL/I. PL/I was IBM's "new programming language"—intended to replace Fortran, Cobol (a business-oriented language which we will not consider here), and Algol by combining the best features of each. The result, of course, was a monster (a camel has been defined as a horse designed by a committee). Still, PL/I has its good points, and there are microprocessor implementations of various subsets of it. Of these the most common is PL/M, available on the Intel 8080.

C.   Probably the most popular language at present (1984) for microprocessors in real-time applications is C[5]. C was developed at Bell Labs, and represents a good compromise between elegance and practicality. It contains a large number of strange and useful constructs, which tend to make programs hard to read, but efficient. Its designer, Dennis Ritchie, took the approach that it was too hard to build a good optimizer, so he included enough low-level constructs in the language to allow the sophisticated programmer to optimize as required.

C is almost unique among the high-level compiler languages in that it does not (usually) come between the programmer and the machine; if something can be done in assembly language, there is usually a way to express it in C. For example, in C you can declare variables that are to be kept in machine registers if possible.

C also has data structures and data types, but unlike Pascal its type-checking is not very strict (some call it promiscuous). C allows pointers to anything (including code, in the form of procedures), arithmetic on pointers, variable-length structures and procedures with variable numbers of arguments. All of these are considered "dangerous" or "ill-structured," and are not allowed in most languages (such as Pascal).

As a result of weak type-checking, mistakes that would be caught by the compiler in Pascal pass unnoticed in C. It is also rather easy to make assumptions about the way data are represented on a particular machine, and to write programs that take advantage of it. The solution to both of these problems is another program, called *lint*, which performs stricter type-checking than the C compiler, and checks for certain potential portability problems. C is *much* harder to use if *lint* is not available.

Ada.   The rising new contender in the language field is Ada[6], the product of an intensive standardization effort by the U.S. Department of Defense. It is designed for use in embedded, real-time applications. Unfortunately, it seems to be less like C and more like PL/I—large, complex, and bristling with features. Still, it should be a good language in which to write real-time programs if compilers become readily available.

Ada allows many of the unusual constructs and operations that C does, but because of its strict type-checking you usually have to go through contortions to do them.

When to Use A Compiler: For big projects; for small projects, especially when space and time are not critical; when you need results quickly; whenever you can. Use C, Modula-2 or Ada if possible.

When Not to Use A Compiler: When you need the ultimate in program compactness or performance; in inner loops—if something is going to be executed ten million times it may be worth optimizing, but remember that saving one instruction ten million times only saves you something on the order of ten seconds. Always ask yourself: is it worth the effort?

Interpreters

An interpreter is a program that takes some language which is not the native language of the machine it is running on, and "interprets" it—examines, decodes, and executes each instruction in turn. Unlike a compiler, which produces a machine-language translation of its input program, an interpreter essentially simulates a machine which directly executes the program.

Since each instruction of the input program may be examined many times (if it is in a loop or subroutine), interpretation tends to be slow. It is at its best for program development and testing; if a program is only going to be partly executed before a bug shows up, the extra time it takes to execute is compensated by the time saved in not compiling the rest of it. More important, a good interpreter will have sophisticated source-level debugging facilities: tracing, single- stepping, and breakpoints.

Another advantage of interpreters is size—the source form of the program being interpreted is often smaller than a compiled version of the same program would be. The advantage is even greater if the interpreter uses a compact intermediate form instead of raw source text.

Basic. Unfortunately, the most common language on microcomputers is a teaching language called Basic (for *B*eginners' *A*ll-Purpose *S*imple *I*nstruction *C*ode), originally developed at Dartmouth (where students had the opportunity to move on to Algol for serious programming). Basic is essentially Fortran, but with two-character variable names (instead of Fortran's six), and line numbers on every statement. Its main virtue is that it is very easy to implement. Although a teaching language, it tends to teach bad habits, as it is very difficult to write well-structured programs in Basic.

Most microcomputer Basics are crude, slow, and suitable mainly for "toy" applications.

Tiny Basic. It is difficult to imagine a language simpler than Basic, but there is one: "Tiny" Basic. The Tiny Basic family was started in response to the *total* lack of software and almost total lack of memory on the earliest hobby microcomputer kits. Tiny Basic has 26 single-character variables, 16-bit numbers, and very little else, but it can be implemented in 2K bytes of code.

Interestingly, this is usually done by writing the actual Basic interpreter in an "intermediate language," optimized for writing Basic interpreters; this intermediate language is then interpreted. Such two-level interpretation makes Tiny Basics *very* slow.

The thing that saves Tiny Basic from a well-deserved obscurity is the fact that several single-chip microcomputers (the National IMS8073 and Zilog Z8071) come with Tiny Basic interpreters on their on-chip ROM's. These interpreters seem to be quite suitable for the quick development of simple controller-type applications, provided speed isn't a requirement.

Although Tiny Basics lack many features of larger Basic languages, they have enough to get by, and are usually *better* equipped for interfacing to special-purpose hardware and machine-language software. For example, Zilog's Z8071 version has single-character constructs for referring to bytes (@ address) and words (^address) in memory, and can call machine language routines either as subroutines (**GO** address statement) or as functions that return a value (**USR**(address, arg1, arg2)).

Forth.   Forth is an oddity. Although an interpreter, it tends to run rather efficiently. It is not a particularly "high-level" language—it is more like an assembler (but for a "stack-oriented" machine). It is, however, a highly interactive interpreter. Programs written in Forth are both compact and relatively fast, making it a plausible candidate for real-time applications.

Forth's reverse Polish (postfix) notation, due to its stack, is a little hard to get used to, and it does require programming at a rather low level, at least at first. Applications are built up as collections of "words" (subroutines), which eventually form an application-specific language. It's much like using a macro assembler.

Forth is very easy to implement on microprocessors; single-chip microcomputers with built-in Forth interpreters, and single-board microcomputers with Forth in on-board ROM's, are starting to make their appearance. They are especially good for "one-shot" controller applications.

Special-Purpose Interpreters.   Writing an interpreter is easy, and is sometimes the best way to solve a problem. Often a program is easiest to write in a special-purpose language, which can then be implemented as a sequence of subroutine calls, or with an interpreter. As an example, consider a process control language whose commands are **TEST**(input), **DELAY**(time), and **SET**(output). You can do a lot with that.

Interpreters also make good user command interfaces, especially if you want provide your user with programming capability. This can be important in, say, a smart instrument.

Other Interpreted Languages. I can't resist, at this point, mentioning four languages that are not presently suitable for real-time applications, but which show the advantages of interpreters as programming systems. These are APL, LISP, Logo, and Smalltalk. Each combines an odd but powerful and elegant notation with a highly interactive programming environment.

APL is a mathematical language with special array-handling operations. It is very rare on microcomputers, and will probably never be suitable for real-time applications.

LISP[7] is a symbol-manipulation language. It is one of the very few programming languages in which one is not restricted to numbers—words and lists of words can be manipulated. LISP has a built-in symbol table, and LISP programs are simply lists of words (and lists of lists), which make it an ideal language for writing compilers and interpreters for special-purpose languages. It is becoming available on microcomputers, but needs lots of memory for real applications.

Logo is LISP with a less arcane syntax, designed as a teaching language for young children. The significant thing about Logo is that children write real-time applications in it! Logo is used for music, graphics with real-time animation, and for controlling a robot "turtle."

Smalltalk[8] is something else. It, too, was designed as a teaching language. Moreover, its basic concept is simulation. It is still in the experimental stage, but has great potential. Its programming environment is highly display-oriented, with multiple, partially overlapping windows. It is probably the best user interface to be developed so far; and is already being copied. Smalltalk is an *object-oriented* language, a concept which we will meet again in Chapter 4.

When to Use an Interpreter: When code compactness is paramount; when you or your user needs interactive programming capability; for ultimate speed in program development (you can re-write using a compiler later, if you must).

When Not to Use an Interpreter: When execution speed is important (this leaves out most of the real-time field).

Special-Purpose Languages

The use of special-purpose interpreters as programming tools has already been mentioned. A few "application-oriented" programming languages are available, usually on process-control computers. Many of them use relay ladder-network notation, with which process control engineers are already familiar. A few use logic gate notation, trying to make a computer simulate a simple logic circuit.

This sort of thing is primarily aimed at process- control engineers, not programmers, and you are unlikely to be using it. However, it is worth keeping in mind that, if the *users* of your system are going to be doing anything complicated with it, they should be giving commands in a language with which they are familiar. They will probably want to write simple programs, too, with tests, loops, and variables. (This is not a consideration for a blender or washing machine, but I have seen some extremely complicated microwave ovens, not to mention digital oscilloscopes with floppy disk drives. Robot languages are already available, with more under development.)

When to Use a Special-Purpose Language: When you can find one that does your (or your customer's) job (you are more likely to be implementing a special-purpose language than using one).

When Not to Use a Special-Purpose Language: Most of the time.

OTHER SOFTWARE TOOLS: UTILITIES

Just as you can't build computers, cars, houses, or anything else without proper tools, you need tools to build software, too. The tool that most strongly influences the shape and texture of your software product is the language you write it in, but there are other important tools as well. These tools, of course, are made of software themselves.

A good reference on software tools, such as the following utilities, is the book of that name by Kernighan and Plauger[9], which includes useable examples of all the programs it describes.

Editors

The program you will spend most of your time interacting with is the *text editor*—the program you use to create and modify the files containing your own programs and documentation. A good text editor is *important*—it can make editing fun, fast, and accurate. A bad editor will make your life miserable. Most microcomputer text editors are rather bad.

A good text editor is display-oriented: the CRT display shows a *cursor* that marks your place in the file, and a screenfull of text around that place. You can move the cursor up, down, and across the screen, and when you insert or delete text, the changes show immediately on the screen. The philosophy of the display-oriented editor is "what you see is what you get;" any change you make in the file is immediately reflected on the screen. Some display editors are better than others, but *all* are better than the alternative, the line-oriented editor, in which you issue commands "blind," and only see the results if you give a separate command to print some text.

With most display editors it is possible to "compose" at the keyboard: translating your thoughts directly into disk files. With a line editor, you usually have to write things down in longhand first. This is also true when making changes; with a display editor you can often avoid making listings (this may have disadvantages, as anyone who has lost a file whose only copy was on disk will tell you).

The best display editors run on machines with memory-mapped displays for fast updating, and keyboards with well-designed function keys that match the functions provided by the editor. There are comparatively few of these. Most display editors are designed to run with any of several different terminals; this restricts them to the set of features that those terminals will support. Also, since all communication with the terminal is via a serial line, updating the screen takes a long time. It is not uncommon for such an editor to have trouble keeping up with a fast typist. This is annoying.

There is no excuse for not having a display editor—personal computers are cheap. If you don't have access to a machine with a display editor, spend a thousand dollars of your own money and buy one. It's worth it.

Word-Processing Software

Not everything you write is a program; even if somebody else writes your manuals for you, you will have to write *something* about your system—maintenance documents (how it works and where the pieces are), memos, proposals, notes to your technical writer, and so on. A good text editor handles all of this.

If you have to prepare your own manuals, there are two other kinds of program in the "word-processing" field you should know about: text formatters and spelling correctors. Text formatters make your document pretty: clean up the margins, number the pages and sections, put in underlining, even (sometimes) prepare a table of contents and index. A text editor closely integrated with a formatter is often called a *word processor*.

Spelling correctors have an obvious and useful function, and are becoming more common. Some are integrated with word processors, for example Spell-Star with WordStar (the most popular microcomputer word processor).

Linkers, Relocators, and Loaders

Large programs are best broken down into "modules:" separate parts that can be edited, assembled or compiled, and (if you are careful) debugged separately. Getting them together again is the job of a program called a *linker*. It is the linker's job to connect *external references* to symbols which are defined in other modules.

If the linker is "incremental," you can take a collection of modules that have already been linked together, and add some more modules to the collection. This lets you build big modules out of smaller ones.

Once the pieces are put together, a program called a *relocator* (often part of the linker) assigns a location in memory to each module, and then a *loader* gets it into memory. When the program is supposed to run on a target system other than the one being used for development, you sometimes find a program called an "imager" that prepares an image of the target system's memory in a form suitable for a PROM programmer. Such an imager is essentially another form of loader.

An effort is under way in the IEEE to develop a standard format for object modules called MUFOM (Microprocessor Universal Format for Object Modules, standard P695[10]). This can be expected to aid in portability.

(Some terminology: the input to a language processor such as an assembler or compiler is a *source file* or *source module*; the output of a language processor and the input to a linker is an *object file* or *object module*, and the output of a relocator and the input to a loader is a *load module* or *memory image*.)

Debuggers

After you get your program written, you have to get it working. This is where a debugger comes in. In the beginning was the front panel, bristling with lights and switches. It was clumsy. But after all, even if your own program doesn't work, the computer (usually) does, so the solution is to have a program, a *debugger*, to help you get the bugs out of your program. Microcomputers have not had front panels since the days of the first hobbyist kits.

The minimal functions of a debugger are those of a front panel: to examine and modify the contents of memory. Most debuggers let you see data in both hexadecimal (or octal) and ASCII. Many also are able to display, and sometimes permit the entry of, machine instructions in mnemonic form (usually with absolute, numeric operands). Some, called *symbolic* debuggers, let you use the symbol table your assembler or compiler generates, and refer to locations by name. Symbolic debuggers are usually capable of assembling and disassembling instructions, so you get to see assembly-language code almost the way you wrote it.

A very few, called *source-language* debuggers, show you your program in the form you gave it to the compiler. Interpreted languages possess this property inherently, which is what makes them so nice to work with. This can sometimes be done by using a compiler option that produces a file which associates addresses in the object program with lines in the source.

Other functions of debuggers include the setting of *breakpoints*, which stop your program at a given location and transfer control to the debugger, and *single-stepping*, which lets you go through your program an instruction at a time to see what is happening. There is a problem here in real-time systems: once you hit a breakpoint or start single-stepping, your program is no longer running in real time! Sometimes it doesn't matter, but computer lore is full of tales of programs that work fine when you step through them, but not when run at full speed (and vice versa!). Later on (in Chapter 5), we will discuss some tricks you can use for debugging real-time programs.

There are also devices called "microprocessor analyzers," a form of logic analyzer, which include many of the features of debuggers. In addition, since they are independent of the computer your program is running on (they simply clip onto the CPU chip and watch what it is doing), they can function in the presence of hardware problems. Perhaps more important, they can store the last few hundred pieces of data to pass in and out of the CPU, and so provide many of the benefits of single-stepping while letting your program run at full speed. We will be seeing more of analyzers in Chapter 5, too.

Operating Systems and Utilities

The *operating system* is the program that lets you load and run your software tools, and also your own programs (this makes it a meta-tool). The operating system includes the drivers for the various I/O devices attached to your system, especially terminals and the disk, and the disk file system, which keeps track of *files*, or pieces of text or program, by name.

More broadly, the term "operating system" usually includes not only the command processor, program loader, and device drivers, but the utility programs as well. Operating systems have, in addition to language processors, text editors, and debuggers, a variety of programs for manipulating files. A minimal set of these includes programs to list a *directory* of file names, to change the name of a file, to copy a file, and to delete a file. (Files are usually created using either an editor, for text files, or a language processor, for binary files.)

Most microcomputer operating systems have a rather simple command interface: the first word of the command is looked up in the file-name directory, and if a program is found with that name, the program is run. This lets you create your own commands, which can be useful. A few systems, such as UCSD Pascal, are "menu oriented," which means that they put up a list of possible commands, and you type a letter to select one of them. If the command has options, it puts up its own menu for your selections. This is very nice for inexperienced users, but can be tedious for experienced users. You often find yourself typing commands to the "wrong" menu, sometimes with drastic effects.

There are two common operating systems on microcomputers and minicomputers which are used for developing software that will run on other machines: CP/M and Unix.

CP/M. CP/M is a "minimal" operating system, having little more than the utilities already described. There is not much more to be said about it, except that it is very common, and therefore there are many programs available that run under it, including assemblers, compilers, and text editors. The original CP/M runs on 8080 and Z80 systems; versions are also available for 8086, 68000, and Z8000 (but unfortunately most of the *application* programs were written in 8080 assembly-language, which also runs on Z80's, but is not portable to the other versions).

Unix. Unix was originally developed at Bell Labs to run on a PDP 11, and was common at universities (who could buy it for $200, instead of the $20,000 Bell charged commercial users). It is a timesharing and multitasking system; users can have several tasks going at once. It is also possible to "pipe" the output of one program into the input of another, and there are many utilities (most with odd names) for transforming files in useful ways. The command processor, called the "shell," is very sophisticated, and in fact can be used as a programming language for writing new commands.

Unix suffers somewhat from obscure command names, inconsistent syntax, and other obscurities. It is terrible for inexperienced users, but superb for experienced programmers (its use tends to be addictive). With new pricing from Bell (binary-only licenses for $150 for a single-user system), it is now competitive with CP/M, and likely to become *very* popular. Another factor in its attractiveness is the fact that it is entirely written in C, and so is highly portable. (CP/M is still more suitable than Unix for small systems; Unix requires a hard disk for its many utilities, and lots of memory, preferably with memory mapping, for its large kernel.)

MS-DOS. Another operating system which is becoming popular on 16-bit machines is Microsoft's MS-DOS. This operating system, similar to CP/M, was adapted by IBM (under the name PC-DOS) for its personal computer. Later versions of MS-DOS have many features of Unix, especially in the file system and the command language.

INSIDE OPERATING SYSTEMS

Operating systems are not just tools to help you get your programs written. Sometimes they can be components of the software running on your real-time product. This kind of thing is called a "real-time operating system," and may or may not be necessary. You probably don't need a real-time operating system in a washing machine. In a smart instrument with a floppy disk for data logging, you probably do.

In any case, it is important to understand the workings of operating systems, because even if you do not incorporate one ready-made into your product, you may end up implementing the parts of one that you need. Besides, in many ways an operating system is the quintessential real-time program: it manages resources, responds to events, and interacts with the real world, and does so in very general ways.

Resources and Objects

An operating system is fundamentally a resource allocator. Various tasks are contending for resources in the form of CPU time, memory, and I/O devices, and the operating system arbitrates among them.

Internally, an operating system has to manipulate several different kinds of so-called *objects*. Tasks are the most obvious of these; others include queues, lists, semaphores, messages, and I/O devices. An object can be defined as a combination of a data structure, and the operations that can be done on it (object-oriented design is considered more fully in Chapter 4).

Since this is a fairly new notion, most operating systems do not go out of their way to handle objects consistently or cleanly. Nevertheless it is useful to consider an operating system as providing the user (or application program) with an extended set of data-types and operations, in addition to those provided by the computer. When considered in this light, the operating system is said to be providing a *virtual machine*.

It is possible to take the virtual machine concept somewhat farther and have the operating system provide each task with what looks like a complete computer. This includes simulating interrupts and I/O instructions, and requiring each user task to run its own copy of an operating system! This is very nice for developing new operating systems, or for running different operating systems simultaneously on the same machine, but is not efficient, nor especially useful for real-time applications.

Multitasking

The primary function of a real-time operating system is multitasking: scheduling and switching the CPU among several tasks. As far as the programmer is concerned, a task is a simple program running on what appears to be a simple computer, all by itself. It is the operating system's job to maintain for each task a "snapshot" of the CPU state at the time that task was last run, so that it can be restored. This is variously called a "task descriptor block," "task control block," or even just a "task" (this apparent confusion of data structure with program is common in "object-oriented" languages, in which, as noted above, an "object" consists of both data and the programs that operate on it).

Synchronization

The whole point of multitasking is for tasks to wait until some "event" happens, at which point they "wake up," or run, and do something. The event may be something in the outside world, indicated by an interrupt, or something inside the computer, such as another task completing an operation.

Semaphores. The best-known method for dealing with such events is the *semaphore*, invented by Edgser Dijkstra. A semaphore consists of a counter which records events which have not yet been processed, and a queue of tasks waiting for events. (If the counter is greater than zero, the queue must be empty; if there are tasks in the queue, the counter must be zero.) The basic operations on semaphores are Wait (for an event) and Signal (an event). Dijkstra called these P and V respectively, which are mnemonics in Dutch, his native language.

When a task does a Wait, it adds itself to the queue if the counter is zero, otherwise it decrements the counter and proceeds. When a semaphore is signaled, if the queue is not empty the first task on it is resumed, otherwise the counter is incremented.

A variant of the Wait operation is sometimes seen in which a task can wait for a given number of signals, rather than just one. This is useful when the semaphore counts the number of identical resources available, such as blocks of memory.

Applications of Semaphores. Semaphores are used in two different ways: signaling, and mutual exclusion. In signaling, the semaphore represents events, timing pulses, characters entering or leaving a buffer, etc. In mutual exclusion (their original application), the semaphore serves as a kind of lock to prevent more than one task from accessing some shared resource (usually data). In this case the semaphore only takes on the values zero (a task is accessing the resource) and one (the resource is free). Such a semaphore is called a binary semaphore.

The resource is accessed within a section of code called a *critical section* (see Fig. 3.2). Each task does a Wait before entering its critical section, and a Signal after leaving it.

Busy-Wait. A simple variation on the Wait operation is to repeatedly test the semaphore's counter, rather than putting the current task on a queue and waiting. This is called *busy-wait* or *spin-wait*. In a multitasking system, of course, it is a very antisocial thing to do, since it ties up the processor while doing nothing. Busy-wait is useful, though, if you are communicating between a sin-

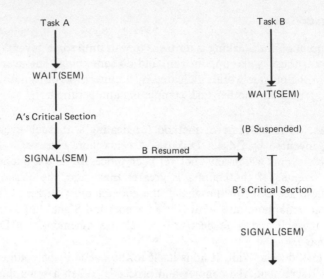

Figure 3.2. Using a semaphore for mutual exclusion.

gle task and an interrupt. It also finds use in the depths of multi-processor operating systems, where it is used to protect very small critical sections against interference by other processors.

Notice that in a single-task environment, mutual exclusion is done by turning interrupts off.

Event Queues.   Another kind of structure found in operating systems is the *event queue*, or *event*. It differs from a semaphore in that if any tasks are waiting for the event, they are all awakened at once, and if no tasks are waiting, the event is not recorded. An event queue thus consists only of a queue, without the semaphore's counter. Event queues are useless for mutual exclusion, but good for some kinds of signaling.

Monitors.   A newer construct for synchronization is the *monitor*, which is essentially a data structure containing a semaphore, and a set of procedures which operate on it. Each procedure is a critical section; it starts by waiting on the monitor's semaphore, and ends by signaling it. This ensures that only one task at a time can be operating on the data structure.

Several newer operating systems have been constructed with monitors as their basic construct. They are not well suited to multi-processor systems, as the monitor's data structure has to be shared. It is also rather easy to get deadlocks if access to monitors can be nested (in other words, if an operation on monitor A involves an operation on monitor B as well).

Messages. As we will see in the next section, messages can be used for synchronization as well as for sending data. Indeed, a semaphore can be regarded as a queue of messages without data, in which the mere arrival of a message is sufficient (not unlike the practice of placing a person-to-person phone call to yourself to let your family know that you have arrived safely).

Inter-Task Communication

Messages. Inter-task communication involves three things: some data, usually called a *message*; a *sender* task; and a *receiver* task. There is usually some additional machinery as well. A message usually has a *header*, including information such as the task sending it and how big the message is, and a *buffer* containing the actual data. The combination of header and buffer is sometimes called an *envelope*.

Messages are usually not sent directly to a task, but to something variously called a *mailbox*, *exchange*, *port*, *channel*, or (especially in networks) *socket*. This consists of a queue of messages waiting to be received, and a queue of tasks waiting for messages (as in a semaphore, at least one queue is empty, unless tasks can wait for a particular type of message).

Message-passing can be either synchronous, in which the sender waits for the message to be received (and usually for a reply to be generated), or asynchronous, in which the sender can proceed immediately after sending a message. Synchronous message-passing is less versatile, but simpler.

Another dimension along which message-passing systems can vary is the size of a message. Many systems insist on fixed-size buffers for their messages, which makes it easy to allocate space for them. Others allow variable-length blocks, which usually take more time to allocate.

Yet another variation depends on where the data are buffered: the buffer can belong to the system, in which case the data have to be moved in and out of it, or can be part of the sender's memory. In this case, the buffer has to be accessible to both sender and receiver (difficult in larger systems with memory mapping and memory protection hardware, whose purpose is in part to keep tasks from accessing other tasks' memory), and the sender has to wait until the message is received before re-using the buffer.

This technique can be regarded either as a fancy way of arbitrating shared memory, or as simple message-passing of fixed-size messages, each containing the address and size of a block of memory.

It is possible to base operating systems entirely on the concept of message-passing; this is becoming increasingly common. Messages can easily simulate semaphores (using messages without data, with the semaphore count being the count of waiting messages), and monitors (performing operations by sending messages to a message-handler attached to each data structure). And, of course, messages are a natural way to implement I/O and multi-processor networks.

Rendezvous. The Ada language uses a form of synchronous message- passing called a *rendezvous* (Ada was designed by a French company). Sending is treated syntactically like a procedure call; receiving is done with an *entry* statement, which resembles a procedure declaration.

Timing and Scheduling

One of the primary functions of a real-time operating system is timing. This includes both scheduling processor time among the various tasks, and timing external events. The timing functions are usually driven by a device which provides interrupts at regular intervals, called a *real-time clock*. It is also possible to use a timer device which can be set to provide an interrupt when the next significant event is about to happen.

The real-time clock, especially on older computers, is often driven off of the 60 Hz (or 50 Hz) power line. The interval between interrupts is called a *tick* or *jiffy*, and ranges on various systems from about 1 to 100 milliseconds.

Scheduling. Real-time operating systems usually allow tasks to be assigned different priority levels, according to their relative need for speedy service. When it is time to run a new task, either because the task that was running has waited for something, or because a new task has become ready, the scheduler finds the task with the highest priority and runs it.

Preemptive Scheduling. If a task can be interrupted to run a higher-priority task, this is called *preemptive scheduling*. In non-preemptive scheduling, task switching cannot be done until the currently-running task explicitly gives up the processor. This is simpler to implement, but means that high-priority tasks may have to wait a long time to run. Scheduling in real-time systems is almost always preemptive.

It is usually possible for a task to wait for a specified interval, or until a specified future time. The operating system maintains a list of times, and things to be done at those times.

Round-Robin Scheduling. When two or more tasks have the same priority, the operating system will often allow one to run for a preset amount of time, called a *quantum*, and then select the next one in turn. This is called *round-robin scheduling*.

Timing. In addition to scheduling, the real-time clock can be used to time events. This can take two forms: computing the interval between events, or providing an interrupt or signal after a given interval. If the purpose of this signal is to wake up a task when some other event that the task was waiting for has not occurred in the given time, it is called a *timeout*. Timeouts are very useful when dealing with the outside world, in which things often don't happen when we expect them to. They can also be used to detect and recover from software *deadlocks*.

I/O and File Systems

All computer systems have inputs and outputs, and most operating systems do something about it, although many real-time systems don't do very much.

Device Drivers.   The minimum service that can be provided is a set of *drivers* for terminals and, usually, disks. These device drivers usually include routines to read and write characters or sectors, control functions such as seeking on a disk, and the necessary buffering and interrupt-handling services.

Terminal drivers usually get quite elaborate. They provide such functions as echoing on full-duplex terminals, automatic linefeed after carriage-return, parity generation and checking, and so on (collectively known as "intra-line editing," "canonization," and even "cooking," as contrasted with "raw" input). They also provide means of turning these functions off if you don't want them.

Logical I/O.   If an operating system treats devices as objects, it is a natural idea to make all devices the same kind of object, so as to make them more or less interchangeable. This has two benefits: code can be shared among many similar devices (such as terminals), and programs can be written without specifying which devices they will be using. This means, for example, that a program can be run one time with its output going to a terminal, and another time to disk.

To properly support this kind of logical I/O, it is necessary for each kind of device to provide a certain minimal set of functions, such as reading and writing single characters. A device or program that reads or writes single characters is often called a *stream*.

Files.   It is possible, of course, to refer to the blocks on a disk simply by their physical addresses, in the same way that it is possible to have a book with page numbers but no chapter headings. Most operating systems provide a *file system*, which allows sets of disk blocks, called files, to be given names. The names are held in a special kind of file—the directory—along with other information such as where the file starts, and usually its size and other attributes.

Some systems, of which Unix is the best-known, treat directories more-or-less as ordinary files, and allow a disk to have many directories. A directory

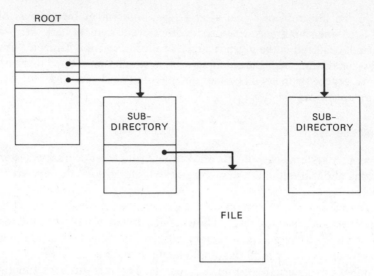

Figure 3.3. Part of a tree-structured disk directory.

can contain files which in turn are other directories, giving a tree-structured file system. This is a good way to organize large projects.

Files can be accessed sequentially, from beginning to end; or randomly.

Files can be organized in any of several ways (see Fig. 3.4). The simplest is to insist that all the blocks of a file be contiguous on the disk. This is the most efficient arrangement for fast data transfer, and for random access. It is the worst possible situation if you want to add to a file, or delete it.

Another method is to chain the blocks in the file together, with each block pointing to the one before it and the one after it. This makes it possible to add or delete blocks anywhere in the file, and to use blocks anywhere on the disk. Random access is very slow, since you have to chain through all the blocks between where you are and where you want to be. This method can be sped up by allocating several contiguous blocks, called an *extent*, at a time. This method is used in CP/M.

Still a third method, a compromise, starts each file with a list of pointers to all the blocks in the file. Since the list is short, it can usually be kept in memory, making random access very efficient. In even larger files, it may take several blocks to store the list; these blocks might be chained together, or possibly listed in a second-level block list.

Pseudo-Files.   It is possible to treat non-disk physical devices as files, as Unix does. It is also possible to treat *programs* as if they were files or devices, giving a method for programs in a multitasking system to communicate at a high level. There are two main ways of doing this: pipes and pseudo-terminals.

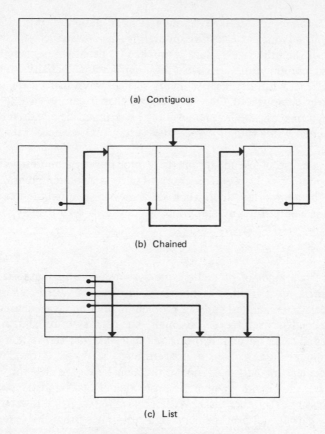

(a) Contiguous

(b) Chained

(c) List

Figure 3.4: Disk file structures.

Pipes. A *pipe*, or pipeline, is Unix's method for connecting tasks. A pipe is a unidirectional pseudo-file that behaves just like a disk or tape file, except that it is a pure stream, and cannot be rewound or otherwise randomly accessed. One task writes characters into the pipe, and the other removes them.

The main use of pipes is to connect the output of one program to the input of another, where each program performs some comparatively simple transformation. For example, a file might be put through a program that copies to its output only those lines containing a particular word, and this output piped into a program that counts the number of lines in its input.

Some single-user systems simulate pipes using temporary disk files. These are a convenience feature only; they use up disk space (in short supply on small systems), and do not result in any time saving. True pipes can save time because both programs can be resident in memory at the same time, so no disk I/O has to be done.

Pseudo-Terminals.   A pseudo-terminal is more elaborate. It is a bi-directional connection, in which one task is simulating an interactive user sitting at the terminal of the other task. Since terminal I/O usually has many options and variations, pseudo-terminals have a high performance penalty. And since programs interact with their users in many strange ways, using a pseudo-terminal can be very complicated. One advantage is that it can be easy to implement, by simply replacing the bottom level of the terminal device driver (where the driver actually reads and writes the serial I/O device) with a message interface.

The main use of pseudo-terminals is probably in situations where a user needs to interact with several programs at once; a switching program can direct input to the appropriate application via a pseudo-terminal, and can direct the application's output to an appropriate window area on a display, or to a file.

Protection

There are two kinds of protection: the system against unauthorized use, and the system against itself. The first kind involves passwords, encryption, and other security techniques, and is a problem mainly on large, shared systems.

The second is useful even on small, one-user systems and in computers embedded in other devices. It means making sure that the system can stay up and running even in the face of program bugs, hardware errors, and user mistakes. Memory management and protection hardware are the most useful device here: they make possible the protection of tasks and the operating system against bugs in other tasks. Without such hardware, a task can "go wild" and write garbage all over memory. In a real-time system this can have results ranging from the amusing to the disastrous.

Timeouts are also a form of protection device. Many real-time systems incorporate a so-called *watchdog* timer. This is a piece of hardware that requires a software response every so often. If it doesn't get it, this indicates that the software has "crashed," and the watchdog restarts the system. Software timeouts are also useful; they can indicate an unresponsive piece of hardware, or a possible software deadlock, and allow a task to take appropriate action for correction or recovery.

Prevention, of course, is the best cure. Most high-level languages provide protection in the form of type-checking, which prevents variables from being mistakenly used in two incompatible ways (say, as a number and as a pointer), and range-checking, which prevents such things as accessing a non-existent array element. (In C, this checking is done by *lint*.)

Object-oriented programming methods, such as Smalltalk's *classes* and Ada's *packages*, are an extension of type-checking in which operations on objects or instances of a data type can only be done by one of the set of subroutines provided for that purpose. This ensures that the object remains self-consistent. (Note that monitors can be implemented this way.) Intel's iAPX432, though generally unsuitable for real-time applications, includes hardware support for objects.

Another object-oriented technique sometimes seen in operating systems is the *capability* mechanism. In such systems, performing an operation on an object requires that the requesting task possess a system-maintained capability for that operation. One problem is that capabilities cannot be revoked, so that objects must have a system-wide unique (for all time!) identifier which can be checked against the capability to make sure that the capability refers to the right object. Such identifiers are generally 64-bit numbers.

When to Use an Operating System

Use an operating system when you have complex multitasking requirements; in interactive systems, especially with multiple users; when several independent processes have to be scheduled independently.

When Not to Use an Operating System

You probably don't need an operating system if your product has only a single process, or if events can be serviced completely in short interrupt routines. Single-chip microcomputers don't have room for operating systems. Really fast processes don't allow time for an operating system's overhead.

OTHER SOFTWARE COMPONENTS

Although a real-time operating system is the largest software component you might consider incorporating into your system, it is by no means the only one. These come in the form of subroutines or programs (tasks). If you have a good linker, it may be able to automatically search a collection of library files for modules that contain names referenced but not defined in your program.

Unix has an extensive library of functions that can be called from C programs; many other C implementations include a large subset of this library.

Mathematical Functions

Functions such as sine, cosine, log, and exponential are obvious and occasionally useful, but by no means the mathematical functions you are most likely to need. Most microcomputers, after all, can't even multiply or divide integers, let alone add floating-point numbers.

Table 3.1 provides a partial list of possible math packages, ranging from

Table 3.1. Mathematical Functions

arithmetic: add, subtract, multiply, divide
  negate, power, max, min
format conversion: fix, float
trig: sine, cosine, tan, cotan, atan, etc.
transcendentals: log, ln, exp
complex numbers
statistics
random number generation
numerical integration
equation solving
filtering and curve smoothing
Fourier transforms

basic arithmetic to advanced functions. Floating point packages are available for most microprocessors, either from the manufacturers or other sources, in both single and double precision (single precision numbers are usually around 32 bits, including a sign, a 7-bit exponent, and a 24-bit fraction).

For integer arithmetic (e.g. multiplication and division) you're probably on your own if you write in assembly language. High level languages supply a library—a file containing compiled functions to be linked in with applications that use them.

Knuth, volume II[11], is a good source for basic arithmetic operations. Collected Algorithms from the ACM is a good source for more advanced functions.

More advanced mathematical packages include procedures for solving simultaneous linear equations, Fourier transforms, numerical integration, and so on.

Data Conversion and Formatting

Another useful set of routines provides *formatting* functions: converting numbers into characters, or vice versa. In high-level languages these are often bundled into the I/O mechanism. It is also sometimes useful to convert to or from character strings in memory, rather than directly to or from an I/O device. Table 3.2 lists some common conversion functions.

C provides the general-purpose input and output formatters **scanf** and **printf**, with several variants depending on whether they are operating on the standard input and output, general files, or strings in memory.

Monitors and Debuggers

Another kind of module you might need is a *monitor*. This is a sort of primitive operating system, and is often found on single-board computers. A monitor is

Table 3.2. Conversion Functions and Their Parameters.

Number-to-String:	base,
	field length,
	signed/unsigned/floating point
	precision (floating point)
	normal/scientific notation (floating point)
	fill character (0 or blank)
String-to-Number:	base,
	field delimiters
	signed/unsigned/floating point
	acceptable notations
	action on bad format
Special: date, time, etc.	

the program to which control is transferred when the computer is reset—it sets up a few control registers in the CPU and some peripheral chips, and transfers control to a debugger which serves as a "front panel" for the system. In addition to the usual debugging commands, there are usually commands to load programs from a serial link, and to "boot" (load, from the old term "bootstrap loader") an operating system from disk (if there is one).

In addition to the debugger, a typical monitor contains terminal and possibly disk I/O routines. Most monitors do *not* support multitasking, which makes them of limited usefulness.

It is also possible to incorporate debuggers into application programs and tasks. This can be very useful in case something goes wrong. It is important, however, not to leave such debuggers in places where a naive user can suddenly run across them! It will do you no good if a machinist using a numerically-controlled lathe with your computer in it suddenly finds the front panel displaying something like

error #24. Debugger Entered. ?

when he was expecting something like "Engage Feedstock." It should take a certain amount of wizardry to get into the debugger, possibly involving a sequence of special commands, or even a physical key inserted into a switch that enables the (hidden) non-maskable-interrupt button.

Other Modules

Other software packages (indeed, software packages in general) are rare in the microcomputer field. Most pre-packaged software is in the form of complete programs for personal computers, not library routines to be built into products. The main exception is software associated with hardware: drivers for interface

Table 3.3. Potential Software
Components

interpretors
command dispatchers
symbol table handlers
scanners
parsers
storage allocators
string-manipulating routines (searching,
    concatenation, etc.)
device drivers

boards of various kinds. If you can use the board in your product, this may be a good deal. Unfortunately, this kind of thing is most common in the S100 bus Z80 CPU market.

Your best source for software packages, in fact, is yourself and your colleagues. *Save old software*! It's remarkable how often you can find yourself dusting off the same old set of formatting routines, the same old symbol table package, the same old command interpreter. It is especially helpful if you design them to be as versatile as possible in the first place.

In other words, when you write a subroutine, think about what other programs it might be useful in. If it looks like a potential component, keep track of it. It may go through several revisions, but at least you won't have to start from scratch each time. Table 3.3 lists some potential software components.

Utility Programs

Some operating systems, especially those (like CP/M and Unix) intended for program development as well as for embedding in products, include a large collection of *utility* programs which can be loaded from disk files just like other applications. Many of these can be useful in a final product. Table 3.4 lists a few of these.

Sometimes an application system need be little more than a few well-chosen utilities, and perhaps a few unusual input and output devices (say, an infra-red spectrophotometer as an input device, and a collection of utility programs to process and plot data files).

Command Processors

Almost all systems that include a file system, and some that do not, include a task which takes commands from an interactive user and executes them. Usually executing a command involves loading a program from a disk file (the

Table 3.4. Utility Programs

file management
    copy file
    rename file
    delete file
    list directory
editors & word processors
programming languages
spreadsheet calculators
data base management
    sort file
    merge file
    search file for string
mathematical utilities
graphical input and output

name of which is usually the name of the command)—this allows the user to create new commands without modifying the system.

Sometimes the command processor occupies a privileged place in the system, but sometimes it is an ordinary program, sometimes called a *shell* (a term which Unix has popularized). The command processor may instruct the operating system to replace it with the command task, or it may create a new subtask. Some systems have more than one command processor.

Command processors range from simple to complex. The simple ones take the first word on a line and run a program of that name, passing it the rest of the command line (after more or less processing). More complex ones add the ability to run scripts from files. Unix (as usual) has some of the most elaborate shells, which are actually interpreters for complete programming languages.

Menus. Other command processors are menu-oriented, offering the user a set of choices rather than waiting for a whole line. Choices can be made from a keyboard, or from a screen equipped with a pointing device. Menu-oriented command processors are better for inexperienced users than for experts— remember that users rapidly tend to become experts.

A multitasking system in an embedded application may lack a command processor, or keep one only for debugging. If the application involves interaction (as in an intelligent instrument), it may have a custom command processor tailored to its front panel.

REFERENCES

1. Naur, Peter *et. al.*, Report on the Algorithmic Language Algol 60. *Comm ACM* 3(5): 299-314 (May, 1960).

2. Jensen, Kathleen, and Wirth, Niklaus. *Pascal User Manual and Report.* Second Ed. New York: Springer-Verlag, 1975.
3. Brinch-Hansen, Per. *Operating System Principles.* Englewood Cliffs, NJ: Prentice-Hall, 1973.
4. Wirth, Niklaus. *Programming in Modula-2.* Second Ed. New York: Springer-Verlag, 1982.
5. Kernighan, Brian W. and Ritchie, Dennis M. *The C Programming Language.* Englewood Cliffs, NJ: Prentice-Hall, 1978.
6. United States Department of Defense. *Reference Manual for the Ada Programming Language.* Washington, DC: The United States Government Printing Office, 1980.
7. McCarthey, John, *et. al. LISP 1.5 Programmer's Manual.* Cambridge, MA: MIT Press, 1962.
8. Goldberg, Adele and Robson, David. *Smalltalk-80: the Language and its Implementation.* Reading, MA: Addison-Wesley, 1983.
9. Kernighan, Brian W. and Plauger, P. J. *Software Tools.* Reading, MA: Addison-Wesley, 1976.
10. IEEE P695 Working Group. The Microprocessor Universal Format for Object Modules. *IEEE Micro* 3(4) 48-66 (Aug. 1983).
11. Knuth, Donald E. *The Art of Computer Programming.* Vol. 2: *Semi-Numerical Algorithms.* Reading, MA: Addison-Wesley, 1969.

II
Design and Implementation

4

Designing Real-Time Systems

THE PRODUCT LIFE-CYCLE

A product goes through several more or less well-defined stages in the course of its existence, from initial planning to eventual obsolescence. These stages are called the *life-cycle* of the product. Various authors break the stages down in different ways, usually according to where in the cycle they feel that design and implementation reviews should take place.

It is important to realize that a product does not progress smoothly from one stage of its life-cycle to another. There are always fuzzy boundaries, parallel development, and feedback. Thus, design and implementation may be going on in parallel, and things learned in the implementation may affect the design. This is especially true in the software parts of the product. (In the past few years articles have been appearing which call attention to this fact, which some of us have always known.)

A simplified view of a product's life-cycle is given in Fig. 4.1. It consists of a series of processes, separated by *milestones* (sometimes called "millstones," especially by the non-management personnel), or significant events.

Each milestone is (ideally) marked by the creation of a document or product which is formally reviewed by all concerned parties. Usually, representatives are present from both marketing and engineering groups, the marketing people to say what they want, and the engineering people to tell them how much it will cost.

Also ideally, any change in the document after the review should require the formal co-operation of both parties.

Design and Implementation Philosophy.

There are two main approaches to designing and implementing a product, only one of which is well described by the process above. This is the "classical" approach: specify the system as completely as possible, plan the implementation carefully step by step, then follow those specifications and plans rigidly until the product is finished.

Unfortunately, this means that if a mistake is made in the early specification and design stages, the project has so much momentum that it will be almost

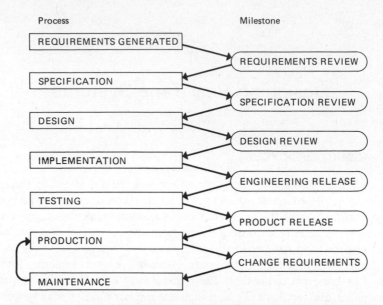

Figure 4.1. The product life-cycle.

impossible to go back and correct it. Since this kind of philosophy is applied especially to large projects (for excellent reasons), the potential for disaster is also large. Large, rigidly run projects are almost always late, over budget, and much less useful than originally expected.

The opposite approach is to get a prototype into the field quickly, with the deliberate intention of following it up with an improved version. Having a prototype in actual use is the best way to find flaws in the original design. This kind of test-marketing has long been used in the consumer field. It is especially well-adapted to software, which is easy to change—there is no large investment in inventory.

There are three dangers with this philosophy: the first is that the prototype, however poor, might become the last and only version; another is that the second version may have so many "improvements," in an attempt to be all things to all people, that it ends up being completely unusable. The third is that if the second version *is* better, the customers who bought the prototype feel cheated. All three results are, of course, particularly common in the computer field; the third can at least be dealt with by providing an inexpensive upgrade path.

Required Reading. The book, *The Mythical Man-Month* by Frederick Brooks (formerly project manager of IBM's OS/360 group) is *required reading* for anyone embarking on a project that involves software, and especially a large project. If you don't read it, you will regret it.

Requirements

The milestone (event) that starts a product on its way is the generation of a set of *requirements*. This is a document (one hopes) setting forth what the customer (or marketing) wants to see in the product. The requirements document is sometimes called the "Design Objectives and Requirements" (DOR) document.

The requirements are the *goals* of the project. They include a general description of the functions to be performed, size, weight, performance, and price limits, and so on. They also include a preliminary schedule and cost estimate for the project. For large (especially military) projects the requirements document can be a large, formal document; for small projects it might be something scrawled on a single sheet of paper (such as a placemat). In any case it ought to be written down and, if possible, formally reviewed.

The review should be formal if for no other reason than to provide a solid basis for later disagreement. If a formal requirements document exists, disputes can be settled by referring to it—it is the ultimate answer to questions like "Why didn't you . . . ?" and "Why did you . . . ?" If it does *not* exist, there is the potential for endless, unproductive finger-pointing.

The requirements document, like the specification, is essentially a contract between the engineering group and the marketing group or the customer. This is true whether or not they are part of the same company. Even within one company, marketing and engineering organizations are separate cultures, with very different ways of looking at the world. (Marketing and sales people solve problems by negotiating and compromising. You cannot compromise with a computer, or negotiate a change in the laws of physics.)

Specification

The next, and probably most important, stage in a product's life is the *specification* stage. This is the stage in which a vague set of objectives are transformed into a concrete specification, saying exactly what the product is supposed to do. The resulting document is the "External Reference Specification" (ERS), which can be regarded as the rough draft of the user's manual for the product. (Sometimes, unfortunately, it is more than a rough draft, and goes directly from the engineer to the user with neither editing nor apology.)

Formal Specification Languages. There is a growing trend toward the use of formal languages for writing specifications. The advantage of formal specifications is that they can be processed using computer programs, both for internal consistency checking and for later verification of the implementation. These formal languages are probably most useful in the later stages of the specification process.

The problem with a formal specification is that it is actually a sort of program, in a very high-level language, with all the problems of programs, including the presence of bugs and the absence of documentation. A formal specification *cannot* be turned into a manual in any reasonable way, and is likely to contain too much detail for it to be obvious whether the product it specifies will actually do what is intended. Formal specification languages are best used with caution, and accompanied by liberal natural-language comments.

One place where formal languages can be especially helpful (and even easy to use) in a specification is in the specification of language syntax. BNF (Backus-Naur Form, introduced in the Algol 60 report[1]) and its derivatives are relatively easy both to write and to read. A closely-related formal technique is that of state-transition diagrams (finite-state machines or regular expressions). More details on both techniques can be found in Chapter 10.

Unfortunately, although the *syntax* of a programming or command language is easy to define formally, the *semantics* (meaning) is much harder to capture, as the virtually unreadable formal definitions of Algol 68 and PL/1 suggest.

The Specification Review.   After the specification document is drawn up, it is reviewed by both the customer (or marketing, or whoever originated the requirements) and the prospective implementers, to make sure that they agree on what is to be done. The document coming out of the specification review is an "External Reference Specification" (ERS).

The specification review is vital. It is at this point that the specifiers, designers, and implementers meet to agree that the design documents describe something that meets two essential requirements: it can be implemented, and when it is done the result will meet the specifications.

The best time for the specification review is after a large part of the design has been done, and part of the implementation! This ensures that, although the implementation details may change, at least the external appearance of the product—its specification—will be fairly stable.

Design

After it is clear what the product is supposed to be and do, the *design* process is begun, to determine *how* to meet the specifications. Often the specification and design process are telescoped together, and the specification and design documents appear at the same time. This is especially common if the product originates in an engineering group.

It is at the design stage that the product is broken down into sections; decisions are made about what to implement in hardware, what in software, and so on. The design documents will be essentially a high- level parts list, describing the major components of the product, and what they are to do. These components or modules can themselves be considered as products; the design documents serve as specifications. The components are then subject to the same life-cycle as the product, but on a smaller scale.

It is important to remember that the documentation is also part of the product, and has to be planned for. There are three kinds of documents that have to be produced: *user* documents (the owner's manual), which tell how to use the product; *manufacturing* documents, which tell how to make it; and *maintenance* documents, which tell how to repair or modify it. The user documents will be derived from the specification, and the maintenance documents from the design. The manufacturing documents are the result of the implementation process.

It is in the design stage that a formal specification of the product can be really helpful, to ensure that parts of the design remain consistent as the details are filled in.

The Design Review. The document coming out of the design review is the "Internal Reference Specification" (IRS)—a complete description of all the parts of the system, how they work, and how they interact. The purpose of the design review is to ensure that the implementation will work, and will meet the specifications. (It is also a chance to change the specifications if they have turned out to be either not what is really wanted, or too costly to implement.) In fact, the implementation has to be compared not only with the specifications, but with the *requirements* of the product, which are sometimes almost forgotten at this point.

As with the specification review, the design review should take place after most of the implementation is done, and testing under way.

Implementation

During implementation, the various pieces of the product are constructed, put together, and made to work. These sub-stages are often referred to as *component implementation*, *component testing*, and *integration*, especially if the product is big enough to require more than one person for implementation. Integrating the hardware and the software components is usually the hardest part.

During the implementation phase, flaws are usually discovered in the design, and sometimes in the requirements (e.g. something that simply cannot be done, or conflicts with other requirements). This requires a feedback loop: some mechanism for getting the design and requirements changed. This mechanism can be more or less formal, depending on the size of the project and the number of people involved.

The end of the implementation phase is marked by an "Engineering

Release" or "Release to Q/A," a formal handing over of the product to an independent organization for final testing. It is important to realize that the product should *not* be totally un-tested at this point. It should, instead, be as thoroughly tested as the implementers can manage.

Testing

The result of the implementation phase is a supposedly-working prototype. At this point, the prototype has to be tested to make sure that it actually does what it is supposed to do. It is best if the testing can be done by somebody other than the implementers. This is the function of a *quality assurance* (Q/A) group, if there is one.

The difference between the testing done at this point by the Q/A group and that done earlier by the implementation group is that the implementers were trying verify that the product *works*, while the Q/A group is trying to prove that it *does not fail*. It is difficult to try to break your own product, and even more difficult to try "impossible" inputs—knowing how the product is "supposed to be" used, it is hard to think of ways to abuse it.

Testing done "in-house" is sometimes called *alpha-site testing*. This is followed by *beta-site testing*, in which a few prototypes are sent to selected, brave customers, who are willing to put up with the hassles of a partially-debugged product in exchange for the opportunity of getting it earlier than anyone else.

Product Release

When the product has been tested, it is *released* to manufacturing (or to the customer, if it is one-of-a-kind). At this point everyone involved agrees that the product can be manufactured, that it meets its specifications, and that it is accurately and completely described by its documentation.

The "release packet" includes the manufacturing, user, and maintenance documentation.

Production

Once the product is released, it is the responsibility of the manufacturing group to churn out copies of it and get them into the hands of customers. This usually involves a *final test* stage, in which the product is put through its paces before it goes out the door. (If the product consists entirely of software, production is particularly simple.)

In the case of complex products, such as large computer systems, the production of a product is followed by *installation* and *acceptance testing*, which is done by the customer. The acceptance test should be agreed upon in advance, especially since the manufacturer is usually not paid until the product is accepted.

Maintenance

Eventually the product will have to be changed. This can be due to flaws which require correction, to changes in the customer's requirements, or to desirable improvements. Each time a change is made, the change goes through the entire life-cycle.

The gradual process of making changes to an existing product is called *maintenance*, or *support*. The computer field has been described as the only one in which adding a new wing to a house is called "maintenance." Often even seemingly small changes can cause major upheavals.

Change Procedures.   It is vitally important to keep track of changes. Once a system is in production (even if it is one of a kind), changes must be made formally, with each change signed off by a *change review board* containing representatives from engineering, manufacturing, and documentation. In software, a source code control system can be useful for tracking changes.

Preparing for Maintenance.   The best way to prepare for maintenance is to assume from the beginning that the system, and especially the software, will change. Knowing that change is inevitable, you can leave "hooks" on which to hang the changes: places where parameters can be changed, additional functions added, programs and data structures replaced. Almost the worst thing you can do is to implement the product's specification exactly, and nothing more. Later in this chapter we will examine modular and object-oriented design techniques, which are helpful in this regard.

In order to do proper maintenance, it is also helpful to have good documentation describing the product. In the case of software, the best documentation is comments contained in the source code. Other forms of documentation, such as flowcharts, are rarely kept up to date. (Sometimes, indeed, flowcharts are prepared automatically from the source code. This makes them accurate, but superfluous.)

DESIGN GOALS

Designing a product is a *goal-oriented* activity: there is a set of requirements which the product must meet. Some of these are explicit, such as the product's function and performance requirements. Others are often implicit or simply forgotten, but are nevertheless important. Such goals as testability and maintainability usually fall into this category.

It is important to get the requirements and specifications as clear as possible before starting the design process. It is hard to hit a moving target, and although a nebulous target is easy to hit, it is hard to say just *what* has been accomplished.

Sometimes, of course, a project starts out with quite general objectives, and evolves into something specific. This is especially true of research projects or experiments. If the project is being supervised in any way, however, it is still important to decide in advance on the limits and directions of its evolution.

Functionality

Obviously, the most important design goal is for a product to do the job for which it is intended. If the thing doesn't work, there is no point in building it. This is, of course, an engineering view of the world. There are other reasons for building systems: for educational experience, for fun, for esthetic effect, or simply to be able to say that you have done it. But I'm assuming that the system in question is intended as a product, a tool, or a toy; in other words, something that works. Even the non-engineering reasons just mentioned are "functional requirements" in some sense.

Performance

In real-time systems, *performance* is also a primary goal, especially when performance is measured as speed. If the system cannot respond in time, it might as well not respond. It is sometimes possible to do an initial prototype without worrying about performance and then optimize it, but this can be risky. Some of the decisions made early in the design process, such as hardware-software tradeoffs, data structure design, and algorithm selection, can make major differences in performance (several orders of magnitude).

The only way to be sure of "optimizing" a prototype design is to allow as much time for the optimization as for the prototype. This gives you time to rebuild the system from scratch, after learning from initial mistakes. (According to Brooks[2] and Knuth[3] you will rebuild anyway. Plan on it.)

Cost

There are two obvious aspects of cost: engineering and manufacturing. Hardware has both, and some attention to detail during the design process can save a lot on manufacturing. This is worthwhile in proportion to the number of systems that will be built—if you are only building one, it doesn't matter. If you are building a million (for example, cars or appliances), it's worth somebody's salary for a year to save a nickel apiece.

Software has essentially zero manufacturing cost, so the amount of attention you pay to reducing its cost should depend on how many systems over which you can amortize the design. Ways of saving software cost are using high-level languages, and using good design practices.

There is another aspect of cost which is often forgotten: maintenance. It is (sadly) not unusual to spend more on fixing something during the course of its lifetime than it cost in the first place. Since this post-purchase cost is usually borne by the customer, it is often ignored by the manufacturer, at least until the next safety recall, or until the customer selects his *next* system.

Manufacturability

It has to be possible to manufacture the system. Not everything that works in the laboratory can be made to work in the field, or even on the production floor. Manufacturability is often a matter of careful *mechanical* design—how many screws it takes to put the thing together, how easy it is to get at the insides for testing, and so on. This aspect is often forgotten in a product which is mainly electronic.

Another manufacturability issue is sensitivity to variations in mechanical and electrical parameters. Parts may work together, or fit together, if they have the values specified for them, but will they work if they have the worst possible combination of almost-out-of-tolerance values? This kind of *worst-case analysis* is (or should be) one of the major points of a design review. (See Chapter 6 for more on worst-case analysis.)

Testability

Testing is one of the invisible cost-savers. If you catch a bad component on incoming inspection, it costs you only the cost of testing the part. If the bad component gets put onto a board, the fault will have to be located and the board reworked. If the board with the bad component makes it into a system, so much the worse. And if the system gets shipped with a bad component in it, you may wind up paying air fare for your best field engineer. (Also see Chapter 6.)

It is possible to design circuitry, and software, so that they are easily tested. It is also possible to design them so that they are essentially untestable. Make sure that important signals can be looked at easily, that clocks can be disabled and supplied externally (most automatic testers want to provide their own clocks), and so on.

Microcomputer-based products can often be made to test themselves. Memory is easy to test. I/O devices are harder—it sometimes requires a test fixture to loop output signals back to inputs. Often this can be built in (for instance, many serial interface chips include a loop-back mode, but this does *not* test any level-converters, cables, or connectors that may come between the interface chip and the real world).

Hardware testability is mainly a matter of putting signals where a tester or the system's software can get at them. This implies that memory on the CPU board ought to be accessible from the off-board bus, and that wherever possible any I/O register that can be written into can also be read. (Many peripheral chips violate this principle, which is unfortunate.)

Reliability and Maintainability

A reliable product is one which doesn't break down often. A maintainable product is one which can be fixed easily and quickly when it does.

Reliability cannot be "tested in"—it has to be designed in. It is not just a matter of using reliable components, but of using them correctly: using worst-case instead of "typical" specifications, avoiding timing conflicts, and generally staying within limits.

Maintainability, also, has to be designed in. Is the system easy to test in the field? Can it test itself? Are the parts easy to get at? Are faults easy to localize?

Parity-checking on the memory is cheap insurance; it tells you for certain whether a fault lies in the memory or in the software. Otherwise, bad memory can be especially difficult to detect. Parity-checking gets you maintainability, but not reliability. Reliability requires error-correcting codes, which are somewhat more expensive.

Software reliability and maintainability are somewhat different from their hardware counterparts, because software doesn't "break down." Any flaws it exhibits were designed in from the start. Reliable software is software that has been designed and constructed so as to minimize the probability of building in a problem. Maintainable software is software that allows faults to be tested for, isolated and modified readily.

Modifiability

The Greek philosopher Heraclitus said it: Everything flows. Sooner or later the product will have to be changed, whether fixed or to improved. Plan for change. In other words, an optimist gets only unpleasant surprises.

Modifiability requires two things: the design has to be easily to understood (by somebody *other* than its designer!), and it has to be easy to change. If there are complex interactions between parts of the system, changes in one part may have unforeseen effects in other parts. If space is tight, it will be difficult to squeeze in new parts. (This goes for software as well as hardware.)

Probably the most important factor affecting modifiability is modularization: breaking the design down into parts that interact in well-defined, limited ways. If the interfaces between modules can be specified exactly (and as simply as possible), it is easy to replace a module with an improved or fixed version without affecting its neighbors.

Hardware modularization is exemplified by bus- oriented design—keeping a single, uniform interface between components. Software modularization is exemplified by object-oriented programming (the Ada *package* concept), in which a data structure can be operated on only by a well-defined set of procedures.

MAJOR DESIGN DECISIONS

Project Scope

In order to design a system, you must first decide just what the system is, and what it is to do. This is not as trivial as it may sound. It is especially important to decide what the system is *not*, that is, what you do *not* intend to attempt. Otherwise, the "creeping features" syndrome, the temptation to add features, change the details of the implementation, and generally keep improving and perfecting, will prevent the product from ever seeing the light of day.

Hardware-Software Tradeoffs

The next thing to decide is what parts of the system are to be implemented in hardware, and what parts in software. Hardware is fast, but expensive and hard to change. Software is slower, but cheap and easy to change. Hardware is usually easier to test, and it is usually easier to prove that a given piece of hardware will do a job, than that the equivalent in software will do the same job. On the other hand, software doesn't break down.

A good way to proceed is to start with the interface to the real world, which *has* to be hardware, and work inward toward the CPU. Assign functions to hardware, with a priority that depends on how hard they would be to duplicate in software.

Speed Considerations. Obviously, any function which cannot be done quickly enough in software has to be done in hardware. There is a less obvious speed tradeoff: the CPU running the software has a finite bandwidth, and the functions assigned to software limit the bandwidth (time) available for other functions.

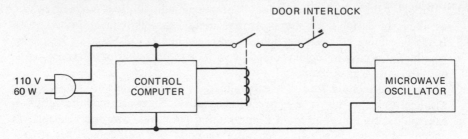

Figure 4.2. Microwave oven control with door interlock.

Safety Considerations.   Functions that affect safety or reliability are best handled by both hardware *and* software. For example, in a microwave oven controller, the magnetron power is usually controlled by two switches in series: one under the control of the software, and the other mechanically interlocked to the oven door (Fig. 4.2).

To take another example, I was told about an effort to write software controlling a daisywheel printer. The print hammer was under direct software control, and it was common for bugs in the controller software to leave the hammer winding energized. This had two effects: the hammer stripped "petals" off the spinning printwheel, and then the hammer winding burned out. This may have been amusing, but was certainly not cheap. The circuitry needed to restrict the maximum length of a pulse to the hammer solenoid would have been minimal. (This sort of protection is especially important in the debugging phase, but it can also keep a freak power-line glitch from doing embarrassing things in the field.)

Versatility Considerations.   Keep in mind that software is easier to change than hardware, which suggests that things that are likely to be changed in the course of product development, and later in the course of product improvement, should be in software.

As a side benefit, the less specialized the hardware is, the greater the variety of products it can be used in without change.

Organizational Considerations.   It is essential for the hardware and software to be designed in parallel, by people or teams that can communicate easily (and frequently!) with one another. This avoids such obvious but common problems as the hardware team putting in (at vast expense) features which the software doesn't use, or leaving out simple things that would have saved the software team weeks of work.

It is best if a hardware team and a software team can build up a close working arrangement over the course of several projects.

Documentation

The time to start the user documentation is as early as possible. (The time to finish it is as late as possible, after all the product changes have been made. But that's another matter.) Starting the documentation early not only keeps future developments on course, but is a good way of catching problems, especially with the user interface. It has often been found that things that are hard to describe turn out to be hard to use as well.

For documentation (both the process and its product) to work well, it is necessary to have a writer who understands the project, and who works well with the engineering staff. As with hardware and software, it is best if such a relationship can be developed over a long period of time. Unfortunately, such writers are rare, and most companies are unwilling to pay for their services. It is also rare for writers and engineers to be together in the same part of the organization.

System Configuration

One of the first things that has to be decided is the structure of the system: the structure of the software and of the hardware, and the tradeoffs between them. Many of these decisions, especially the hardware configuration, will be made as much on practical, political and personal grounds as on technical ones. For example, the choice of CPU will usually depend not on the true merits of the CPU chips on the market, but on which chips are already in use in the organization, and which instruction sets the programmers are familiar with.

Software Configuration.   The major decisions to be made here are the general structure of the software and the language it will be implemented in. In a large project, the software is also partitioned into modules that can be implemented by different programmers or programming teams.

Software Structure.   Decide what the overall structure of the software is to be: polling loop, foreground-background, or multitasking. Consider the limits imposed by processor bandwidth, operating system overhead, and your implementation language.

If you decide on multitasking, determine whether tasks should be station-oriented (one per processing step) or item-oriented (one per item being processed). In a continuous-flow process tasks will necessarily be station-oriented. Station-oriented systems tend to be simpler because they do not have to create and destroy tasks dynamically.

Software Partitioning.   Software partitioning should be done to make interactions between parts as limited as possible. In the design phase the interfaces are designed and documented, with as few restrictions on the implementation of each part as possible. (Obviously in some cases, such as time-critical inner loops, it may be necessary to implement something just to prove that it is feasible.)

If the software is to be written by a single person or small team, the partitioning can be less well-defined, because it will be easier to shift the boundaries around. But this should be guarded against in excess; it is all too easy to spend more time moving the boundaries than filling them in.

Hardware Configuration.   As a rule, the hardware is best designed with the help of advice from the people doing the software. Often seemingly trivial things, such as which bit in a register indicates a given condition, can be totally indifferent to the hardware design, but highly significant to the software. For example, it is often easier to test the high-order bit of a word than any other, because that is the sign bit. This could mean the difference between using a single test instruction and having to do a load and a bit test. In a tight loop, it could make the difference between being fast enough, or too slow.

Logical Structure.   The major hardware decisions are the choice of CPU, the amount and type of memory in the system, and the I/O structure. These form the *logical* architecture of the system, that is, the system as the programmer sees it.

These matters should be decided as early as possible in the design process so that the programmers can get to work. Although a high-level language and modular design can isolate hardware-dependencies to a large extent, they cannot be avoided forever. A "programmer's guide" is a major part of the hardware design.

Physical Structure.   The *physical* or mechanical structure of the system is usually a matter of only minor importance as far as the functionality of the system is concerned; it mainly affects manufacturability, maintainability, and, of course, the price. However, the latter are very important matters for the success of the total system.

The major decisions that determine the physical structure of the system are how (and whether) to partition the system into boards, the type of bus that interconnects them, and the physical packaging.

The Hardware-Software Interface.   Anything already said about partioning holds even more strongly for the hardware-software partition. It is especially important to get this nailed down early in the design process, and well-documented in language that both sides can understand (which is usually the hard part).

Implementation Strategy

Finally, you have to decide how you are going to proceed. This is usually the point at which a schedule can be drawn up. (Unfortunately, the schedule is often decided earlier than this.) Scheduling is especially tricky if both the hardware and the software are new; some software will have to be available for testing the hardware, and some hardware will have to be available for testing the software. Both sides have to make adjustments.

Implementation strategy includes both organizational aspects: who does what; and scheduling or planning aspects: what gets done first. It also includes planning the implementation milestones and other methods for tracking and controlling progress.

SOFTWARE DESIGN TECHNIQUES

In this section we will examine and compare two major software design techniques: top-down programming, and object-oriented programming. The two are in many ways complementary: both can be used on a single project. They are more a difference in philosophy or emphasis, with top-down programming concentrating on the algorithms, and object-oriented programming on the data.

Top-Down Programming

Basic Principles.   The idea behind top-down programming is simple: fully define the program in general terms, and then fill in the details until the program is complete. The guiding principle is to insure that the design at all stages is *complete* and *correct*, in the sense that when all the details are filled in, the program will fulfill its design goals.

Obviously, it is important that the design goals be precisely defined at the outset. It would be nice if these goals could be specified in some formal language. This would let us write computer programs to ensure first that the goals contain no contradictions, and then that the program (at all stages of refinement) meets the goals.

Such formal design languages exist, but they are rarely found in the microcomputer environment. Apart from being expensive to implement and difficult to use, there is a further problem: they are essentially programming languages! Formal design languages are most useful on large, multi-person projects, since they allow many people to work on a program without the danger of inconsistencies developing.

Hardware designers will recognize the top-down approach as the usual technique of drawing a block diagram of a system, then filling in the blocks.

How to Program Top-Down. Top-down programming proceeds in the following way:

1. Make sure that the design is complete.
2. Decide what data structures will be common to all parts of the program. This includes inputs and outputs and, if the top level of the program is a loop (in real-time systems it almost always is), whatever information needs to be carried over from one iteration to the next.
3. Write the program, at a high but meaningful level. This is the hard part. The program should have enough detail to suggest a natural division into sub-programs at the next level. The program at this point is sometimes said to be written in *pseudocode*.
4. Verify the program, making sure that it will perform its function.
5. Fill in detail, taking each division of the main program as the specification for the next level. Repeat until all the details are filled in.

Subroutines, Testing, and Stubs. It is usual to actually write each level in the target programming language. The high-level descriptions of detailed action (the next level) are expressed as comments, but the control structure (tests, loops, and so on) is usually expressed in the syntax of the language in use. In assembly language you can either write macros for the control structure, or use your favorite high-level language in comments.

The "detail," especially at the top levels, is usually supplied in subroutines. This makes it possible to replace subroutines not yet written with *stubs* (fakes), and to test parts of the program at an early stage. Since all the higher levels presumably work, there is always a "driver" for the lower parts, and the subroutines are always tested in their proper context.

Stubs are a powerful tool: stubs representing a section of the program you don't expect to get to in your test can print an error message; stubs that you do expect to get to can announce their presence, and supply "fake" results to their caller to let the test proceed. Stubs can even be interactive, and ask for the proper response.

Limitations. The biggest limitation of top-down design is that you have to have the problem completely specified at the start. This is always a laudable objective, but it is not always possible. In general, top-down design is *not* very flexible: you tend to make decisions early on that limit your ultimate choices.

This can be devastating if a design change is made, or a bug found, that conflicts with one of your early decisions. Large parts of your program may have to be rewritten.

The top-down approach is also not very good at recognizing common operations that ought to be done in subroutines. It is easy, especially if several people are working on the project, to do essentially the same thing in slightly different ways in different parts of the program.

Finally, top-down program design tends to focus on the procedural aspects of the problem, and to ignore the data. Since real-time work is usually a matter of sequencing, control, and responding to simple events, this is usually not a problem. Sometimes, however, a more data-oriented approach is desirable.

Object-Oriented Programming

Rather than concentrating on the program, with its control flow, object-oriented programming concentrates on the data and the operations performed on it. It is, in fact, top-down programming applied to data structures rather than to control structures. As such, object-oriented programming is not so much in conflict with top-down, as complementary to it, being simply an elaboration of step 2, above.

How to Program with Objects.   Object-oriented programming proceeds as follows:

1. Determine what "objects" in the real world need to be represented inside the program. An object might, for example, be a motorized joint, with a position, velocity, and desired target position.
2. Determine, for each object, what its components are, what data are needed for its representation, and what operations need to be performed on it. The components of an object are treated as objects: a robot arm might have several joints. Objects themselves are divided into *classes*, according to their structure and behavior.
3. For each class of objects, decide the details of its representation (usually a record structure), and the details of its operations. Each operation is a subroutine, one of whose parameters is a pointer to the data structure representing the object (unless the object is literally in a class by itself). Ordinary top-down programming can be used to write the subroutines that perform the operations.
4. At this point, the program is practically written. Simply perform the desired operations on the set of objects. Again, this is a case of top-down programming. It is usually fairly simple if the initial problem is specified in terms of real-world objects and their interactions.

Advantages.   Object-oriented programming reflects the structure of the real world, which is made up of interacting objects. It is only natural to take advantage of this structure in writing a program to control a part of the world.

Object-oriented techniques are especially suited to interactive programs.

Here, the user is issuing *commands*: asking the computer to perform operations on some set of objects. The multiple-window display-oriented user interface of programming systems like Smalltalk or Apple's Lisa computer is an excellent example.

Of course, the computer does not need to be interacting with a human; many real-time control applications can be interpreted as operations on an object. A smart controller for any peripheral device, be it disk drive or robot arm, is simply interpreting commands from some outside source.

Object-oriented programs are usually easy to debug and later to modify, because everything specific to a class of objects is encapsulated in one module. It is possible to completely change the representation of a class of objects, or the algorithms that operate on them, without affecting anything outside the object's handler module. It is also easy to add new classes that behave like old ones, or to add new operations to old classes.

Limitations.   Object-oriented programming is not suitable for problems with simple data and complex control structures.

Object-oriented programs also tend to be inefficient, because the style lends itself to complex data structures accessed via pointers, and to subroutine calls to perform operations which often turn out to be simple loads and stores.

Comparison of Top-Down and Object-Oriented Methods

To see the difference between top-down and object-oriented programming style, we will consider a simple example. We are given a set of ten sensors, each with an identifying number, and a port from which a value can be read. Also associated with each sensor is a limit value. We need a procedure to read each sensor in turn, and to print the sensor identifier and value if its limit is exceeded.

Top-Down.   Proceeding top-down, we get the following structure for the program:

```
for (each sensor) {
    read value from port
    if (value > limit)
        PRINT value, identifier
}
```

It seems natural to store the ports, limits, and identifiers in three parallel arrays. This gives us the following C program fragment:

```
#define N_SENSORS     10

Test_Sensors(port, id, limit)
int     port[N_SENSORS],
        id[N_SENSORS],
        limit[N_SENSORS];
{
    int     sensor,
            value;
    for (sensor = 0; sensor < N_SENSORS; sensor++) {
        value = Read_Port(port[sensor]);
        if (value > limit[sensor])
            printf("sensor %d = %d\n", id[sensor], value);
    }
}
```

Object-Oriented.   Approaching the problem from the point of view of objects first, we decide that a sensor is an object whose state includes value, limit, port number, and identifier. Obvious operations are

Test_Sensor()—compare value with limit, and print if too high.

Get_Sensor_Value()—return the sensor's current value.

It seems natural to represent a sensor as a record, and we get the following C program fragment:

```
#define N_SENSORS     10

struct Sensor {
        int     port;
        int     id;
        int     limit;
};

/* Operations on sensors */

int Get_Sensor_Value(s)
struct Sensor *s;
{
        return(Read_Port(s->port));
}

Test_Sensor(s)
struct Sensor *s;
{
    int     value;
```

```
        value = Get_Sensor_Value(s);
        if (value > s->limit)
            printf("sensor %d = %d\n", s->id, value);
}

/* Main Program */

Test_Sensors(sensors)
struct Sensor sensors[N_SENSORS];
{
    int     index;
    for (index = 0; index < N_SENSORS; index++)
        Test_Sensor(&sensors[index]);
}
```

Comparison. Note that the object-oriented version is considerably more verbose, and contains two "extra" levels of procedure calls. In such a simple example, these are plainly disadvantages. If running time or program space are important, the top-down version is clearly best.

On the other hand, suppose getting a sensor's value were at all complicated, and suppose that other parts of a larger program needed to do so. Then the object-oriented version, which already has this operation, starts looking better. We would have to add essentially the same subroutine to the top-down version, and unless we were careful we might end up defining two slightly different versions in different parts of the program.

Now suppose we wanted to change the representation of sensors in the top-down version to match that of the object-oriented version. Large portions of the main procedure would change. But if we changed the representation in the object-oriented version to use arrays, the only thing that would change in the main procedure is that the type of a sensor goes from a record to an integer. Now the advantage becomes clear: the object-oriented version is easier to modify.

In fact, with the use of **#define** macros in C (or a macro preprocessor and some other language), we can avoid the overhead of subroutine calls for common operations, so that the efficiency penalty of the object-oriented program is not as great as it seems.

REFERENCES

1. Naur, Peter *et. al.*, Report on the Algorithmic Language Algol 60. *Comm. ACM* 3(5): 299-314 (May, 1960).
2. Brooks, Frederick P. *The Mythical Man-Month*. Reading, MA: Addison-Wesley, 1975.
3. Knuth, Donald E. *The Art of Computer Programming*. Vol. 1: *Fundamental Algorithms*. Reading, MA: Addison-Wesley, 1968.

5

Implementing Real-Time Systems

Once a system is designed comes the difficult part: getting it up and running. This is not simply a matter of drawing schematics and writing programs—these, in fact, are really part of the design process. (This can be seen more clearly in the case of hardware than of software, because there is a clear separation between the design—a piece of paper, and the final product. In software, the completed design *is* the product.) Implementation, then, is largely the process of debugging a partially-completed design.

HARDWARE IMPLEMENTATION

The Wire-List

If at all possible, a machine-readable *wire-list* should be generated before building the hardware. This is a file listing all the wires (connections) in the product, usually by listing each pin of each device, the name of the signal it is connected to, and the type and location of the device. Ideally, the wire-list can be generated automatically from an automated drafting system (Computer-Aided Design, or CAD system), but it is worth entering by hand with a text editor if a CAD system is unavailable (CAD systems are mostly expensive, although small ones are starting to appear on personal computers).

Once a machine-readable wire-list is available, it can be used to

Automatically check the design;
Drive a simulator;
Help build a prototype;
Verify the final PC board.

Design Checking. A good CAD system will have programs to check design rules: short circuits, outputs connected together (other than buses), inputs without outputs or vice versa, power and ground to the right pins, and so on.

It is possible to perform some such checks even without special-purpose software, given a good sorting program. Simply having a listing of the wire-list sorted by signal name, and another sorted by device and pin number, is enough to reveal shorted signals, unconnected pins, and other such faults. For example, suppose we have a file with entries like

SIGNAL	DEVICE	PIN	I/O	LOCATION
Addr1	7400	7	I	A–9

We can sort this in various useful ways. Sorting first by signal, then location, then pin produces a file that can be used to check signal loading by counting the entries for a given signal. It can also check for multiple outputs driving the same signal.

Sorting by location, then pin, then signal can be used to find any pins connected to two different signals, and can also show up missing or extra pins. By looking at the device field we can also show up cases of devices given wrong locations. Sorting first by device type, then location, gives us a parts list and placement list.

Programs can be written to do all of these things; on Unix or similar systems they could also be done using shell scripts. It is worth the investment to write some design-checking software of your own if you intend to do hardware designs regularly.

Simulation.   Simulation will be discussed further below, but here it should be noted that one important use of machine-readable wire-lists is to drive software for logic simulation. Simulation can be used not only to test a design before it is implemented, but to generate test data after implementation.

Many board-level test systems use a simulator both to compute the test stimuli which will exercise all the components on a board, and to predict what results will be produced by faulty components. It is worth noting that these techniques are more common in IC testing—IC's, after all, are specified at the level of individual transistors, and are considerably simpler than whole boards full of IC's.

Less expensive board testers usually use a "known good" board as a reference, and "learn" the board's responses by applying random stimuli to it. This does not produce as thorough a test as a full simulation.

Prototyping.   Probably the most useful thing to be done with a wire-list is to drive an automatic or semi-automatic wire-wrapping machine. Prototypes can then be generated quickly and very reliably. Even if hand wrapping is used, a wire-list sorted by wire length and pin number will considerably speed the process.

Verification.   Automatic printed-circuit layout programs are still rare, and do not produce as tight a design as can draftsmen. However, it is relatively easy for a program to verify the equivalence of a PC board and a schematic, using the corresponding wire-lists as an intermediate form.

Breadboarding

The basic hardware implementation technique is breadboarding: putting together a prototype piece of hardware in some form that is easily modified as the design evolves. The most common breadboarding system at present is wire-wrapping.

Wire-Wrapping.   Wire-wrapping is so well-known as almost to need no explanation. The end of a piece of insulated wire is stripped and wrapped tightly around a sharp-cornered square pin to make a connection. Wire-wrapping is reliable, fast, and relatively cheap. It can be automated for limited production runs, or for reliable prototyping from a machine-readable wire-list.

Wire-wrapping has problems. The sharp corners of the pins eventually wear through the insulation on the wires, producing shorts which are extremely hard to locate. In addition, there are often cross-talk and capacitance problems. Many of these can be avoided by suppressing the impulse to keep the wiring "neat," and running wires directly from point to point. This eliminates long parallel runs of wiring, with their associated crosstalk.

Insulation-Displacement.   Recently, the insulation-displacement techniques pioneered in telephone systems and later applied to mass-terminated flat cables have been applied to prototyping. Sockets and socket boards are available with insulation-displacement connectors, which are U-shaped metal contacts into which an insulated wire is forced. The metal displaces the insulation to make a solid connection to the wire inside. This technique is faster and simpler than wire-wrapping, partly because a single piece of wire can connect more than two contacts.

Another advantage is that the insulation-displacement contacts are considerably shorter than wire-wrap pins, so that an I-D prototype takes up little more space than a PC production version. Wire-wrapped prototypes usually take up two slots in a card cage.

Other Breadboarding Systems.   Two other breadboarding systems are worth mentioning: "breadboarding sockets" and automatic wiring systems. Breadboarding sockets are sockets which accept both IC's and 22-gage solid wire for interconnections. Their use is largely confined to hobbyists, but they can be used for very small interfacing or prototyping projects. A typical prototyping socket will hold a half-dozen IC's, which is sufficient for a custom interface between a parallel I/O chip and almost anything. Breadboarding sockets are useful for *testing* new circuits rather than for permanent installations, or even for prototypes that will be used for a long time.

Automatic wiring systems include, besides wire-wrapping, various numerically-controlled wire-welding systems. In these systems, wire is automatically spot-welded to special contact pads, forming a board which is as compact as a PC board, and even less expensive in short runs. Tooling costs (including layout, usually the most expensive part) for PC boards are avoided, and the prototype is also more reliable than a wire-wrapped board. A machine-readable wire-list is, of course, essential.

Some companies, blessed with CAD equipment and fast-turnaround PC manufacturing lines, simply go directly to PC boards (which may even be laid out automatically or semi-automatically) for their prototypes.

OEM Boards

Often the hardest part of bringing up a new computer-based system is getting the CPU and memory sections up and running. It is also the least productive—no hardware can be tested until there is something to control it, and no software can be tested until there is something to run it on.

The obvious solution is to let someone else do the hard part. Most manufacturers of microcomputers, and many other companies besides, produce a line of PC boards. Just plug two or three of these into a backplane and you have an instant microcomputer, waiting for your special-purpose peripherals. It is even possible to get rather specialized I/O boards—parallel I/O with either TTL interfaces, opto-isolators, or solid-state relays; analog input and output; and more.

Since using OEM boards gives you a CPU and some of the necessary I/O right at the start, you can then move directly to developing any software and special-purpose hardware without worrying about making the computer work. Meanwhile, if your product in its final form cannot use the OEM boards (due to space constraints, price, or company politics), you can develop your own compatible microcomputer in-house. Some manufacturers also offer deals whereby you get manufacturing rights to the design after buying several hundred boards.

Buses. The most important part of selecting a set of OEM boards is deciding on the bus. This includes not only the names and descriptions of the backplane signals, but the form factor of the cards. There are four major buses in use at the moment: Multibus, STD Bus, VME, and S100. All are in various stages of standardization, and are available from multiple sources.

The decision of which bus to use is probably more difficult and more important than that of which CPU to use. Most CPU's are available on most buses, besides which the the use of a high-level language can hide the details of the CPU. The bus, however, has a major effect on the performance, physical configuration, reliability, and price of your product (among other things).

Single-Board Computers.   The heart of an OEM board-based system is the CPU board, which in most modern systems has evolved into a single-board computer, with most of the memory and I/O you need for development. It is possible to fit a CPU, 64K of memory, a serial interface, and a floppy disk controller onto a single card (in any common form factor, including STD bus and single-sized Eurocard). At this point, all you need to add is the specialized I/O your application requires.

Almost all single-board computers come with a debugger or monitor program in PROM, and those with disk controllers include a bootstrap loader. Some come with more: Forth and Tiny Basic are common. Such boards thus include all the development software you need for a small application, if you don't need the speed of assembly language.

Test Equipment

The test equipment used for debugging real-time systems is the same as that used for any electronic systems, with the possible added twist that real-time systems tend to involve both analog and digital circuitry. The discussion of test equipment here will be restricted to a brief review.

Oscilloscopes.   Oscilloscopes are, of course, the "old standby," and remain indispensable. Contrary to what the makers of logic analyzers and in-circuit emulators may try to tell you, it *is* possible to debug a computer system with nothing but a dual-trace, triggered-sweep 'scope. It is not, however, much fun.

Make sure that any oscilloscope you get has triggered sweep, dual trace, and at least enough bandwidth to display the system clock as a reasonable facsimile of a square wave (20 MHz is marginal in most modern microcomputers). A storage scope is helpful but not essential. A scope works well in conjunction with a logic analyzer, which can provide a digital trigger for just the event you want to see. (For example, you can look at the signal going into an A/D converter at exactly the moment the CPU reads it.)

Logic Analyzers.   The logic analyzer is essentially a multi-channel digital storage oscilloscope (Fig. 5.1). In its basic form, it consists of a fast RAM for storing the signals, a counter, and a multiple-input gate for a trigger. Logic analyzers can, almost without exception, be programmed to stop any number of clock cycles after receiving a trigger. They can thus display information about what came before an event, as well as what comes after.

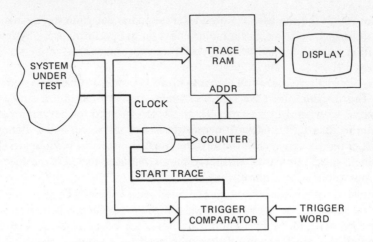

Figure 5.1. Logic analyzer block diagram.

Logic analyzers are available with from eight to sixty-four or more channels. It is advisable to get one that can watch all of your processor's address and data lines simultaneously. This means 24 channels for the typical 8-bit microcomputer, and 32 or more for a 16-bit machine. Working with a 16-channel unit (a rather typical size) is intensely frustrating, since you are continually having to decide which signals not to look at.

Most analyzers give you the choice of either a timing diagram display, which is useful for debugging hardware, or a mass of ones and zeros which is more useful for software. Recently, analyzers are providing even more formatting options, including hexadecimal, ASCII, and even disassembled opcode mnemonics. These are usually provided by analyzers tailored to specific microprocessors. Someone should provide a completely software-formatted logic analyzer, which could be tailored by the user to display not only CPU signals, but those on I/O chips (where the problem usually is).

Specialized Analyzers.   In contrast to general-purpose analyzers, which generally take their signal inputs from a large number of single-wire clips, logic analyzers are available that are specialized for particular situations. For example, there are analyzers specialized for microprocessors, getting their inputs from a probe that clips over the CPU chip. (These analyzers perform most of the functions of in-circuit emulators, which will be discussed later.)

Analyzers are also available for the common I/O interfaces: RS-232 (the ubiquitous serial interface) and RS-488. Such analyzers are almost indispensable if you are trying to build a product that makes full use of these interfaces, especially the 488 bus. (The difficulties of using "standard" RS-232 ports to connect devices are well-known; hardly anyone implements the full standard correctly.)

There are also *bus analyzers*, which take their inputs from cards that plug into various buses, mainly S100 and Multibus. Some of these have a built-in display of LED's; others are simply a RAM which is accessible to the main CPU. This is a case of a processor incorporating its own in-circuit emulator.

Emulators.   Emulators are one step beyond analyzers—they not only allow you to look at what a circuit is doing, but to influence it. An emulator is essentially an externally-controlled simulation of a digital circuit element (although in the case of CPU's, the most common target for emulation, the "simulation" is the CPU chip itself running in a controlled environment).

CPU emulators.   CPU emulators, or "in-circuit" emulators (Fig. 5.2), allow you to look at and modify the internal state of a CPU chip while it is actually running your application on your hardware. In this it differs only little from a purely software *debugger* (which we will describe later on), the main difference being price. The additional expense of an emulator gets you two advantages: it works even when none of your hardware is working, and you get the usual benefits of a logic analyzer—complex triggering and a history trace.

Emulators often include built-in memory that can be "mapped" in place of your system's memory (which may not be working, or which may be ROM in the final version). They almost always include a facility to load programs into your system's memory from whatever computer you have developed them on.

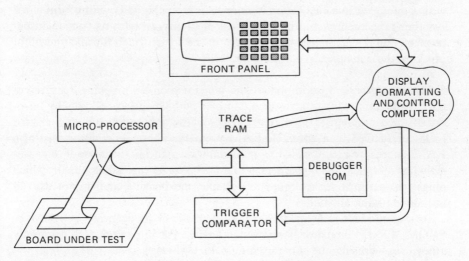

Figure 5.2. Microprocessor emulator.

The disadvantages of an emulator are that its analyzer looks only at the CPU, and that the additional circuitry required to stop and examine the state of the CPU may introduce timing problems. It is possible to have problems that go away when you look at them with an emulator, or conversely to have a circuit that stops working when the emulator is attached.

Emulators are mainly useful when the CPU board and memory are first being debugged. After that it is usually possible to add more memory to hold a software debugger. Note that it is possible to connect the "external trigger" output of a logic analyzer to an interrupt line, to get the logic analyzer features of an emulator. Unless your company is doing enough hardware designs to keep an emulator in use, it is probably better to rent one.

For all their problems, CPU emulators are a major innovation in the debugging of real-time systems. Many of the bugs that plague real-time, multitasking systems are rare, transient events that may cause the program to "blow up" and destroy the contents of memory. The triggering and history features of an emulator or logic analyzer let you capture the events leading up to a crash. The ability to trigger on, for example, a store into a particular data location is invaluable.

A few microcomputer systems include a trace and trigger board that looks at the computer's bus, and provides an interrupt that invokes a debugger. In older generations of computers this was a set of front-panel switches called the "address stop."

Once the hardware is running, a software debugger is almost as good as an emulator. A simple substitute for an emulator, in systems that don't have enough on- board memory to keep a debugger, can sometimes be a small board with a debugger in a PROM on it, connected over the CPU with a "dip-clip." Another refinement would be to add a logic analyzer, with its trigger output connected to the non-maskable interrupt of the CPU, which is usually used for invoking the debugger.

ROM Emulators. In addition to the general memory-mapping features of CPU emulators (which make them complex and expensive, and usually introduce timing problems), there exist devices whose only function is to replace a ROM or PROM by a writeable RAM memory. These generally consist of a RAM, some circuitry for loading it (usually a small microcomputer, but possibly just a UART and a counter), and a DIP plug on the end of a cable, which plugs into a ROM socket. They are simple, inexpensive, and do *not* usually introduce timing anomalies.

If your product is going to have most or all of its software in ROM or PROM, a ROM emulator is well worth having. It will pay for itself after only a few uses—erasing and programming a PROM takes about half an hour.

Other Test Equipment. Although counters and signal generators are not generally useful for debugging digital equipment, they can be quite useful in real-time systems. For example, a counter set to measure frequency can be used to determine the accuracy of a real-time clock, or the bandwidth of a signal-processing routine. Measuring a time interval or period can be used to determine response times and throughputs.

A signal generator can be used to generate known waveforms for sampling, and a variable pulse generator can be used to determine the effect of varying a clock rate.

Software Test Aids

Once the CPU and some of its memory are working (and in a system built from boards they are from the start), the most useful tool for debugging the hardware is software.

Scope Loops. One easy thing to do is to write a two- or three-instruction program that generates a recognizable signal in some output device. It can, for example, turn a signal alternately on and off, or count. The resulting signal can then be examined with an oscilloscope. Incrementing a count in a register and sending it to a DAC, for example, will produce an easily-verified staircase ramp if all goes well.

This technique can be elaborated considerably. With a dual-trace scope, you can generate a recognizable triggering pulse just before doing something that needs looking at. This is the real-time programmer's equivalent of the old technique of inserting PRINT statements into a program being debugged.

If a suitable output port is not available for such a pulse, other techniques can be used, such as reading from a nonexistent memory location to pulse the high-order address line. The main thing is to have a loop that produces a repeating signal.

Scope loops are usually the province of hardware designers and technicians, who often hand-assemble them and enter them in absolute machine language via a debugger or emulator. Most hardware designers have acquired at least this level of programming skill out of self-defense.

System Exercisers. It is possible for software to run elaborate checks, and to put a system through some of its paces. What this means in detail depends on the system, of course; the idea is to produce results that are simple and obvious to verify. If there are moving parts, for example, write a program to move them slowly back and forth. If there are analog inputs and outputs, connect an output to an input and see whether you can read what you think you are writing.

Self-Test Software

One step beyond the simple exerciser programs used to verify that a system is working is software that actually checks as much of the system as possible. This kind of self-test software may be used only in final test, but it is usually a good idea to build it into the final product. This gives the user confidence that the system is working every time it is turned on. (On the other hand, you have to balance this confidence against the possible annoyance of waiting for an extensive series of tests to be completed.)

Processor Tests.   The first thing a self-test program has to do is to verify that the processor is working. This is not a trivial problem, and it is usually necessary to make assumptions (for example, that instructions are being fetched correctly from memory) that may later prove invalid.

Informing the user of a problem, in the absence of a fully-functional system, may also be difficult. The usually method is to produce some result after the test is successfully completed; absence of the result (e.g. lighting an LED on the front panel) means that something is wrong. If there are several tests, it is necessary to perform a series of actions. One elegant method, on systems with an alphanumeric display, is to output a single character of a greeting message after completion of each test. By elimination, the characters successfully displayed tell which test failed.

Memory Tests.   Another indispensable piece of software is the memory test. It is not at all uncommon to spend days chasing a mysterious problem that turns out to be a bad bit in memory. Having parity-checking or error-correcting memory helps immensely, but tests are still necessary. Here is a minimal set:

1. Write all one's into memory and read them back. Do the same for all zero's. This tests for stuck bits.
2. Write the address of each memory location into that location, and read it back. This checks for stuck or shorted address lines. In byte-wide memories, write first the high-order byte of the location, then the low-order byte.
3. Write all zero's into memory, and "walk" a single byte of ones through it, checking *every word*. Then do the same thing complemented. This checks for "pattern sensitivity," especially leakage from one bit cell into its neighbors. (This one takes a long time. There are faster versions, but they require knowledge of the topology of the RAM chips.)

The corresponding program (in C) is

```
/************************************************
** char *mem_test(low_address, high_address)
**       Returns with 0 if successful, otherwise
**       a pointer to the offending byte in memory.
***********************************************/
char *mem_test(low, high)
char *low, *high;
{
        register char *addr;
        register char *addr1;

        /*
        ** Solid one's and zero's
        ** to test for stuck bits
        */
        for (addr = low; addr <= high; addr++)
               *addr = 0xFF;
        for (addr = low; addr <= high; addr++)
               if (*addr != 0xFF) return(addr);

        for (addr = low; addr <= high; addr++)
               *addr = 0;
        for (addr = low; addr <= high; addr++)
               if (*addr != 0) return(addr);
        /*
        ** Write low and high bytes of address
        ** to check for addressing faults
        */
        for (addr = low; addr <= high; addr++)
               *addr = (char)addr;
        for (addr = low; addr <= high; addr++)
               if (*addr != (char)addr)
                       return(addr);

        for (addr = low; addr <= high; addr++)
               *addr = (char)(addr >> 8);
        for (addr = low; addr <= high; addr++)
               if (*addr != (char)(addr >> 8))
                       return(addr);
        /*
        ** Walking one's and zero's
        */
        for (addr = low; addr <= high; addr++)
               *addr = 0;
        for (addr = low; addr <= high; addr++) {
           *addr = 0xFF;
           for (addr1 = low; addr1 <= high; addr1++) {
```

```
                    if (addr1 == addr && *addr1 != 0xFF)
                            return(addr);
                    else if (*addr1 != 0)
                            return(addr);
            }
            *addr = 0;
    }
    for (addr = low; addr <= high; addr++)
        *addr = 0xFF;
    for (addr = low; addr <= high; addr++) {
        *addr = 0;
        for (addr1 = low; addr1 <= high; addr1++) {
            if (addr1 == addr && *addr1 != 0)
                    return(addr);
            else if (*addr1 != 0xFF)
                    return(addr);
        }
        *addr = 0xFF;
    }
    return(0);
}
```

It is possible to try to "simplify" this program by checking each byte immediately after writing it. Doing the test in a separate loop gives the memory more time to fail. In practice, of course, this program would be written in assembly language. Machines like the Z80 which have block-move instructions can use them for filling on the solid one's and zero's tests.

An interesting (and practical) game is to try to write a memory test program which uses no RAM memory itself, residing instead in ROM and keeping all its state in registers. Another test which at least checks all of the bits and has the advantage of not (permanently) changing any data in RAM is to replace each word by its complement, then complement it back and verify that the result is equal to the original value.

In dynamic memory, an extremely good test is to run the above tests while refreshing at a reduced (out-of-spec) rate. This gives "early warning" of marginal bit cells, and gives them a chance to fail solidly. A cell which may fail one time in a million under normal conditions may fail 100% of the time if refreshed at a lower rate. The scaling rules for MOS device behavior make lowering the refresh rate, raising the clock speed, and raising the temperature all roughly equivalent as ways of pushing marginal parts to their limits. This is a modern revival of the *marginal checking* once common on large computers, especially those built with vacuum tubes.

ROM Integrity Tests.   Read-only memory, of course, cannot be tested this way. In this case, a checksum or CRC check will verify the contents to a high degree of confidence. The usual checksum is an exclusive-or of all the bytes in the ROM.

I/O Tests.   Finally, I/O devices have to be tested. This is usually the hardest part, since the CPU does not have complete access to the I/O. In many real-time systems, in fact, fully testing the I/O may be dangerous or impossible—if the computer is launching a rocket, you do *not* want to test the complete ignition sequence beforehand!

In most cases, however, it is possible to build feedback into the system by connecting outputs to inputs. This can either be done via permanently- installed gates or relays, or by external connectors or cables (for example, to connect a serial output to a serial input). Some serial I/O chips have loop-back tests built in, but although these may test a large fraction of the *chip*, they don't test the line drivers or the connectors.

Diagnostic Software

Beyond self-test software is diagnostic software—software that attempts to identify and isolate a problem in malfunctioning hardware. This is usually not built in to the system, and may require special feedback cables or test equipment. Indeed, it often resembles the scope loops and system exercisers used to debug the system in the first place, and may even be derived from them (if the original exerciser programs were saved, which is an excellent idea).

There is a difference between self-test and diagnostic software: self-test software has only to prove *that the system works*; diagnostic software has to find out *why it fails*. Other than that, however, there is considerable overlap, and a good self-test is a large part of a diagnostic package.

SOFTWARE IMPLEMENTATION

Implementation Aids

There are a few programming aids that greatly assist implementation: these include *cross-reference generators, include* and *macro pre-processors, configuration control* programs, and program analysis systems. *Software Tools*, by Kernighan and Plauger[1] is an excellent source for such programs.

The Cross-Reference Listing.   The software equivalent of the wire-list is the *cross-reference*: a listing of all the symbols in the program, the files and lines where they are used, and the place they are defined. Ideally, the cross-reference should also include their data type, and their location in memory.

Cross-reference listings are, sadly, falling into neglect as assembly language becomes less popular—most compilers, and most modern (i.e. microcomputer) assemblers don't produce them. The use of relocating linkers also makes it harder to get at the address of a symbol—the address is not known at assembly or compilation time.

In the absence of a cross-reference program, you can often make good use of a utility that searches files for a string (such as a symbol whose uses you want to track down). This is a kind of interactive cross-reference. An example of such a program can be found in Kernighan and Plauger.

In a large project, say with five programmers and lasting a year, it would probably be worth a month of somebody's time to write a cross-reference program.

Include Files.   One of the most useful tools for controlling a software configuration is the use of *include files*. An include file is a source-language file which can be inserted (included) into another source file in place of a statement which specifies the file to be included. Many assemblers, and the C language compiler, have such a facility. In C, an include statement takes the form

```
#include "filename"
```

The advantage of include files is that a set of declarations for constants, data structures, and external variables and procedures, can be written once, and included in all the modules that use them. The include file thus becomes a standardized description of the interface to a module. (Ada package descriptions serve a similar function.)

An include pre-processor is easy to write, and well worth the effort if you don't have one. (Kernighan and Plauger have one in *Software Tools*.)

Macros.   Macros, which we have already met in connection with assemblers, can have uses similar to those of include files. They are good for standardizing interfaces and common sequences of code that are too complex to be written in-line, and which would be inefficient if made into subroutines. Macros can also be used for constructing data structures, or to make up for deficiencies in the local programming language.

(C, recognizing its deficiencies, includes a macro facility in its compiler. Macro invocations look just like variables and procedure calls, so they can be used to implement named constants and efficient in-line procedures.)

Macros do not have to be built into a language—they can be handled by a "pre-processor" program, at some cost in disk space and time. As usual, Kernighan and Plauger have one.

Configuration Control Programs.   *Configuration control* is the problem of keeping track of which versions of what components have been used to build a particular instance of a product. The problem tends to be particularly acute in software; industries that deal with physical objects have already learned their lesson. Fortunately, there are some programs which can make your life easier by tracking software configurations. Two typical such programs are the Unix *make* command, and the Unix Source-Code Control System.

Make.   *Make* is a utility program in the Unix system; it has analogues in several other minicomputer operating systems but is not yet common on microcomputers. Its function is configuration control: making sure that all the modules that make up a software system are up to date. It does this by means of a file, the "makefile," which lists all the files in the system, the files that they depend on (for example, an object file depends on a source file, and possibly on some include files), and the commands required to make them. (Sometimes *make* can deduce dependencies based on the last character in the file name.)

When the *make* command is issued, the program compares the last-modified date and time of each file with the dates and times of each file that it depends on. If any of the predecessor files is more recent, the dependent file is remade.

If a program similar to *make* is unavailable, it is possible to use a script file to at least keep track of the commands required to construct a system, but you lose the advantage of automatically tracking dependencies. Thus it's always possible to forget to remake one module in a system when something it depends on changes.

Source-Code Control.   Another kind of configuration-control program is used for tracking different *versions* of a set of programs. This is exemplified by the Source-Code Control System of Unix. It is most useful after the first version of a system has been released, and work has started on the second version.

Program Analysis Systems.   A more advanced kind of cross-reference system would not only produce a listing of symbols and where they are used, but could extract other information, such as which modules depend on which other modules, and which variables are used by subroutines. This kind of *program analysis system* is, unfortunately, rare on microcomputers. These systems do exist on larger machines, and so can be expected to appear on the larger microcomputer systems, such as Unix.

Most program analysis systems are interactive, and so include a data base (built by analyzing the program) and a query language. Some of the questions that can be asked are

Which variables are used by subroutine A?
Which subroutines are called by subroutine B?
Which modules use variables from module C?
And so on.

Software Breadboarding

There *can* be a software counterpart of hardware breadboarding. For many reasons, the production version of the software, the version that actually gets shipped in working systems, should not be the first version you produce. As Brooks[2] points out, you are likely to do the equivalent of a complete rewrite, even if you *don't* plan on it.

The first version of the system's software, then, is a prototype. Corners can be cut, and rough edges left on. Perhaps it is not as fast as the final version. Perhaps some features are missing, or else the software takes twice as much space as it should. Perhaps the user interface, if there is one, is crude. There may be some debugging hooks, the software equivalent of test points, left in in case something goes wrong. Even if the eventual product will be shipped in ROM, the prototype is in PROM or RAM. And even if the eventual product will be written in assembly language, the prototype will probably be in a high-level language.

BEWARE! It is easy to look at a "working" software prototype and think that the job is finished. Just because loose wires, paper clips, and chewing gum don't show on the PROM package or the disk doesn't mean that they aren't there in the software, waiting to fall apart in the field. It is *vitally* important to finish the job, and get the final production version finished. It is not unusual for this to take considerably longer than writing the prototype.

It is especially common for *management* (or marketing) to say "It works— ship it!" With eager customers breathing down their necks, this is easy to understand. Well-established companies usually have rigid controls on the release process, which make it difficult for a product to get into the field until engineering is done with it. In small start-up enterprises, however, it may be wise to make sure that *something* in the prototype doesn't work so that it can't be shipped. A message on the console (if there is one) saying **PROTOTYPE— NOT TO BE SHIPPED** is always a good idea.

Debuggers

The software equivalent of an emulator or logic analyzer is the debugger. The interactive debugger is the successor to the late, unlamented front panel. It is a program which allows you to take control of the computer (usually via an interrupt, or a *breakpoint* instruction planted in the program), examine and modify registers and memory locations, and resume or single-step your program.

Types Of Debuggers.   Debuggers come in four general levels, distinguished by the way in which they display programs and data: *absolute*, in which every-

Register Display

```
af=0000  bc=0000  de=0000  hl=0000  af'=0000  bc'=0000  de'=0000 hl'=0000
ix=0000  iy=0000  sp=3ff0  id=0000  ms=0000  pc=0000  "............................"
```

Hexadecimal and ASCII

```
000003e8:  3e 0a a6 32 64 00 00 00 00 00 00 00 00 00 00 00  >..2d..........
000003f8:  00 00 00 00 00 00 00 00 00 00 00 00 00 00 00 00  ..................
```

Disassembly

```
000003e8:  3e  0a              ld      a,00a
000003ea:  a6                  and     (hl)
000003eb:  32  64  00          ld      (00064),a
```

Figure 5.3. Typical debugger displays.

thing is displayed as hexadecimal or octal numbers; *mnemonic*, in which instruction mnemonics are displayed but operands are still numeric; *symbolic*, in which the variables and labels of the original program are available; and *source-language*, in which the program is displayed in its original high-level language, either by "de-compiling" the code, or by making the actual source file available.

Symbolic and source-language debuggers require co-operation from the program-development system. For a symbolic debugger, the symbol table must be available (usually a linker function); for a source-language debugger, the compiler has to make some information available, such as the correspondence between line numbers and program addresses. De-compiling is very uncommon except in interpreter-based programming systems—the transformation performed by a compiler is too drastic to be easily reversed. (Fig. 5.3 shows several typical debugger displays.)

Debuggers can also be categorized by their relationship to an operating system: *stand-alone* or *dependent*. Stand-alone debuggers perform their own I/O and have full control of the computer, while dependent debuggers rely on an operating system for I/O, and are usually restricted to debugging application tasks. Debugging an operating system is tricky—both it and the debugger are fighting for control of the machine. There are few good solutions to this: either build the operating system and the debugger together, or drag out the emulator. Some real-time kernels come with a specialized debugger.

The problem with debuggers in a real-time system is that, although it is usually possible to transfer control into the debugger, missed interrupts and lost time usually make it impossible for the debugger to resume your program after looking around. This problem can even happen with emulators: it takes time to read out and display the CPU's registers, and this time may be too much to allow the system to continue. Fortunately, some debuggers (and most emulators) have a "snapshot" mode in which they display the CPU's state at a given point and then proceed without stopping for user interaction. This mode can be used to watch what is going on without disturbing the timing too much.

Debugger Features.   All debuggers let you examine and modify data and registers, and at least examine your program (source- language debuggers might not let you change the program, as this would require a mini-compiler as part of the debugger). Data can always be displayed in hex or octal; usually decimal and ASCII are available. Table 5.1 shows a typical set of debugger commands.

Almost all debuggers provide *breakpoints* and *single-step* operation. Breakpoints are special trap or call instructions inserted into a program to return control to the debugger if the location of the breakpoint is executed. Single-step is the ability to execute a program a single instruction or high-level statement at a time. Often a "trace" mode is provided, in which the processor's state is displayed after each instruction is executed; but execution proceeds automatically unless the user stops it.

A useful variation of the single-step and trace commands allows all or selected subroutines or system calls to proceed at full speed. A useful variation on breakpoints takes control only after the breakpoint has been executed a given number of times (which allows you to grab control just before leaving a loop, for example).

Another variation on breakpoints is the snapshot, already mentioned, which displays the registers or other information when executed, but proceeds without giving control to the user.

Many debuggers include commands to fill memory with a constant pattern, to move a block of memory from one place to another, and to compare two blocks of memory. You can perform a crude memory test by filling blocks of memory with the same pattern, and then comparing them.

Two rare but extremely useful features are a built-in calculator, and the

Table 5.1. Typical Debugger Command Set

Display	address bytes
Set	address data . . .
Jump	address
Go	(to current program counter)
Break	address
Step	number-of-instructions
Registers	
Move	from to count
Compare	address address count
Fill	address count data

ability to define data-structure formats. The calculator is especially useful for doing addressing calculations, either to find out what variable or routine corresponds to a location, or vice versa. User-defined formats are especially useful in programs, such as operating systems, that use complex linked data structures.

Monitor Features.   The line between a debugger and an operating system's command processor is sometimes thin. (In fact in the ITS timesharing system at MIT the debugger *was* the main command processor.) Many debuggers, especially the ones provided in PROM on single-board computers, are also what are called *monitors*. They contain commands to load programs either from the console's serial port (a leftover from the days many terminals had paper-tape readers), or from disk.

There is usually a simple command to load and execute a disk operating system (a *bootstrap load* command), and there may be commands to save memory images on disk files.

Hardware Test Aids

Just as software can be useful in debugging hardware, so a little hardware can make life easier for the programmer.

Address Comparators.   A simple piece of hardware is a set of comparators which provide an interrupt whenever the address bus of a system matches the value in a register. This gives a debugger a "hardware breakpoint" which is especially useful because the address in question can be that of some data instead of an instruction.

History Buffers.   One step beyond the address comparator is a buffer that records the last thousand or so bus transactions, and which stops recording when the address comparator generates an interrupt. The system should also include a counter, so that a preset number of events can be recorded *after* the trigger point. This is, in fact, a built-in logic analyzer, with all its advantages.

Single-Step Hardware.   It is not always easy for a debugger to "single-step" a program on the machine it is running on, that is, to execute a program one instruction at a time. In general, this means having to simulate all or part of the instruction set of the computer, which is not an easy job. Single-stepping is also needed for a useful implementation of breakpoints: if a breakpoint is to be left in place after being activated, the debugger has to restore the instruction replaced by the breakpoint, single-step it, and then put back the breakpoint instruction before going on.

Some newer CPU's (the 68000, Z800, and 16000) have a single-step bit in their control word; if set, the bit causes the processor to interrupt after executing a single instruction. Most CPU's lack this capability, but it can usually be added with some extra hardware. An address comparator is one form of hardware that will do the job, and probably the best for the purpose. Many systems use a counter chip which is set to count memory references or instruction fetches—this can be set up when leaving the debugger to generate an interrupt just after the target-program instruction is fetched.

Useful Tricks

There are a few useful tricks for using or supplementing debuggers that deserve to be better known. These are the software analogs of the test points and jumpers built onto PC boards to make them easier to debug and test.

All of these tricks occupy space, and may have to be removed from the final version of your software. This is easiest if your development language supports conditional assembly or compilation, which lets you leave the code around. Some day you are likely to need it again. (It is best, of course, to leave the debugging aids in permanently if you have the space. You never know when something may go wrong after the product is in production.)

Data Tags.   One simple trick is to tag each piece of data in your program with a few ASCII characters that identify it. This makes it easy to find with a debugger which displays memory in both hex and ASCII (as most do). You don't have to make tedious and error-prone calculations to locate important data. It also works for subroutines, which can be preceded in memory by their name. This is almost as good as having a symbolic debugger, and sometimes even better. The results are shown in Fig. 5.4.

If the program is in ROM, or in a language like PASCAL, which does not allow pre-initialized variables (or like C, which separates initialized variables

```
A Z80 assembly language fragment:
two 2-byte variables with tags.

         defm    'FOO:'
foo:     defs    2
         defm    'BAZ:'
baz:     defs    2

The same, as seen with a debugger:
------------------------------------------------------
1000      46 4F 4F 3A 00 00 42 41 5A 3A 00 00    FOO:..BAZ:..
```

Figure 5.4. Debugging with ASCII tags.

from uninitialized ones), you have to add code to store the tags. This is tedious, but the results are worthwhile.

Event Buffers. Especially in interrupt-driven systems, it is useful to know what sequence of events lead up to a crash. Write a routine that stores a number or a few characters in a circular buffer, and call it every time something significant happens. The overhead is small, and you can look at the buffer with the debugger to figure out what has happened.

```
#define bufsiz 100      /* # of events to save  */

int buf[bufsiz];        /* the event buffer     */
int ptr;                /* pointer into buffer  */

event(tag)              /* put tag in buffer    */
int tag;
{
    if (++ptr == bufsiz) ptr = 0;
    buf[ptr] = tag;
}
```

Some things you can put in the buffer are: simple event numbers, input data (i.e. characters from a serial port), ASCII tags (two to four characters are usually enough), addresses (some versions simply store the address from which the event routine was called), and times.

History Files. If your system has interactive inputs, it is useful to record them in a history file. This can give you a record of what the *user* did that led up to a problem. (In the days of teletypes this was not a problem—the user just handed you a roll of paper containing everything he had done, and what the system said about it. The lack of hard copy is one of the few disadvantages of the display terminal.) History files are sometimes called "dribble files."

Scripts. The inverse of a history file is a *script*—a file of characters used in place of interactive input. This is an immensely powerful tool. Not only can a user employ it to save long, complex set-up procedures, but the developer can use it to simulate an interactive user. This guarantees that tests can be repeated exactly. (By making it easy to reproduce tests, it also helps ensure that *all* test scripts will get run every time a change is made. Such *regression testing* is needed to catch bugs introduced by the fixes to earlier bugs.)

Scripts and history files together provide a form of crash recovery in transaction-processing or editing systems; the history file can be read back as a script to duplicate an abnormally terminated interactive session.

Debugging Style

There are three main styles of debugging. One is active: some people like to set breakpoints, single-step, and otherwise attempt to observe the program at work in hopes of picking up clues. The second is passive: cogitating on the nature of the symptom, and its possible causes. The third way is called "desk checking:" mentally simulating the program, looking for something odd to turn up (when done formally in a group, this is called a "structured walkthrough"). (Fans of mystery stories will recognize, respectively, the styles of Sherlock Holmes, Nero Wolfe, and Father Brown here.)

The active method, grubbing around in the bits and machine instructions, is often the only way to turn up compiler or hardware problems, which are not apparent from the source code. It is *very* hard for an experienced programmer to find one of these bugs, since the tendency is always to expect bugs in one's own code.

The passive and desk checking methods are sometimes looked down upon in these days of emulators and interactive debuggers, but someone familiar with the program (or the nature of the problem being solved) can often spot the bug immediately. Passive debugging and desk checking are useful in spotting subtle race conditions and other interactions among tasks and interrupts, because timing relations can be changed by the presence of a debugger or emulator (a sort of software "uncertainty principle").

Often a change in tactic helps, as does calling in another programmer, who may be able to provide a different approach. Another advantage of calling in someone who is not familiar with the program is that he or she can spot trivial mistakes that you have long since stopped looking for because you know what the program is "supposed" to be doing. Examples are incorrect addressing modes in assembly language (using direct instead of immediate addressing is an especially common one), and incorrect operators or operator precedence in high-level languages (a classic bug in C is to use = for comparison when you mean = =).

SIMULATION

Hardware Simulation

It is possible to use software to simulate hardware. This fact can be used in three general ways: one can simulate a CPU and its memory, the I/O devices attached to a system, or both. Unfortunately, such simulations are usually slower than the hardware itself, typically by a factor of 100 or more. This means that hardware is rarely simulated when the real thing is available.

There is an important exception to this: it is worthwhile simulating hardware that already exists, if the simulation can be used to study effects that are difficult or impossible to observe in the actual hardware. For example, the interior of a single-chip microcomputer is inaccessible; it may be easier to debug software using a simulation. Software simulations are also useful for evaluating things like cache memory usage and pipelining, which are also inaccessible from outside a chip.

It is also possible to simulate hardware with different hardware—a breadboard. Such a simulation need not function exactly the same as the hardware it replaces, as long as its interface is the same. For example, a terminal could be simulated by a *word generator*—a device that continuously sends a single character or a repeating sequence of a few characters.

CPU Simulation.   Software simulators for most common microprocessors are available, mainly running on the VAX and similar large computers. These are often called *instruction-level simulators*, to distinguish them from the *gate-* or *transistor-level* simulators used in designing the chips in the first place. Their main purpose is to allow software to be written and debugged before the actual chip is available.

(It is worth noting that a second, older function for such simulators has once again made its appearance. Simulators were once common [and are still used] in the mainframe data-processing world, to allow old software to run on new, faster machines. A few Z80 simulators are now being used to run new microprocessor software, especially interactive spreadsheet programs, on old mainframes.)

Instruction-level simulators do offer some advantages over real hardware—they allow complex breakpoint conditions to be set, and allow complete access to all of a processor's internal state. Since I/O is usually simulated via a script, it is also possible to generate interrupts and other I/O events at carefully controlled times. This can be important in debugging device drivers and operating systems. Apart from this ability, most of the functions of instruction-level simulators can be performed by in-circuit emulators, and much more quickly.

The need to simulate I/O using scripts or data files is severely limiting. Generating such scripts is difficult, and the randomness of the real world is lost—race conditions that may show up in reality may not be detected in the simulation.

I/O Simulation.   It is also possible to use software to simulate an I/O device. This can be done by means of a software replacement (stub) for a device driver, running on the target system. It can also be done by a separate piece of hardware (usually microcomputer-controlled) that plugs into the socket intended for the actual device. For example, a human sitting at a terminal can be simulated by a microcomputer plugged into the terminal port.

This second kind of I/O simulation may require considerable effort if a device simulator is not commercially available. Simulators for communication devices, IEEE 488-bus devices, and disk drives are fairly common. If your system involves expensive, delicate, or dangerous peripherals, however, it will usually be worth building a simulation of them even if it takes more resources than the final system itself.

One advantage to I/O simulators is their ability to simulate worst-case conditions. It is, for example, very difficult to deliberately misalign a disk drive until it is just on the verge of being out of specification, in order to verify that the controller you are building will still accept data. A good simulator would be able to do it.

Software Simulation

It is impossible to simulate software completely! A piece of software that perfectly simulated some other piece of software, in the sense of performing all of its functions, would be equivalent to the software it is simulating.

This said, it is still true that software can be simulated, in the sense of performing some *subset* of its functions, or performing its functions too slowly or in too much space to be of use in the final product. We have already mentioned this limitation under the heading of software breadboarding.

High-Level Language.   One obvious way to simulate the production version of the software is to write a preliminary version in a high-level language (assuming that the final version will have to be in assembly language for speed or compactness). The program can then be tested with the system running slower than normal.

Stubbing.   A less obvious form of simulation is the use of stubs to replace parts of a program not yet written. If stubs provide pre-calculated results, or some useful nominal result, large parts of the software (and the hardware) can be tested. For example, a stub for a limit-checking routine can always report a within- limits condition to test nominal operation (to be handled with caution, and a fast hand on the power switch in case a limit *is* exceeded), or the stub can report an out-of-limits condition to check fail-safe tests.

Some linkers (on mainframe computers) are able to replace undefined external subroutine references with the address of a predefined stub that simply reports the fact that it has been called, and the caller's location. This idea does not seem to have caught on in the microprocessor world yet.

Environment Simulation

A special case of stubbing is software simulation of the computer's environment—the real-world system in which it is embedded. This has already been alluded to in the simulation of I/O devices.

There are two reasons to simulate your system's environment: to debug the system before its environment exists (or before the system is ready for it), and to put the system through its paces more rigorously than the actual environment could do it. A nuclear reactor controller provides excellent examples of both reasons: you can't put an untested computer in charge of a real reactor, and you don't want to use a real reactor to test the controller's response to a meltdown.

Environment Simulators.   An environment simulator is usually a blend of hardware, simulating the sensors and effectors that interface to the environment, and of software, generating stimuli and monitoring responses. Such a simulator is, in fact, a real-time system itself—often a bigger and more elaborate one than the system under test.

Automatic test equipment (ATE) for IC's and boards is a good example of this. Although ATE is usually found in a manufacturing context, verifying the operation of products coming off an assembly line, it is also possible to use such equipment for initial testing of new products. You may have to fight the production people for time—these testers are expensive.

Simulation Tools.   In many cases you will have to build your own environment simulator, but there are some good places to start. Automatic test equipment, as suggested above, is the most versatile (and expensive); both digital and analog testers are available in a wide range of capabilities. If you have access to one, and it will fill your needs, by all means use it.

Automated systems built using the IEEE 488 instrumentation bus are another good starting point. Almost every imaginable kind of test equipment is available with a 488 bus interface that allows it to be controlled and monitored from a central computer. Unlike ATE systems, which often have their own specialized languages, most 488-bus controllers are microcomputers programmed in Basic. The entry-level cost is also less: you buy only a controller (which may be a $2000 personal computer) and just those instruments you need.

Scripts.   Scripts have been mentioned before—they are still the easiest way to simulate the behavior of a complex device. The script need not be a literal copy of an input text; it can be a set of commands to a simulation of any I/O device. In particular, it might be a list of commands for a set of devices connected to an IEEE 488-bus controller.

A script, then, is really a program written in some command language. Some operating systems, notably Unix, allow commands to be either compiled programs, or scripts. Script command languages may allow parameter substitution, conditionals, and loops, and are indeed programming languages. Since they are languages specialized for controlling other programs, they are a good tool or model for controlling a program being debugged.

Programmed Simulations.   Scripts have two limitations: they are slow, and they are big. If the environment is sufficiently simple and predictable, it is possible to generate a large number of test cases with a simple program. For example, a ramp waveform can be generated by a simple loop, rather than by listing successive output values. Other waveforms are similarly simple. So are test patterns for character-oriented devices: just step a variable through the character set.

System Simulation

It may be possible to simulate a real-time system in a more global way by constructing a mathematical or computational model of its behavior. In some cases, of course, the mathematical model describes the *desired* behavior of the system (for example, the function of a computer-controlled waveform generator is to produce an output that approximates a set of mathematical curves). This also applies to signal processing and servo-control applications.

In other cases, however, the function the system is performing may be complex, and a mathematical approximation will help verify that its behavior will be correct. For example, in a system involving buffers for inputs that arrive at irregular intervals, statistical modeling may be needed to determine the optimum size for the buffers.

Continuous Simulation.   Continuous simulation is the simulation of a system via the construction of a set of continuous functions that describe its behavior. Usually differential equations are involved. Opportunities for this are rare in the real-time world; as suggested earlier, if a continuous function describes a system, then usually the system has been designed to approximate the function, not the other way around.

Discrete Simulation.   Discrete simulation applies to systems that process discrete objects or events—it involves preparing a list of events, and putting them through a computer model of the system. Event or object tokens are followed through a network of abstract functions: processing steps with appropriate delays between input and output, decision points that direct different kinds of tokens to different processing steps, and buffers with various capacities. The goal is either to determine timing parameters such as expected response time, or the expected sizes of queues and buffers, by observing the behavior of the simulation.

There are languages and programming systems, such as Simscript, Simula, and GPSS, which provide special constructs for processing steps, and so on, and for generating events according to various statistical distributions. They also provide mechanisms for keeping track of events and of simulated time (scheduling), and for gathering statistics on performance. These systems tend to be large and expensive, and run on large mainframe systems.

A reasonable alternative to discrete simulation is to take the program itself, replacing the processing steps with delays, the input handlers by random event generators, and the output handlers by simple data loggers. Then just to watch it. If interrupts are involved, a real-time operating system can be used to simulate them by signaling semaphores at appropriate times.

This reveals discrete simulation for what it is—an extreme case of stubbing, with all actual processing and I/O replaced by stubs, leaving only data paths and buffers. It also reveals the difficult part about discrete simulation: correctly estimating input distributions and processing times.

Statistical Simulation.   There is an alternative to discrete simulation—analyzing the system statistically. The applicable branch of mathematics is called *queuing theory*. A good discussion of queuing theory, if you need it, can be found in Martin[3] and other works on "old-style" real-time processing, as well as newer books on operating systems. Unfortunately, as in digital filtering, digital control, and parsing, the theory is often studied for its own sake rather than because of any practical significance.

REFERENCES

1. Kernighan, Brian W. and Plauger, P. J. *Software Tools*. Reading, MA: Addison-Wesley, 1976.
2. Brooks, Frederick P. *The Mythical Man-Month*. Reading, MA: Addison-Wesley, 1975.
3. Martin, James. *Design of Real-Time Computer Systems*. Englewood Cliffs, NJ: Prentice-Hall, 1967.

6

Testing Real-Time Systems

After being debugged, a typical system goes through four different kinds of test: *quality assurance* (Q/A) testing, which is done by the manufacturing organization to ensure that the system's design is sound; *production* testing, which is done by manufacturing to ensure that a system being shipped is functional; *acceptance* testing, done by a customer to ensure that the system as delivered is capable of performing its task; and *field service* testing, which is done to diagnose and repair a broken system.

QUALITY ASSURANCE TESTING

The Quality Assurance Group

Any sufficiently large organization should have a group devoted to quality assurance. This group has two main functions: making sure that a system (new or revised) is capable of meeting its specifications, and making sure that it is manufacturable. The first function is usually performed by testing the system against its specifications, the second by doing a "worst-case analysis" on the design. The Q/A group should have the power to keep a system from being shipped until it works.

It should be noted that the Q/A group's function is a combination of both testing and design review—many things can be seen from the design, without having to determine them from the actual hardware.

The Q/A organization has to be separate from the group that actually designed and implemented the system—it is difficult to find flaws in one's own work. Sometimes the system is tested by the group that specified it in the first place. This works when there is a separate implementation group. It is better, however, to have a completely separate Q/A group, because the talents required for designing and for testing systems are different.

It is also possible to get Q/A done by outside consultants (at a high price). This is recommended for a small company, especially if its product must work very reliably, or meet other unusual requirements. Table 6.1 is a checklist for quality assurance.

It is important to realize that the existence of a Q/A group is no excuse to

Table 6.1.   Q/A Checklist

Does the system meet its specifications?
Does the documentation accurately describe the system?
Is the system manufacturable?
Is the system testable?
Is the system repairable?

avoid thorough testing by engineering. In fact, engineering usually gives Q/A the test cases they have developed and the worst-case analyses they have done, along with the product itself. Ideally, this simplifies the Q/A task to first verifying that the test cases and analyses are adequate, and then verifying that they are reproducible.

Testing

Test Plan.   The Q/A organization should get the specifications of the system well in advance of its completion, so as to have time to develop a test plan. In fact, a test plan should also be developed as part of the implementation of the system, and the test plan and all engineering test cases should be supplied to Q/A along with the rest of the system's documentation. It is part of Q/A's job to determine whether the test cases already run are sufficient, and to devise new ones if they are not.

Regression Testing.   Every time a change is made to a system, it is a good idea to run all previous tests on it, to make sure that no new problems have been introduced. This is called *regression testing*. Naturally, if something has been changed rather than added, earlier test cases may have to be modified to accommodate it.

This, naturally, means that old test cases have to be saved. To be practical, it also means that some means of running test cases mechanically has to be available. Scripts and environment simulators (including automatic test equipment) are both useful here.

Test Case Generation.   The only way in which testing can prove that a system is fully functional is to try it on all possible inputs. Since the range of possible inputs to even simple systems is immense, this is impractical. (A "simple" one kilobit RAM chip is capable of holding 2^{1024} different patterns. Testing them all at the rate of one per microsecond would require considerably more time than the age of the universe.) Therefore, a way has to be found to generate a set of test cases that will be sufficient, in the sense that if the system works on these cases, it will work for all inputs. It turns out that for most interesting systems generating a sufficient set of test cases is not a computable problem, so in the end it is necessary to rely on a combination of intuition and a few systematic techniques.

There are two basic ways of generating test data, and both should be employed. The first is *functional* testing: treating the system as a "black box," and testing it against its intended function. The second is *structural* testing: generating a set of test cases intended to exercise each component of the system.

Functional Testing.   The problem in functional testing is to find a set of test cases that will be effective in probing for the system's probable weaknesses. There are three kinds of test cases, based on the input values they present, or output values they generate: *extremal*, *non-extremal*, and *special*. Testing using extremal values is also called *boundary value* or *stress* testing.

Test inputs should lie at the extremes of the input range, at "typical" values, and at any special intermediate values (zero, for example). Test cases should also be chosen to force the output to its extreme values, and to generate special output values. If the system does error-checking (and it should, if erroneous inputs are possible), test inputs should also be chosen just beyond the range of acceptable values.

For example, if a routine is supposed to convert ASCII-encoded decimal numbers into 16-bit binary numbers, good test values include 0, 9, 10 (extremal and special input values), 65535 (extremal output value), 65536 (one beyond acceptable range), and "/" and ":", (the ASCII characters on either side of the digits).

Good test cases for a digital filter include impulse and step functions, and sine waves at the limits of its bandwidth. A clock can be stress-tested by setting it to one second before midnight and ensuring that all the carries happen correctly. Systems involving data structures should be tested using null- and single-element structures, as well as maximal-sized structures or arrays.

Hardware is also subject to this kind of testing: signals at the extremes of voltage or frequency, mechanical parts at the limits of movement and load, and so on. Experimentally determining the parameters of a device is called *characterization*; the word is applied mainly to new semiconductor devices, which are tested to determine their actual parameters, as opposed to their intended design parameters. Stress-testing a computer system by running it at the extremes of its power-supply voltages is called *margin* testing, and is an excellent way of finding unreliable components.

Structural Testing.   Structural testing is a matter of identifying, and then (functionally) testing all of the parts of a system. It is complicated by the fact that not all of the parts (especially the software modules) are directly accessible, and further complicated by the difficulty of identifying a "part." In the case of software, it is necessary to have a *metric* that measures the number of parts in a program, so that the *test coverage* (the ratio of number of parts exercised by a test to total number of parts) can be determined.

The simplest software metric is number of statements. This is not particularly good, since branch and loop statements have parts which might not be counted. For example, in the program fragment

```
if (x > 0) x = x / 2;
```

there is a null **else** clause which does not appear in the program. Will it be tested? A better metric is the number of *segments*, or decision-to-decision paths. This catches both branches of the **if** above, even though one is empty.

Test cases for software are usually derived by hand, although a few automatic aids exist, then the cases are evaluated for coverage by means of instrumentation in the program. The most common instrument is a compiler option that causes a "profile" of statements (or, better, branches) and execution counts to be generated when the program is run. This usually results in a program listing annotated with execution counts for each statement.

In the case of hardware, simulator-based automatic test-case generators are available, although they usually do not handle microcomputers very well. A self-test program is essentially a built-in test case generator with high hardware coverage.

Some components of the hardware or software may be difficult to test, either because the sequence of inputs required to exercise them may be extremely long, or because their effects on the output may be difficult to identify. In such cases, a "test mode" can be useful, that is, special logic to grant direct access to the inputs or outputs of internal modules. Typical examples include internal registers (in hardware) and data structures (in software). Programs often incorporate a "debug mode" which can be turned on to display information about what the program is doing.

WARNING: many bugs are due to *missing* logic: cases not covered by the program or the hardware. These are invisible to structural analysis, although they may be revealed in the course of the analysis by their effect on the functioning of other parts of the system. This is why *both* structural and functional testing are important.

Worst-Case Analysis

Worst-case analysis is the technique of determining whether the system will work even if all manufacturing tolerances are in the "wrong" direction. If this is not done, it may be necessary to select parts in order to build a system. This can be done in engineering (though it's a bad idea), but is deadly in production. There are actually systems on the market which are produced by swapping boards in and out of a card cage until a set is put together that works! This always indicates bad design.

Naturally, analysis of this kind is part of the design process, as well; it is a truisim that quality has to be built in, not tested in. It is the function of the Q/A group to make sure that this has been done.

Hardware.   The worst-case analysis of hardware is a well-known and well-understood process. More experienced engineers do it almost habitually, out of self-defense (against their own mistakes). Unfortunately, in the microcomputer field almost everything is being done by someone who has never done that kind of thing before, so the same mistakes keep being repeated.

Component Tolerances.   Manufacturers of electronic components generally provide two values on their data sheet for every parameter of interest: a "typical" value, and a minimum or maximum value (sometimes both, but usually variation in one direction is harmless). It is tempting to use the typical values in the design, since they are inevitably more favorable. Don't. It is best to assume that components will be closer to an extreme value of their range, rather than in the middle.

It is also a good idea to allow for aging and drift, especially in analog components.

Logic Fan-Out.   An obvious thing to check for is that each logic gate is driving no more inputs than its specifications allow. In the TTL families, an output can usually drive up to 10 "standard" inputs. Some inputs on some parts (especially older designs), however, are non-standard, and present larger loads. This is especially true of clock inputs. Fan-out is easy to check automatically.

Timing tolerances.   Timing is all-important in digital systems, and most of the important specification parameters of devices are times. In memories the important considerations are access time and cycle time; in logic parts they are response times and gate delays. It is important to also check data set-up and hold times, as they are often overlooked; set-up time is the time for which a signal must be valid before it is sampled, and hold time is the time it must remain valid after sampling. (See Fig. 6.1.)

Clock speed variation is usually not much of a problem in digital equipment, but it can become important in real-time systems, where the system must interface with the outside world. It is usually unwise to make anything depend on the cycle time of a microprocessor (in other words to use software loops for timing). Even if interrupts are disabled, there can be variations in memory

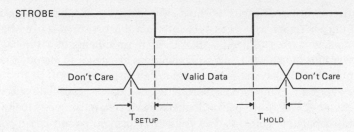

Figure 6.1. Data set-up and hold times.

speed if DMA devices are present and, more important, if a faster microcomputer is used the software will have to be rewritten. Worse, CPU's with the same instruction sets may have different internal implementations, resulting in different timing for the same instructions. This is especially true if a manufacturer introduces an "improved" version.

Variation in device signal delays can lead to race conditions and glitches. These occur mainly when signals go through several levels of gating along different paths. Glitches can also occur when PROM's are used in place of combinatorial logic; after an address input changes, the outputs may go through several intermediate states before settling down.

Power.   It is elementary to determine the power consumption of a system, by adding up the power consumption of each of its parts, and to provide a sufficient supply. It is also tedious, and so power consumption is often determined experimentally after the fact. This can be risky—some parts (such as dynamic RAM chips) have different power consumptions under different conditions. In the case of RAM's, the memory usage patterns of the software can also make a sizable difference in power consumption. (Typically, the stand-by power consumption of such parts is small, and power consumption rises as the part is accessed more often.)

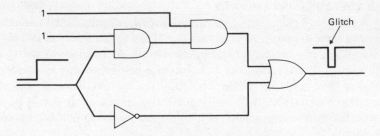

Figure 6.2. A glitch: cause and effect.

One often-overlooked factor is the power-handling capability of backplane wiring and connectors, as well as I/O interfaces. Most standardized buses use enough connector pins to handle the power requirements of a typical board, but it never hurts to check. (Your specifications are going to include the power consumption, so you have to make the determination anyway.)

Power distribution lines are also prone to noise spikes, especially when many parts (such as RAM's) are being clocked or selected in unison. Liberal use of decoupling capacitors helps, as does four-layer printed circuit board construction with heavy internal ground-planes.

Software. Software as well as hardware is subject to worst-case analysis, especially in real-time systems. Real-time systems are often called upon to be highly reliable, more so than most computer systems. Software is usually the weak link in the reliability chain; it is usually more complex than the hardware, and it is more difficult to ensure its correctness.

There are, however, a few definite things that can be verified as part of the Q/A process. These, plus thorough testing of the parts that are not susceptible to analysis, will have to do, until software for mechanical program verification becomes more available.

Timing Considerations. It is necessary to determine the worst-case throughput in operations per second, the response time, and the recovery time (the interval between servicing one event, and the time when the next event can be serviced). Determining the time it takes to execute a complex series of loops and conditionals is difficult—the software should be as simple as possible in places where fast response is required. Interrupt routines and high-speed polling loops, in particular, should be simplified.

In computing software timing, allowance has to be made for non-standard clock speeds (a nominal "4 MHz" CPU may actually be running at 3.58 MHz (the TV color-burst frequency) or some other speed related to something in the system. It is also necessary to allow for memory wait cycles (including dynamic-memory refresh), cycle-stealing by DMA I/O devices, and interrupts (which can be difficult to allow for).

Software timing can often be measured directly, usually be executing a particular sequence of code a large number of times to bring the total time up to something that can be measured on a stopwatch or timed using the system's real-time clock. Short sections of code can also be timed using an oscilloscope, counter, or logic analyzer. Before applying this method, however, you should be sure that the software will be executed the same way as it will be in the field. Possible differences include, as above, memory waits, DMA accesses, and interrupts.

Memory Considerations.   Memory usage also needs to be considered. At this point in the development of the system, the program presumably exists, so its size is known. However, the sizes of buffers, stacks, and so on may have been chosen arbitrarily—it remains to ensure that they are adequate.

Buffers have to be provided to contain enough data at the maximum expected rate, for the maximum expected time. In other words, $B = RT$, where B is the necessary buffer size, R the data rate, and T the time over which the data has to be buffered. Usually the difficulty is in determining T, which may be unpredictable (and is often data-dependent, with different inputs taking different times to process). It may be necessary to apply queuing theory, or simply to overestimate and hope (the usual method, alas).

Stacks, which are buffers of a sort, also have to be allocated. There are two cases to consider: subroutines and interrupts. Maximum subroutine nesting depth is usually simple to determine, although the use of recursive algorithms may make it data-dependent. Maximum interrupt depth is harder to determine, if interrupts can be nested. If the routines that service interrupts can never themselves be interrupted, the problem is simple—provide for the routine that uses the most stack.

Interrupt nesting can be controlled if interrupts can have different priority levels, with interrupts only able to interrupt service routines of lower priority. Then the total worst-case stack depth is the sum of the worst-case depths of each level. This reduces a potential problem in queuing theory to one of simple arithmetic.

Correctness.   It seems elementary, but the software should perform its intended function correctly. Unfortunately, software correctness is a difficult notion, and automatic verification techniques are still in their infancy. Moreover, the software in a typical system is its most complex part, and the Q/A group rarely has enough time to understand the software, let alone verify it.

Software correctness, then, is usually a matter of thorough testing. Software in life-support or other high-reliability applications should be verified mechanically, if possible. An intermediate solution is an exhaustive series of tests, making the program go through as many branch paths as possible. Part of the Q/A process is ensuring that test coverage is adequate. An instrumented compiler generating an execution-count profile is useful; a similar effect can be obtained in assembly language by built-in test instrumentation, or by an external logic analyzer.

Putting a real-time system through all of its control paths will often require special-purpose hardware to simulate its environment, which may be difficult.

Interface consistency should also be verified. There are systems that maintain a data base of interface definitions, and ensure that procedures, variables, and data types are used consistently. (The Ada language requires this kind of inter-module checking.) Other assumptions can be also be checked. Automated design-checking packages are not yet available on microcomputers, but some microcomputer software development is done using cross-software on mainframes where they are available.

One intermodule type-checking system that *is* available on (larger) microcomputers is *lint*, a syntax- and type-checker for for the C language running under Unix. It does not check everything (since C is rather lax about type-checking), but it is better than nothing. It also checks for possible machine dependencies and portability problems.

Packaging. An often-overlooked part of a system's design is its physical packaging. This is too often left till the end of the project (like the documentation), and, also too often, is done poorly.

Ease of Assembly. First of all, the system should be easy to assemble. Somebody has to pay for the time it takes to install every screw (a sum that vastly exceeds the price of the screw itself). One example of good design is a terminal, with its main electronics housing consisting of three subassemblies: an electronics board, a power supply, and the top and bottom plastic castings, all held together by molded plastic clips, a two-piece power connector, and one screw.

Ease of Disassembly for Repair. Eventually, the system will probably have to be taken apart and fixed. Time is money in field service just as it is on the assembly line, so disassembly also has to be simple. It is particularly important to make sure that parts requiring periodic maintenance or adjustment (such as disk drives) are easily accessible.

One infamous example in this regard is a car on which the engine had to be removed in order to change one of the sparkplugs. Aligning a floppy disk drive on some microcomputers can be nearly as difficult.

Mechanical Tolerances. Any system with mechanical parts that fit together has to be checked for tolerances—will the screw fit through the holes in both pieces if the holes are off- center by the maximum amount in opposite directions? Absurd as it seems, systems are still being made in which this is not checked, leading to covers being custom-matched to enclosures, for example.

Environment. The system's intended environment also has to be considered. It is here, more than anywhere else, that governmental and other standards come into play. Environmental considerations fall into three major categories: stresses such as temperature, electromagnetic interference (EMI), and safety.

Along with temperature, environmental stresses include humidity, vibration, dust (especially that brought in by the cooling system), and corrosion. Special hazards in industrial environments also include power-line spikes and explosive or corrosive atmospheres. It is worth noting that the home environment is considerably harsher than the office, and sometimes worse than the factory floor; temperatures range from 40° to 110°F, humidity from 10 to 90%, line voltage is variable, and treatment varies from rough to bizarre (including cockroaches and spilled drinks). The life of a computerized home appliance is not an easy one. Automobiles are even worse—Mil-Spec parts are usually required. Temperatures range from −40° to nearly 200°F, and the ignition system puts 1000V spikes on the power supply. (Roberts[1] recounts many appalling anecdotes about the industrial environment, and is a good introduction to the problems encountered there.)

Designing and testing to meet the various requirements, especially for EMI and safety, is worthy of a book or two in itself, and any sufficiently large company must have a person or group whose sole function is to keep track of such things. The problem is worse for products that may be sold in other countries— the solution usually involves different configurations for different countries, and not just because of differing power-line voltages.

There are firms that specialize in testing against the various environmental and safety specifications. In some cases, certification by a government agency (e.g. the FCC for the EMI specifications) is required. (It is worth noting that the EMI specifications are stricter for the home than for the office environment. It is also worth noting that European and Japanese specifications are different from American ones, and that trying to meet all of them can be a nightmare.)

Cooling System.   Along with the external environment, the system's internal environment must be considered. Cooling is a necessity in any system that uses power. The basic principle of heat transfer is $T = P\theta$, where T is temperature rise (usually expressed in degrees Celsius), P is power dissipation in watts, and θ is *thermal resistance* in degrees Celsius per Watt.

As usual, there is a catch: thermal resistance is difficult to measure and to control. Thermal resistance values are published in the specifications of most power semiconductors and heat sinks, but are harder to come by for ordinary logic IC's on PC boards. Ceramic packages have lower thermal resistance than plastic ones, and the leadless chip carriers now being used for some VLSI parts are even better. There are also heat sinks which can be applied to DIP packages.

Most microcomputer systems are air-cooled. If a fan is used, it should not work against convection (in other words, it should not try to make air flow from top to bottom). If convection cooling is used, it should work. It works better if PC boards are mounted vertically, with intake vents below and outlets above. All this seems obvious, but it is amazing how often it is ignored.

Table 6.2. Worst-Case Analysis Checklist

Hardware	Software (cont.)
Component tolerances	Memory considerations
component values	buffer sizes
possible drift	stack space for maximum interrupt
Timing tolerances	depth
clock speed variation	stack space for maximum subroutine
clock skew	depth
device delay variation	program space
glitches	Correctness
race conditions	
Logic errors	Packaging
fan-in and fan-out	Ease of assembly
power-on reset problems	Ease of disassembly for repair
lockup	Mechanical tolerances
metastable states	Environment
Power	temperature
power supplies	humidity
connector ratings	vibration
component ratings	dirt and corrosion
distribution	EMI
Testability	safety
uncontrollable nodes	Cooling system
unobservable nodes	power dissipation
	air/coolant circulation
Software	outside clearances for ventilation
Timing considerations	Strength
throughput/bandwidth	weight
response time	vibration
recovery time	

Vents need outside clearance, which should be clearly specified in the system's installation guide. A fan does little good if it is jammed up against a wall. Computers should also not be mounted too close to other head-generating equipment.

Strength. It almost goes without saying that a system's packaging should be strong enough to support its weight, but surprising things can be overlooked. In systems with heavy I/O devices such as disk and tape drives, which are usually mounted on slides, it is also important to make sure that the cabinet will not tip over when the slides are pulled out. It may be necessary to install a stabilizer that pulls out from the bottom of the cabinet. This is often an afterthought, and usually looks the part.

The package also has to withstand vibration. Delicate components should be shock-mounted. Vibration can shake boards loose, causing unreliable connections—in severe cases locking bars or other measures may be necessary.

Table 6.2 is a checklist for worst-case analysis.

PRODUCTION TESTING

The Economics of Production Testing

The economics of production testing are simple, though often overlooked: the earlier in the production process a defective part can be found, the less it will cost to fix. (This argument can be found in the marketing brochures of any manufacturer of test equipment.)

For example, consider a defective PC board. The bare board may cost $10. Testing it for shorts and opens on an automatic tester will take perhaps a minute, and cost another $1, so if you find a defect at this stage you lose $11. (You also add $1 in testing to the cost of every board. As we will see, this can be justified.)

After the board is stuffed with parts and soldered it is worth, say, $100. Now, testing it will take a more complex tester, and more time. If it doesn't work, and is too expensive to throw away, it will now take from several minutes (with a tester capable of fault isolation) to several hours of a technician's time to locate the problem, and even more time to fix. It may be necessary to unsolder and replace parts. A defect at this stage can easily cost $50 or more (up to the cost of the board, if you have to throw the whole thing away).

After the board is put into a system, it may take minutes or hours of testing to reveal the problem, and more hours to locate the problem among many boards and subassemblies. It will be more expensive time, too; the job requires an engineer or super-technician. The cost of the defect has risen to $500 or so.

After the system is shipped and installed, finding a defect will probably mean sending out a field service representative. With travel time and expenses, the cost could be as much as $1000, not counting bad feelings and lost time (and possibly other damage) to the customer (which may mean a lawsuit).

The moral of this little story is simple: an ounce of prevention is worth $1000 of field service. Test early and often. Naturally, the exact numbers and trade-off points depend on the cost of your parts, the sizes of your boards and systems, and especially on your expected failure rate (i.e. how much you trust your suppliers and your factory).

Burn-In

Failure rates in integrated circuits and most other semiconductors (and many other things) follow a "bathtub-shaped" curve (Fig. 6.3): high rates of failure

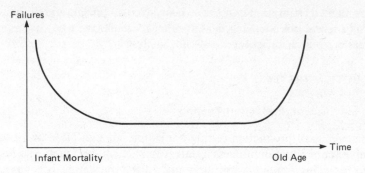

Figure 6.3. Failure rate vs. time ("bathtub curve").

in the early and final stages, separated by a long period of comparative reliability. In other words, they will tend to fail either early, or much later, after "wearing out." Early failures (also called "infant mortality") are usually due to slight, not-quite-fatal imperfections, which become fatal when stressed by the temperature changes of operation, or possibly by vibration or applied voltage.

The solution to this problem is to "burn in" parts—run them with voltage and input signals applied, usually at an elevated temperature. IC's are usually burned-in in large batches of many parts in parallel. Power and inputs are applied, but there is usually no testing of the outputs; instead, the parts are re-tested after burn-in. This avoids tying up expensive test equipment.

One important consideration in burn-in is to isolate the inputs, and especially the power pins, of each part, so that a short in one part does not keep the rest from being burned in. A series resistor is sufficient.

It is also possible to burn in boards and systems. This is a good idea even if they are made with burned-in parts, because the boards, connectors, and backplanes also need to be burned in. System burn-in is usually done by running diagnostic programs for times ranging from 24 hours to a week or more. This is a good time to run extensive memory or disk diagnostics, which tend to be very time-consuming.

Outside Test Organizations

If automatic test equipment is too expensive, it is possible to send equipment outside for testing. This is especially common with IC's; there are organizations that specialize in burning-in and testing parts. The cost of this service is about the same as the chip being tested. If your boards are manufactured or stuffed outside, it may be possible to get them tested by the same source.

An alternative is to buy parts already burned-in and tested. Most OEM boards are sold this way, as are Mil-Spec IC's and other parts. As usual, there is a price; as usual it may be worth it. (Military-grade parts also have to meet more severe temperature and other specifications, so the cost is usually excessive unless your system is going into an extreme environment. Of course, many real-time systems do.)

ACCEPTANCE TESTING

Acceptance testing is similar to Q/A, only it is done by the customer instead of the manufacturer. It is complicated by the fact that the customer usually does not have access to all of the internal documentation of the system, so that the system may have to be studied and tested as a "black box."

Unless the customer is buying a large number of systems, ATE is rarely used for acceptance testing. The customer may run his or her own diagnostics, but the test usually consists of running the manufacturer's diagnostics, and then running the system in its intended application for a while. (Usually the time allowed for acceptance testing, and sometimes the nature of the test, is specified in the contract or purchase agreement.)

If rare and unusual conditions can affect the system, some effort should be made to make them happen or to simulate them, to make sure that the system responds correctly. This may be difficult, especially in large process-control systems—nobody is going to stage a real disaster just to test the new computer. If this is the case, there should at least be some evidence that the manufacturer has considered the possibility.

FIELD SERVICE TESTING

Once a system is installed in the field, it will have to be maintained and repaired. It is usually impossible to bring automatic test equipment and complex environment simulators to bear; field service testing techniques have to be designed for a minimal amount of portable equipment.

Self-Test Programs

As we have indicated before, one substitute for automatic test equipment is to have the system attempt to test itself. This is usually done automatically on power-up. Such tests are rarely thorough; some tests take too much time, while others require a special set-up (for example, testing a disk write function properly requires putting a blank disk into the drive being tested). However, the self-test can be a useful tool if its limitations are made clear.

Diagnostic Programs And Techniques

Once it is clear that problems exist, more elaborate diagnostics can be run (if the system runs at all). The purpose of the diagnostic software is to isolate the fault to some part of the system that can be repaired or replaced. This software can be run either by the user (which usually requires a large investment by the manufacturer in documentation), or by a manufacturer's field service representative. If the system is portable, testing can also be done on the manufacturer's premises.

The ancient technique of "board swapping" is usually effective for locating faults, if software is incapable of it or unavailable. Its disadvantage compared with diagnostic software is that it can take a long time to isolate the problem, especially if the problem shows up toward the end of a long sequence of operations. The system has to be powered down, the next board has to be swapped, then the system powered up and the test sequence run. It is better to test things directly if possible.

Signature Analysis

One specific hardware diagnostic technique deserves mention: signature analysis. Developed by Hewlett-Packard, the technique requires software to place the system into a completely known state (if this is not done by hardware reset), to generate a start signal, then to execute a series of operations that exercises every component and signal in the system, and finally to generate a stop signal. This is similar to a self-test, except that no checking needs to be done.

Checking is done by means of a probe connected to a shift register with

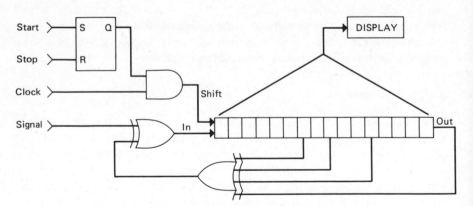

Figure 6.4. Signature analyzer block diagram.

feedback (Fig. 6.4). Between the start and stop signals, data on the probe are clocked into the shift register. The feedback causes the shift register to contain a pseudo-random function of the bit sequence presented to it—its signature.

Each signal on the system's schematic is annotated with its signature, which is essentially a checksum for the bit-stream at that point. The signature analyzer's probe is placed on the signal, the test program is run, and the signature on the schematic is compared with the contents of the shift register. A bad component can be identified because it will have good signals with correct signatures on its inputs, and incorrect signatures on its outputs. The signatures are the digital counterpart of waveforms and voltages annotating an analog circuit diagram.

Signature analysis does *not* locate problems with interfaces to the real world (being a purely digital technique), software problems, or timing glitches. It is also not much good at detecting infrequent, intermittent problems (but then, nothing else is, either).

REFERENCES

1. Roberts, Steven K. *Industrial Design with Microcomputers*. Englewood Cliffs, NJ: Prentice-Hall, 1982.

III
Techniques and Examples

7
Uniprocessing Systems

Uniprocessing systems are systems whose software consists of a single process or task, usually a simple loop that periodically performs some function or set of functions. They are the simplest kind of real-time system. The task may either *poll* its inputs to find out whether any events are waiting to be serviced, or external events may *interrupt* the main loop. Systems in which a single main task is combined with interrupts are called *foreground-background* systems.

Because any multiprocessing system can be regarded as a collection of uniprocessing tasks, anything said about uniprocessing systems is likely to apply to most other real-time systems.

POLLING SYSTEMS

Applications

A slight paradox makes polling systems suitable for both the slowest applications, in which plenty of time is available for inefficiency, and the fastest, in which there is no time to waste on such luxuries as interrupts. In both cases, simplicity is the prime consideration.

Also because of their simplicity, polling systems are often found in applications based on single-chip microcomputers, in which space is at a premium.

General Program Structure

The general structure of a real-time polling loop is some initialization followed by an infinite loop.

```
initialize();
while (TRUE) {
    process();
}
```

The second level is usually a series of tests. If the corresponding conditions (usually input conditions or time tests) are true, then some appropriate action is taken. This repeated testing of conditions is called *polling*.

```
initialize();
while (TRUE) {
    if (condition1) { action_1(); }
    if (condition2) { action_2(); }
    /* etc. */
}
```

(Of course, some actions are performed unconditionally, every time around the loop. This is especially useful if the loop takes a fixed, known amount of time, or starts off with a synchronization operation.)

In systems which include an interpreter for Basic or some other user-level language, the polling is done in the main loop of the interpreter (once for each statement, or possibly more often depending on the interpreter's structure). This organization provides "interrupts" at the interpreter level.

Scheduling

One problem with the organization above is that the time it takes to execute a loop depends on how many conditions are true. Moreover, the tests are always performed in the same order, with no way to adjust their priority.

Priority Scheduling.   Some of these limitations can be overcome by means of explicit scheduling. One way is simply to test the more important conditions more often:

```
initialize();
while (TRUE) {
    if (condition1) { action_1(); }
    if (condition2) { action_2(); }
    if (condition1) { action_1(); }
    if (condition3) { action_3(); }
}
```

This can also be done using a table of pointers to subroutines. (Each subroutine has to include its condition, if any.) This way, each time around the loop a single condition may be selected for testing, with more important conditions being selected more often. Another advantage of this technique is that since the scheduling information is in a table instead of in the program, the priorities can be adjusted at run-time.

```
act1()
{
    if (condition1) { action_1(); }
}
```

```
act2()
{
    if (condition2) { action_2(); }
}

#define N_ACTIONS 3                    /* number of entries    */
(*actions[N_ACTIONS])() = {           /* action routine table */
        act1,
        act2,
        act1,
};
int action_ptr;

main()
{
    other_initialization();
    action_ptr = 0;
    while (TRUE) {
        (*actions[action_ptr])();
        if (++action_ptr == N_ACTIONS) action_ptr = 0;
    }
}
```

Note that the only difference between this technique and a multitasking system with non-preemptive scheduling is that each "task" runs to completion, so that its program counter, subroutine stack pointer and registers need not be saved.

If the action routines can store into the table, they can each do *part* of their action and save a continuation entry point for the next time around the loop. This turns them into coroutines instead of subroutines, and brings the system even closer to true multitasking.

Sub-Polling.   If there is an action that takes a long time, it may be necessary to intersperse it with tests on higher-priority conditions. If the action involves a loop, polling can be put inside the loop. For example, if an action involves printing a message on a slow output device, a test for high-priority conditions could be done while waiting for the device to become ready after each character is output.

```
print_msg(msg)
char *msg;
{
    while (*msg != END_CHAR) {
        if (READY_FLAG & input(PRINTER_PORT)) {
            output(PRINTER_DATA, *msg++);
```

```
        } else {
            poll_others();
        }
    }
}
```

Action-Splitting.   Another (and usually better) technique is to break the
lengthy action into several sub-actions, and execute each in turn. In the mes-
sage-printing example, the message could be put into a buffer, and a test
inserted in the main loop that puts out a character if a message is being printed
and the device is ready.

```
/*
** The following action routine can be inserted
** into a polling loop to print the message
** pointed to by msg.
*/
char *msg;                    /* message pointer */

put_msg_char()
{
    if (*msg != END_CHAR &&
        (READY_FLAG & input(PRINTER_PORT)) {
            output(*msg++);
    }
}
```

This kind of action-splitting is another disguised form of multitasking.

Software Timing.   Although usually bad programming practice, sometimes it
is necessary to base the timing of the system on the amount of time it takes to
execute the main loop. This kind of software timing is usually done in very
simple, high-speed tasks in which interrupt response time is too slow, or in
systems where the signals used for synchronization come too far apart or at the
wrong time. Examples include I/O controllers for high-speed devices, signal
processing, and some applications of single-chip microcomputers.

Accuracy in software timing requires a stable clock, and the absence of
interrupts. Memory timing must also be stable—waiting for a separate controller to refresh a dynamic memory, or to perform a DMA transfer, will throw
your timing off.

In order to control the amount of time to go through the loop, it is necessary
for each branch of an **if** statement to take the same amount of time. Intel's
2920 signal processing chip has an ingenious solution to this problem (suitable

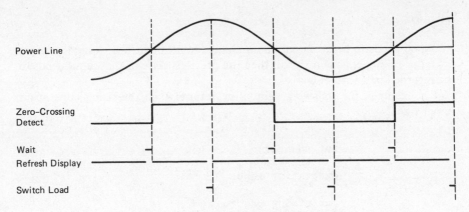

Figure 7.1. Timing for microwave oven controller.

only for special-purpose processors)—the test instruction skips over a sequence of instructions at the same rate that it would take to execute them. On normal microprocessors, though, it is necessary to count instruction cycles, and add padding where necessary.

Since software timing depends on the CPU's clock and cycle time, redesigning the system with a faster CPU becomes a major undertaking. Also, even minor software changes become extremely difficult, since they affect the timing. Software timing should be avoided wherever possible.

One example of software timing occurred in a microwave oven controller which got a timing signal on the zero-crossings of the 60 Hz power line (120 interrupts per second), but had to refresh a display more often than that, and also had to switch an inductive load 90 degrees out of phase. (The timing diagram is shown in Fig. 7.1) The solution looked like the following:

```
while (TRUE) {
    wait_for_crossing();
    refresh_display();
    /*
    ** Takes slightly under 1/240 sec.
    ** We are now at the peak of the waveform.
    */
    switch_load();
    refresh_display();
}
```

A better solution would have used an RC network to shift the timing signal 90 degrees, but the programmer had no control over the hardware.

Edge Detection

If action needs to be taken only on a change in an input, for example, on the rising or falling edge of a signal, then the previous state of that input needs to be recorded in a variable.

For example, the following subroutine returns 1 on the rising edge of an input signal.

```
int counter;
int this_input;
extern int input();

int rising_edge()
{
        int last_input;

        last_input = this_input;
        this_input = input();

        if (this_input > last_input) {
                return(1);
        } else {
                return(0);
        }

}
```

This technique is frequently used to synchronize the start of a loop with an external clock signal (often derived from the 60 Hz power line).

Note that the processing associated with a change in an input must be completed before the next change, otherwise the transition will be missed. Indeed, missing a transition because processing takes too long is a common bug in real-time systems, and especially in uniprocessing programs.

Hardware Edge Detection. The edge-detection algorithm above is easily implemented in hardware (Fig. 7.2). This simplifies the program, eliminates a state variable, and speeds up response time. It is necessary for the act of reading the corresponding input port to reset the hardware, which means that reading the same port twice in a row gives different results. This kind of side-effect can make debugging difficult, since it is impossible to take a "snapshot" of the state of the system—attempting to observe the system's state will change it!

Most devices that generate interrupts are edge-sensitive. This can be used to advantage even in a system without interrupts, since the edge-detection circuitry can usually be used independently.

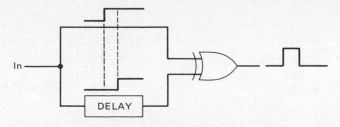

Figure 7.2. Edge-detection in hardware.

De-Bouncing. Another problem arises when an input is generated by a device, such as a mechanical switch, which does not generate a "clean" edge. This kind of behavior is usually called "contact bounce," because one major cause is the mechanical bouncing of the switch contacts (Fig. 7.3a).

Hardware De-Bouncing. Contact bounce is usually easiest to eliminate using hardware. There are two main hardware techniques for controlling bounce: treating it as noise to be filtered out, usually by an RC network (Fig. 7.3b) or possibly even a simple digital delay line (Fig. 7.3c), and using a flip-flop circuit and SPDT switch (Fig. 7.3d). Note that the gate in Fig. 7.3b is shown as a "Schmitt trigger." This eliminates a secondary problem caused by noise superimposed on a slowly changing input (Fig. 7.4).

The "bounceless switch" of Fig. 7.3d is simple and reliable, but requires a mechanical SPDT (single-pole, double-throw) switch, an extra wire to the switch, and two extra gates. An interesting development is the "solid-state" switch with built-in de-bouncing.

Software De-Bouncing. Software can also be used for de-bouncing, although this is sometimes wasteful. The usual technique is simply to insist that the input be stable for a given length of time, enough for the bouncing to stop. This is an extremely simple form of low-pass filtering. Of course, if the input is sampled infrequently enough (say, ten times per second), de-bouncing is unnecessary.

This technique can also be implemented in hardware using a delay element and an OR-gate (Fig. 7.3c). The Motorola 14490 puts six such debouncers on a single chip.

FOREGROUND-BACKGROUND SYSTEMS

A *foreground-background* system is one in which a single task runs continuously in the "background," while real-time events cause *interrupts* which are

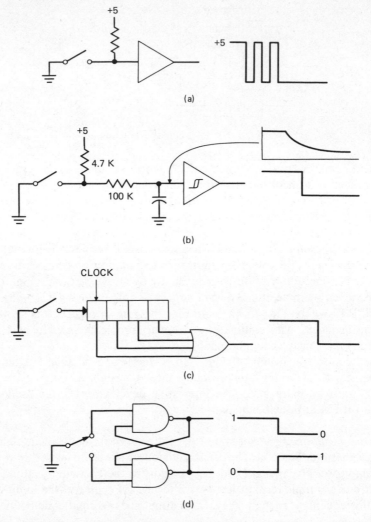

Figure 7.3. Switch contact bounce and de-bouncing techniques. (a) Simple switch. (b) R-C filter. (c) Digital delay line debouncer. (d) R-S flip-flop.

serviced in the "foreground." The foreground is often called *interrupt level*, and the background *task level*. Other terms for foreground-background systems are *interrupt-based* and *event-driven* (a term which is also applied to some multi-tasking systems).

Interrupts are essentially a kind of subroutine call which are executed in response to external events rather than by explicit instructions. Since interrupts

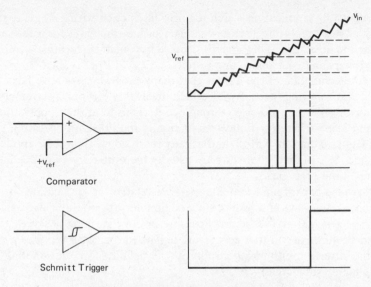

Figure 7.4. Comparator and Schmitt trigger.

occur asynchronously with respect to the background program, rather than at points which can be specified in advance, care has to be taken when information is shared between an interrupt routine and the main program.

Since the time required to respond to an interrupt is short, operations that require fast response time can be moved to interrupt level, freeing the background task for lengthy computations and user interaction. Then response time would no longer be a major consideration in the background task, enabling it to be written in a high-level language, even an interpreter-based language such as Tiny Basic.

Applications

A foreground-background system can handle any but the most complex real-time applications. Most single-user computers also have foreground-background operating systems; application programs run in the background (which is all the user ever interacts with) while I/O devices such as disks and terminals are serviced by interrupt routines.

One typical advantage provided by interrupts is the ability of an interactive user to "type ahead" of a program. An interrupt routine can collect characters from the terminal (or the front panel of an instrument or machine) while the main program is still working on the previous command or data. This eliminates the annoying (and potentially dangerous) habit of some computer systems which "drop" characters when the software isn't listening.

Certainly any application which requires interaction with a single user, plus control of some real-time I/O devices, is a prime candidate for a foreground-background structure. This includes smart instruments, terminals, programmable timers and controllers, and so on.

It is the contention of the author that many programmers have been brainwashed into believing that software which involves interrupts is extremely complex. As a result, they either go through contortions to fit their application into a polling loop, or buy (or build!) an elaborate multitasking operating system that does more than they need (and usually more slowly than their applications have time for). In fact, interrupts are usually the simplest way of dealing with most real-time problems.

Foreground-background systems are *not* suitable for applications in which the time taken to save and restore state on an interrupt would be excessive (e.g. a high-speed signal-processing application), or in which each of several devices or users requires substantial computation. The former case requires a polling loop, the latter a multitasking structure (the definition of "substantial" is, of course, highly subjective).

General Program Structure

An interrupt is essentially a subroutine, called not by a program but by external hardware at an unpredictable point in the execution of the main (foreground) program. Since a condition that causes an interrupt can be handled immediately, a foreground-background system can respond quickly to many different events. (See Fig. 7.5.)

Interrupts differ from ordinary subroutines in that they are "called" at unpredictable times. Thus, it is impossible for subroutine parameters or results to be passed in the usual way. All communication between the interrupt and the background routines must be done by means of shared memory. This raises the possibility of conflict if both routines are trying to access (and possibly change) the same data structure at the same time.

The background task usually handles the sequencing of operations, and user

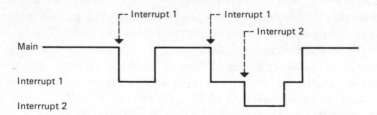

Figure 7.5. Program instruction stream with interrupts.

interface functions such as command decoding. Interrupts handle I/O and timing functions.

In the limiting case, the background task disappears entirely, becoming a simple loop, and all processing is done by interrupt routines. This, like the polling loop with scheduling, is a simplified form of multitasking. The difference is that the interrupt routines are "scheduled" by the events they service, and are executed only upon demand. As noted above, such a system is called *event-driven*, a term which also applies to general multitasking systems in which tasks are scheduled by interrupts from external events.

Context Switching.   It is the combined responsibility of the hardware and the interrupt routine to save any registers or other machine state used by the interrupt routine, and to restore them on exit. All microprocessors at least save the program counter (by pushing it onto a stack), and most save the flag register as well. The combination is often called a *program status word*.

Some microprocessors also save the rest of the registers, the Motorola 6800 and its offspring being typical examples. This simplifies the interrupt routine, at the expense of sometimes saving more state than necessary (which takes both time and stack space).

Other microprocessors have alternate sets of registers which can be used to speed up the business of context switching. Most 16-bit microprocessors have two modes of operation: *user* or *normal* mode, for the foreground, and *system mode* for interrupts and operating system functions. These processors usually have separate stack pointers for each mode. Interrupts and a *system call* instruction, which functions as a software interrupt, switch the processor into system mode.

The limiting case of alternate registers is where there is a complete alternate set of registers. The Zilog Z8 and TI 9900, for example, both accomplish this by keeping their registers in a block of ordinary RAM, with a register to point to them. Changing context simply requires moving the pointer. The Zilog Z80 is an intermediate case—some of its registers are duplicated, once, on the chip itself. These can be used either by the program, or by an especially privileged interrupt routine which requires fast service.

Re-Entrancy.   One hears a lot about subroutines or programs being "re-entrant," often with the adjective "fully" attached. A routine is *re-entrant* if it can be invoked (or re-entered) from an interrupt while simultaneously executing in the background. A routine is guaranteed to be re-entrant if it accesses no statically-allocated (local or global) variables; in other words, if all of the memory it uses is either on the stack or in registers. Most high-level languages make it fairly easy to determine whether a routine is re-entrant in this sense, although if it calls subroutines, it will be necessary to check them as well.

Re-entrancy should not be confused with recursiveness. A subroutine is *recursive* if it *calls itself*, or is called by a subroutine that it calls. A recursive routine need not be re-entrant, although confusing things can happen if it is not.

A re-entrant routine has no side-effects—it affects no memory or other objects that can be accessed from outside it, *or* that can be accessed if it, itself, is re-invoked. Programming without side- effects is generally considered desirable; a language in which side-effects are impossible is called *applicative* or *functional*, since the only construct in it is the application of a function to some arguments. Unfortunately, purely applicative languages do not permit communication between parallel processes (such as interrupts and a background), so they are of purely theoretical interest here.

A routine can be re-entered safely if interrupts are disabled while it is accessing static variables (or in other words, if the non-re-entrant parts cannot be re-entered). This less restrictive kind of routine is, of course, *necessary* if we are to communicate between interrupt and background levels, but it is not, strictly speaking, re-entrant. We will be meeting this kind of routine further on in the chapter.

Performance.   The time required to respond to an interrupt-causing event is the sum of three times: the time between the event and the start of the interruption sequence (*latency time*), the time required to save the state of the interrupted process, and the time required to actually service the event. The recovery time after that is the time required to restore the state of the interrupted process and to return control to it. (See Fig. 7.6.)

Latency Time.   Latency time occurs because an interrupt cannot happen instantaneously, but usually only after the "current" instruction has finished execution. (Some processors allow certain lengthy instructions, especially block-move instructions, to be interrupted.) Moreover, interrupts may be dis-

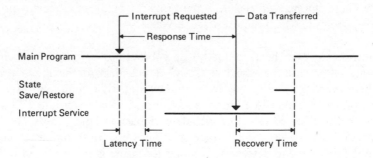

Figure 7.6. Interrupt timing.

abled, either because the background task is accessing some data structure that it shares with an interrupt routine, or because another interrupt is being serviced. Such latency time is a large contributor to the response time.

The time listed on a microprocessor's data sheet for responding to an interrupt is misleading—it is actually only part of the state-saving time. The rest of that time is spent saving registers and other data not saved by the hardware. If interrupts from different events share the same code, additional time will be spent determining which event caused the interrupts. Similarly, the time required to execute a "return from interrupt" instruction is usually only a small part of the recovery time.

Throughput. Similarly, the throughput or cycle time of an interrupt-level process is determined by the response time, and the time required to restore the state of the interrupted process.

Because of the considerable hidden time penalty of interrupts, they cannot be used for processes that require really high throughput. Such processes must be handled either by special hardware (such as DMA), or in a fast polling loop (usually with interrupts disabled).

Nested Interrupts. A large part of the latency time for responding to an interrupt is often due to the servicing of other interrupts, which in some cases may be less important. For this reason it is often desirable to allow an interrupt routine itself to be interrupted. This situation is called *nested* interrupts.

Usually, interrupts can be prioritized, and enabled in such a way that higher-priority interrupts can interrupt lower-priority ones, but not vice versa. One simple way of doing this is *daisy-chaining* (Fig. 7.7). In order for a device to generate an interrupt, it has to receive an enabling signal from the processor. This enable signal is "daisy-chained" from one device to the next, and when a

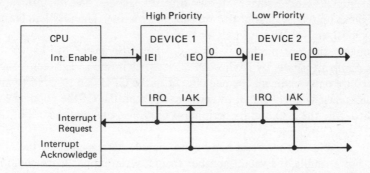

Figure 7.7. Interrupt daisy chain. A device will only generate an interrupt if its IEI line is high. If a device is requesting an interrupt, it will hold its IEO line low.

device decides to generate an interrupt, it blocks the enable signal to the rest of the chain. After the interrupt has been serviced, the processor sends a signal to the device that tells it to pass the signal on once more. In this way, devices closer to the processor on the chain have higher priority.

Many processors also have several interrupt lines that can be disabled (*masked*) separately, and almost all have one such line of very high priority that cannot be disabled. Such a non-maskable interrupt can be used to signal catastrophic events such as power failure or memory parity errors. It is also commonly used for debugging, since it can interrupt any process immediately. A button labeled "Break" on the front panel of a microcomputer is usually connected to the non-maskable interrupt line.

Vectoring. If more than one event in a system can cause an interrupt, there has to be some way of determining which one has caused a particular interrupt. There are two basic ways of doing this: polling and *vectoring*. Polling means reading a status bit from each potential interrupt source to determine which one is active. This is slow. Vectoring involves somehow associating a number with each possible interrupt source, and looking the number up in a table to determine the address of the routine that will handle the interrupt. (Such a table of subroutine addresses was once called a "transfer vector;" these days every manufacturer calls it something else.)

There are several ways to get such a number. One is to use a "priority encoder" chip such as the 74148. This device has eight input lines and three output lines; its output is the binary index of the highest-numbered active input line. A single I/O read can then determine the interrupt source with the highest priority, and software can use this as an index into a transfer vector. Some manufacturers now sell interrupt priority encoders specifically for their microcomputers (e.g. Intel 8259 and Motorola 6828).

Another method is to incorporate several interrupt lines into the CPU chip itself. The CPU then provides its own priority encoder, and the interrupt hardware picks up the address of the appropriate routine. The problem is that pins are expensive, so there are rarely enough.

Probably the best method is for each interrupt source to "know" its own index number (usually by having the CPU write it into a register). When such devices are daisy-chained, the one closest to the CPU can respond to an interrupt acknowledgement signal by sending the number. Of the popular eight-bit families, only the Z80 and its peripheral chips use this method; all of the popular 16-bit CPU's use it.

It is possible for the vector number to include data, especially in 16-bit systems. For example, the vector number from a serial input device could include the received data in the high-order byte. (I am not aware of any peripheral chips that do this, but an intelligent controller board could do it easily.)

Interaction Between Levels

Interrupt routines interact with the background process (and with each other) in two general ways: by transferring timing and synchronization signals, and by transferring data. These two are closely related: a timing signal can be considered as a single bit of data, and access to data requires timing signals that announce their availability.

Synchronization. Synchronization involves a single bit of information: "It's time!" Usually it is an interrupt that sends the information, and the background program that receives it. This is usually accomplished by setting some flag variable to one when the time comes.

Naturally, an acknowledgment is sometimes required, and in any case the variable has to be cleared in preparation for the next signal. This is usually done by the receiving task after the condition has been handled (or at least noticed).

This kind of flag variable is called a *binary semaphore*. (Semaphores have been mentioned in Chapter 3, and will be discussed further in Chapter 8.)

Often it is possible for an event to happen more than once before the background program gets around to handling it. In this case, a counter must be used instead of a flag. The interrupt routine increments the counter when the event happens, and the background program decrements it. The semaphore has now become an *integer semaphore*. The counter is usually good for something besides a signal; it is now the number of data items in a buffer, or the number of timing pulses received.

A subtlety arises: consider the background operation of decrementing the counter by one. In machine instructions, it might look like

> **load** register with counter
> **subtract** 1 from register
> **store** register into counter

What prevents an interrupt from happening sometime between the load and the store, resulting in an undetected event? This can be an extremely hard bug to find, since in a program with several thousand instructions, the probability of an event's occurring within the two-instruction window is quite small. Worse, depending on the length of the main loop and the timing between events, it may *never* happen, until years later when the logic of the program is changed to put the decrement in a different place!

The solution is to ensure that an interrupt *cannot* happen in this place. If necessary, instructions can be included to disable and re-enable interrupts, but most microcomputers have single instructions to increment and decrement variables in memory. These are sufficient if no other processor is sharing memory (and we'll get to that problem two chapters from now). Most compilers will not generate an increment or decrement instruction, so you may have to write assembly-language semaphore routines. A few C compilers *will* generate them, in response to the + + and − − operators. But this is highly implementation-dependent and not to be counted on.

When an increment or decrement operation has to be uninterruptable, we will use the following subroutines, which take the address of a variable being used as a semaphore, and increment or decrement it.

```
increment( sem)
int *sem;
{
    disable();
    *sem += 1;
    enable();
}

decrement( sem)
int *sem;
{
    disable();
    *sem -= 1;
    enable();
}
```

Notice that unless the interrupt routine is interruptable, and unless *that* interrupt routine uses the same semaphore, it is not necessary to worry about interruptions while *incrementing* the counter.

Of course, nothing prevents the opposite situation, in which the background program increments the counter, and the interrupt routine decrements it. This corresponds to, for example, a foreground process that is trying to print characters, and an interrupt process that sends them one by one to a serial port. A further subtlety develops here: when the counter goes to zero, the interrupt routine has nothing more to do. Usually, whatever is generating the interrupts then stops generating them. The background routine has to detect when this has happened, and restart the interrupt source.

Simply detecting that the count has gone from zero to one is sufficient if the interrupt source was actually disabled when the count went from one to zero, that is, when the last data item was handled. This is not always the case—sometimes the interrupt source is allowed to run on in hopes that by the time the next interrupt happens, another data item will have appeared. (This often happens with serial interface chips, which generate an interrupt when they are ready to transmit another character.)

This requires another (binary) semaphore that indicates whether the interrupt source is running. The following pair of programs does the trick:

```
int      running;          /* interrupt process is running */
int      count;            /* event counter                */


/* main program fragment */

    increment(&count);
    if (! running) {
        running = 1;
        start_interrupts();
    }


interrupt() {

    if (count == 0) {
        running = 0;
        stop_interrupts();
    } else {
        count--;
        handle_data();
    }
}
```

We will examine this problem again in the next chapter, where the presence of other tasks will make it somewhat more complicated.

Mutual Exclusion. The "subtleties" above are special cases of the *mutual exclusion* problem, which arises wherever a data structure is shared between two processes. The classical solution to this problem is the use of a semaphore to signal the data's availability. A binary semaphore is sufficient.

In the case of interrupts, the problem is simplified by two facts: we can always disable interrupts while operating on a data structure, and even if we do not, the interrupt routine must run to completion before resuming the background program. This last point can sometimes be used to advantage—it is often possible to make a sequence of code interruptable if we know that the interruption is "clean," in the sense of always leaving the shared data in a consistent state. As we will see in the next chapter, it is not always possible to guarantee this in a system with multitasking.

Buffers

When a piece of data is passed between an interrupt and a background process (or another interrupt), it has to be placed in some piece of shared memory.

Such a piece of memory is called a *buffer*. A buffer generally holds more than one data item, since data may be sent by one process faster than the other can accept it. Semaphores are needed to signal the availability of data.

The general case of buffering data between tasks will be treated in the next chapter. The case with interrupts is simpler, and will be treated below.

Ring Buffers.   The simplest kind of buffer to implement (and use) is the *ring buffer* or *circular buffer* (Fig. 7.8). The ring buffer is an array with two pointers (indices) into it, one for writing and the other for reading. The pointers are incremented modulo the size of the buffer, making it look like a continuous ring, with the read pointer following the write pointer around the ring.

The following are the declarations for a ring buffer, and the read and write routines. In the example, the buffer stores character data (the most common case).

```
#define BUFSIZE 100
struct buffer {
    int count;              /* number of data items present */
    int size;              /* total size */
    int readp;             /* read pointer */
    int writep;            /* write pointer */
    char data[BUFSIZE];    /* the data itself */
} a_buffer = {0, BUFSIZE, 0, 0, 0};

/* write routine.  Returns 0 if buffer full, */
/*                 otherwise returns 1        */

int write(item, buf )
char item;
struct buffer1 *buf;
{
    if (buf->count == buf->size) return(0);
    increment(&buf->count);
    buf->data[buf->writep++] = item;
    if (buf->writep == buf->size) buf->writep = 0;
    return(1);
}

/* read routine.  Returns 0 if buffer empty,   */
/*                otherwise returns next item */

char read(buf)
struct buffer *buf;
{
    char item;

    if (buf->count == 0) return(0);
```

```
    decrement(&buf->count);
    item =buf->data[buf->readp++];
    if (buf->readp == buf->size) buf->readp = 0;
    return(item);
}
```

There are a couple of things to notice in the routines above. First is the fact that they implement an abstract data type, and so are a good candidate for inclusion in a separate module. Second is that uninterruptable increment and decrement operations do not have to be used for the pointers, because each routine operates on its own pointer. The routine called from the interrupt does not need to protect the increment or decrement of the count, either, unless it can itself be interrupted by something that operates on the *same* buffer.

Variations.   The count is not strictly necessary—the pointers can be tested for equality to see if the buffer is empty. This is a little trickier: if the write pointer is *one less than* the read pointer, the buffer is full. At least one array cell is always unused (otherwise equal pointers would mean that the buffer is *either* empty or full!). Then, too, pointer comparisons usually take longer than comparisons with zero (and the count can be a single byte if the buffer is small), and finally the method does not generalize well to the use of semaphores between tasks.

Yet another variation (and a common one) is to make the two pointers actual addresses rather than array indices. This is sometimes faster, although if the buffer is at a known place in memory and the data are characters, indexed

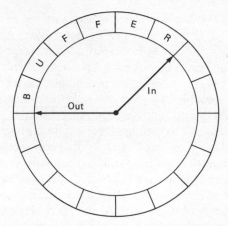

Figure 7.8. A ring buffer. The string "BUFFER" has been written into it and is waiting to be read.

addressing may be nearly as fast. Another variation is to make the read routine wait (loop) if the buffer is empty.

Block Buffers. When the data are arranged in blocks which are transferred only on request (for example, disk sectors or network packets), the ring buffer is unnecessary, and a simple array is sufficient. The buffer is filled by one process, and emptied by the other.

A pair of binary semaphores could be used to indicate that the buffer is empty and full respectively, but if one of the processes is interrupt-driven only a single "busy" flag or semaphore is necessary. When the background process is finished with the buffer, it sets the "busy" flag and starts the interrupt process. When the operation is complete and the buffer available again, the flag is cleared. Before using the buffer again, the background process must check the flag to see whether the interrupt process has finished.

Double Buffering. When blocks can arrive at unpredictable times (as in a network), or when speed is desired (operating on one block while another is being transferred), two or more buffers can be used. This ancient practice (it is one of the earliest ways of managing I/O) makes the set of buffers into a large ring buffer, whose data items are whole blocks. Usually the buffers are linked by pointers, and each buffer has its own "busy" flag.

Each process has its own pointer, to its "current" buffer. These correspond to the read and write pointers of the ring buffer. As usual, if the background routine is writing (filling buffers) and the interrupt process is reading (emptying them), there will be complications having to do with stopping the interrupt process when there are no more buffers to be processed, and restarting it when a new buffer is filled.

If there are only two buffers, it is not necessary for each buffer to have a busy flag; a single "I/O complete" flag or test will do. As we will see in the next chapter, buffers can also be managed using message-passing operations. In this case, message headers replace the links between buffers, and exchanges (mailboxes) replace each process's "current buffer" pointer.

For some reason, double buffering has fallen into disuse, possibly because none of the popular microcomputer operating systems support it, possibly because it is rarely obvious to the high-level language programmer that double buffering is being done. The "read" and "write" operations of most high-level languages assume that the operation runs to completion before the program is allowed to proceed, or at least that any buffering is done by the system, not by the programmer. (Fortran is an exception, but Fortran is uncommon on microcomputers.) It is rarely possible to start an I/O operation and then proceed, getting an indication back when the operation is complete.

Modern language and operating-system designers seem to feel that the user should not be bothered with such complications, and indeed this is generally true. But real-time work, with its performance constraints, is an exception. (So is business programming, which tends to be I/O intensive.)

Passing State Between Interrupts

It is often necessary for an interrupt process to retain some state from one interrupt to the next. This may be as simple as a buffer pointer telling it which byte to output next. Sometimes, however, not just data but control needs to be passed from one interrupt to the next, making the interrupt process more like a continuous task than like a series of calls on the same subroutine.

There are ways of doing this without going all the way to a multitasking kernel. The simplest method works if the interrupt task is essentially a *series* of subroutine calls, each interrupt calling a different subroutine. In this case, each interrupt routine can modify the interrupt vector before it gives up control, so that the next interrupt will invoke the next routine in the series. Another way of looking at this is that the interrupt task is a coroutine instead of a simple subroutine.

If this is impractical (for example, if the interrupt vectors are in PROM), the main interrupt routine can simply dispatch through a pointer to the appropriate subroutine. The effect is the same. This technique works when the interrupt process is a sequence of "wait-for-event," "handle-event" operations. Both versions are variants of the table- driven polling loop, except that the table is the interrupt vector list, and the scheduling is event- driven instead of loop-driven.

I first encountered this trick in the driver for a floppy disk controller—the interrupt routine would wait for a sector hole, then set a timeout. The next interrupt would occur a set time later, when the next interrupt routine in the series would read a sector number from the disk. At this point it would either transfer data, or point the interrupt vector back to the first routine to wait for the next sector.

If the interrupt task is sufficiently complex that a "wait" operation can occur in the middle of a subroutine, this method will not work. In this case, the interrupt task needs its own subroutine stack, and the stack pointers of the background and foreground tasks have to be exchanged whenever control is passed between them.

This is a true multitasking system, but it is not feasible to have more than two tasks (foreground and background) going simultaneously. (There may still be other interrupts, but they should not have their own stacks.) In this case, it is still possible for the background task to treat the foreground as an interrupt process, with busy waits in the background, and with simple solutions to mutual exclusion problems.

8
Multitasking Systems

INTRODUCTION

Definition.

A *multitasking* system is one in which a single computer switches its attention between several sequential programs (tasks). In the real-time field, such a *context switch* is usually caused by an external event that generates an interrupt. In addition, usually present is a device (sometimes called a *real-time clock*) that generates interrupts at regular or specified intervals, for timing purposes.

Multitasking differs from foreground-background operation in that control is passed freely among the various tasks—there is no single background task to which control always returns. Interrupts occur, indeed, but an interrupt may cause the state (registers and stack pointer) of the task it has interrupted to be saved, and that of a different task to be restored.

The part of a multitasking system that manages the tasks and the communication between them is usually called the *kernel*, and the rest of the system is built around it. Sometimes, the kernel is augmented by the addition of routines to manage memory, I/O, and named disk files. This is called a *multitasking operating system*. It may also be called a *timesharing* or *real-time operating system*, depending on its intended use.

Timesharing. A *timesharing* system is a kind of multitasking system designed to support multiple, interactive users on terminals. The goals of timesharing systems are usually not compatible with those of real-time control systems, and timesharing systems in general make poor real-time systems unless they have been specifically designed for it. There are two main problems: scheduling and memory management.

Both problems arise from the timesharing system's need to divide the resources of computer time and memory "fairly" among the users (tasks). Scheduling is usually simple, sometimes making distinctions between interactive and compute-bound tasks. Memory management involves moving users' programs (or parts of them) between main memory and a "swapping" device, usually a disk.

Real-time situations, however, are not "fair." Often a task will have to stay locked in main memory, doing nothing, because it will eventually be needed to respond to some high-priority event. At that point the task will have to be run immediately. Most timesharing systems are not set up to handle this kind of situation, although a few are beginning to appear.

Another difference between timesharing and real-time systems is interaction between tasks. Timesharing systems attempt to isolate the users from one another, to give each the illusion of "owning" the machine. Tasks in a real-time system, on the other hand, need to interact in many ways, since they are presumably working on parts of a single problem.

Applications.

Multitasking is useful when the situation is too complicated to be dealt with by a single background task and interrupts. This can happen when several ongoing processes of roughly equal importance exist; for example, several motors on a robot arm. It also happens when real-time control is mixed with the support of one or more interactive computer users.

Other applications include logging or processing data from several asynchronous sources. In this case, a task would be assigned to each source, to process data as they arrived. Any application requiring a disk and a file system is likely to involve a multitasking operating system.

It is not always necessary (or even desirable) to purchase or write a complete operating system for multitasking. Single-chip microcomputers such as the Z8, with its multiple register sets, can support multitasking rather simply. Some languages, such as Ada, also provide support for multiple tasks, in effect including a simple multitasking kernel in their run-time library. Moreover, general-purpose multitasking systems often impose a large performance penalty.

An operating system *is* desirable, however, if the application includes a disk file system, or if the interaction between tasks is in any way complex (for example, involving messages or monitors). It is rarely desirable to build a custom operating system; they are obtainable from both microcomputer manufacturers and other sources at a price considerably less than the one or more man-years it would take to write one. A general-purpose real-time operating system may have to be customized, however, and this has to be taken into account.

The remainder of this chapter is divided into three parts: a brief, general description of multitasking system structures and performance; a detailed description of the programming techniques used in building a multitasking kernel and techniques for application programming.

GENERAL DESCRIPTION

General System Structure

A multitasking system takes the form of a number of more or less independent uniprocessing programs called *tasks*, tied together by a "glue" consisting of the context switching and other services provided by the operating system. Multitasking systems are usually built in layers, with each layer defining the abstract objects used by the outer layers (Fig. 8.1). It is sometimes useful to look on each layer as a "virtual machine," a computer with extended data types, on which the outer layers are implemented. (See the section in Chapter 5 on operating systems for a more general description.)

Communication between layers is more or less restricted. If the host computer has a "system call" instruction (a special kind of subroutine call that includes part of a context switch), it will be used for communication between tasks and inner layers of the system. Otherwise, subroutine calls must be used; usually an "operation code" parameter is passed to a single entry point that serves for all system functions. The system entry point is usually at a known, fixed location in memory; this saves the effort of relinking when the system changes.

The Kernel

The innermost layer of a multitasking system is the kernel; in some real-time systems this is the only layer. The fundamental service provided by the kernel is task (context) switching. Usually, it also provides operations for scheduling, synchronization, and inter-task communication. (Kernel operations are sometimes called "primitive operations" or simply "primitives," in a vaguely sociological analogy.)

The fundamental tool of the kernel-builder is the *queue*, which we have already met in connection with buffers. Almost everything in a kernel involves a queue—queues of tasks waiting for events, a queue of ready tasks waiting for the processor, a queue of timed events waiting to happen. These queues may be linked lists (usually doubly-linked for easy insertion and deletion), ring buffers, or other structures; linked lists are the most popular.

Other System Services

An operating system has to manage other resources besides the CPU, mainly time, memory, and I/O devices. Timekeeping includes delays, timeouts, and scheduling. Memory management may be as simple as allocating blocks of

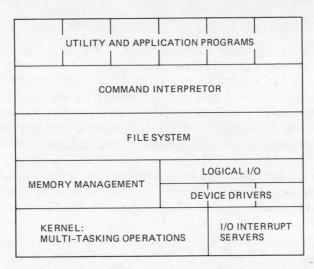

Figure 8.1. The structure of a typical multitasking operating system.

storage for buffers and other uses, but may be complicated by such problems as paging and virtual memory (which we will discuss later in this chapter). I/O is usually managed by means of *logical devices* and *files*, abstract I/O devices that serve as connections between a task and a real (*physical*) device.

Whether these services are implemented as separate tasks or as part of the kernel is a matter of implementation choice. Implementing them as tasks is "clean" in a theoretical sense, but often imposes a considerable burden in context-switching time. When implemented using tasks, each resource has a "manager" task, and other tasks needing the resource send messages to the manager. This implies at least two task-switches per operation, which is why cleanliness is often sacrificed for expediency.

Application Programs

The ultimate goal of a real-time operating system is to run *your* application programs that control real-time processes. (Note that this is *not* the goal of a timesharing system, whose goal is either to help you *develop* programs, or to allow many users to run interactive, not real-time, applications.) A real-time application usually consists of a number of co-operating tasks. In a system with a disk, the applications are loaded from files.

Application-level programs in systems with disks usually include a command processor (which may occupy a privileged status, but need not), and various utility programs for managing files and other purposes.

Interrupts

Strictly speaking, interrupts are not necessary for multitasking—tasks could politely resume one another at appropriate intervals. This is rarely either possible or desirable, so in fact it is interrupts that cause most of the task-switching in a multitasking system. Although it is possible for every interrupt to immediately resume a task in order to service it, the overhead for this is high. (This is one reason why "toy" operating systems developed in academic environments often fail miserably in the field—elegant, clean implementations are rarely efficient.)

In fact, a multitasking system looks more like the background task of a foreground-background system. Interrupts do their work in the foreground, as usual, and occasionally signal a task with the news that something needs further attention.

Performance

Task-switching is expensive. It is more expensive in a multitasking system than in a foreground-background one, because of the extra bookkeeping required for scheduling. Protection, virtual memory, and other refinements add to the context-switch time by providing more things to save and restore for each task. As a result, task-switching usually takes on the order of a millisecond (i.e., from .1 to 10 mSec, depending on the system).

Latency Time.   Interrupt latency may be considerably less than this, if the system is designed so as not to disable interrupts for long periods. (Unfortunately, it is easier to disable interrupts while executing system calls than to figure out when they *really* need to be disabled, so in many systems interrupt latency is also on the order of a millisecond.)

Task-switching latency (the time required to preempt a low-priority task when a higher-priority task is resumed due to some event) is at least equal to the sum of the interrupt latency and the task-switching time, but is often more. As with interrupts, this is due to the fact that task switching may be disabled while performing operations on system data structures shared by several tasks.

Response Time.   Because of the possible difference between interrupt latency and task-switching latency, there are two possible values for response time, depending on whether the response requires a task switch, or can be handled by an interrupt. When a system is specified, it is necessary to distinguish between the two.

SYSTEM PROGRAMMING TECHNIQUES

Queue Management

As we have seen, the basic building-block for kernel-builders is the queue. Indeed, almost everything in an operating system is associated with a queue of some sort—tasks waiting for semaphores, events waiting for their time to happen, messages waiting to be received, and so on. It is not surprising that some operating systems have been built whose only operations are "enqueue" and "dequeue."

A queue is a collection of objects which is accessed in roughly a "first-in, first-out" (FIFO) order, although in operating systems the objects on queues may be ordered by priority or another criterion other than time.

Queue Structures. A queue can be implemented using a ring buffer, and usually is when the objects in it are characters. For more general queues, however, the most common structure is the doubly-linked list. (Single links with pointers to the first and last element are sufficient if objects are never deleted out of sequence; this turns out to be rare. A doubly-linked list also lets us use the same structure for the queue header as for a node.)

A queue element, or *node*, then, will look something like this:

```
struct q_node {
    struct q_node *next,      /* pointer to next item */
                  *last;      /* pointer to last item */
};
```

The node structure could be separately allocated, but this is rarely a good idea—it takes too much time to allocate and de-allocate nodes. It is better to make the node part of the data structure for the object that is being put on the queue. If possible, the queue node should be the first thing in the object's data structure, so that a pointer to the object is also a pointer to the queue node.

If items on a queue are prioritized, the node must include the priority. On a microprocessor, it is usually a good idea to make the priority the first element of the node structure, since it is usually easier to operate on the word a pointer is pointing to than a word at an offset from it.

A queue *header*, the data structure by which the queue is referenced, needs to have pointers to the first and last objects on the queue. This, conveniently, is provided by an ordinary queue node linked in between the first (next) and last objects. The header of an empty queue points to itself; deleting an item from an empty queue will have no effect, which is also convenient.

It is also sometimes desirable for an object on a queue to include a pointer directly to the queue header. This is especially true if the queue header contains other information which must be updated when an object is deleted out of sequence. (For example, a semaphore would have to have its count updated if a waiting task is removed out of sequence due to a timeout.)

Queue Operations. The basic operations on a queue are to insert and delete nodes. A little cleverness in defining their parameters helps. Let's suppose that we are passing them a queue header. The **insert** operation wants to make the object being inserted the *last* one in the queue; **delete** wants to delete and return the *next* one. Assuming that we want delete to return NULL (zero) if the queue is empty, we have:

```
/***********************************************
** q_insert(queue, node)
**        insert node as last element of queue
**        (or the element before a given node)
***********************************************/
q_insert(q, n)
struct q_node *q,      /* the queue header */
              *n;      /* the node to insert */
{
    n->next = q;
    n->last = q->last;
    q->last = n;
    n->last->next = n;
}

/***********************************************
** q_node *q_delete(queue)
**        delete and return the next element
**        of the queue
***********************************************/
struct q_node *q_delete(q)
struct q_node *q;
{
    struct q_node *n;   /* the deleted node */

    if (q->next == q->last)    /* empty        */
        return(NULL);
                               /* not empty    */
    n = q->next;               /* ... delete   */
    q->next = n->next;
    q->next->last = q;
    return(n);                 /* return node  */
}
```

These may be used to insert an object before, or delete an object after, any object on a queue. Sometimes, however, we want to delete a particular node.

In this case, we do not need to worry about whether the queue is empty, so there is nothing to return. We add the further refinement (also possible in **q__delete**) of making the deleted node point to itself, so that if we should try to delete it again, nothing will happen. This is not as unlikely as it sounds— suppose the node is a task, and we want to remove it from any queue it happens to be waiting on before resuming it. It might *not* be waiting! In any case, we get the following routine:

```
/***********************************************
** n_delete(node)
**      delete a node from its queue
***********************************************/
n_delete(n)             /* delete node */
struct q_node *n;
{
    struct q_node *nl, *nn;

    nl = n->last;       /* relink neighbors */
    nn = n->next;
    nl->next = nn;
    nn->last = nl;

    n->next = n;        /* point node at self */
    n->last = n;
}
```

There are, of course, many other ways to implement these routines. For example, we could have implemented **q__delete(q)** using **n__delete(q -> next)**. These routines are also good candidates for writing in assembly language for speed, since they are done often.

Mutual Exclusion. If a queue might be accessed by more than one task (which applies to almost all queues in an operating system!) it will be necessary to exclude access by other tasks when one of the above queue operations is being done. A superficial analysis might suggest that a semaphore could be used in the classical manner, but a semaphore has a queue in it!

The usual solution in a multitasking system is to disable interrupts while the queue operation, and any associated processing, are going on. With only a single processor, this is sufficient to ensure that no other task will try to access the queue. With multiple processors, the solution is to busy-wait if another processor is using the queue.

Some operating systems take the rather drastic step of disabling interrupts whenever a system call is being serviced, but this can degrade performance considerably. It is possible to avoid disabling interrupts almost entirely by simply setting a "lock" flag, and having interrupt routines that want to execute system calls queue their requests when the lock is set. Then when the lock is cleared by the task that set it, all of the queued requests are done. This is rather elaborate and somewhat tricky. Even more elaborate and tricky schemes are possible if we try to lock particular data structures.

For the remainder of this book, we will assume the existence of operations called **lock**() and **unlock**() that do whatever is necessary to prevent other tasks from accessing a data structure.

Task Management

Task Control Blocks.   The data structure that the kernel uses to keep track of a task is sometimes called a *Task Control Block*, or TCB, although terminology varies considerably from system to system.

A TCB must contain the task's stack pointer, at least. Sometimes it also contains the task's registers and program counter, but it is often easier to save these on the task's stack, since most processors have special instructions for doing this. The information that has to be saved when switching tasks is essentially the same as that which an interrupt routine has to save, and indeed most system call instructions are software simulations of interrupts. (In fact, in the 6800 family the system call instruction is called "software interrupt," and like a hardware interrupt it automatically saves all the registers on the stack. This makes task-switching especially easy. Task-switching is also easy in machines like the TI 9900 and Zilog Z8, which keep their working "registers" in memory and refer to them using a pointer.)

A TCB also contains whatever other information the system needs for keeping track of the task, including scheduling priorities, pointers to other tasks, and pointers to the blocks of memory used by the task. It is also usual, as we have mentioned before, for the first thing in a TCB to be a queue node for whatever queue the task is waiting on. (If the task might be waiting on several queues simultaneously, for example a semaphore and a clock timeout, it may be necessary to have several queue nodes embedded in the TCB.)

In systems with separate stacks for "system" and "normal" or "user" modes, it is usual for tasks to run in "normal" mode, with a stack for each task, while all interrupts and kernel operations share a single stack. It is also possible to allocate a separate system stack for each task, which allows tasks such as device drivers to run in system mode. This means that they can perform I/O and other "privileged" instructions, which is useful in real-time systems. The disadvantage is that more memory is required for each task.

In any case, assuming a suitable structure "cpu" for holding the task's CPU registers (possibly just the stack pointer), a typical task control block structure might look like this:

```
struct task {
    struct q_node t_queue;      /* queue to wait on */
    int           t_priority;   /* scheduling priority */
    struct cpu    t_cpu;        /* task's CPU state */
    unsigned      t_delay;      /* timing delay */
}
```

A real task control block will usually have much more in it than shown here.

Again, this is not the only possibility. Before structures were popular, and most data structuring was done using arrays, a "task" was simply an index into each of several arrays, one for each element of the TCB structure. Thus, the priority for task **n** would be in **priorities[n]**. This has its advantages—it may be faster (depending on the CPU), and a task can be referred to using a small number instead of a pointer. It does, however, have a somewhat archaic flavor, and the disadvantage that the total number of tasks is fixed when the system is linked.

Saving the CPU State. As we have mentioned, the CPU state may be as simple as a copy of the stack pointer or a pointer to a set of "working registers" in memory. It is also possible to save the complete set of CPU registers, or at least as many as the language you are writing in expects to be saved when calling a subroutine. Having all the registers of a task in one place may make debugging easier.

Some operating systems save the complete state of the CPU at the point a system call is given or an interrupt occurs, putting the state in the task control block. Saving state immediately, rather than waiting for a task switch, means that the operating system code does not execute as part of a task, and so cannot make use of the same synchronization and other mechanisms that are available to tasks. A similar problem applies on two-stack machines like the Z8000 if tasks run exclusively in user mode and all interrupts and system calls share the same system-mode stack.

Task States. A task can be in any of three basic states: *running*, *ready*, and *waiting*. A *running* task is in control of the processor and is executing instructions. A *ready* task is waiting for the running task to release control of the processor, but is otherwise able to run. A *waiting* task will become ready only after some event external to it occurs. (Some systems split some of the states, or add states such as "nonexistent" and "killed." It is also possible to merge states by treating running and ready as the same state, or to consider a ready task as waiting for the CPU.) These states and transitions are summarized in Fig. 8.2.

Scheduling

The activity of allocating the processor among the running and ready tasks is called *scheduling*, and usually involves assigning each task a priority. Scheduling can be either *preemptive*, in which a task of higher priority can interrupt (preempt) a running task of lower priority when it becomes ready, or *nonpreemptive*. Most real-time systems use preemptive scheduling.

There are three basic scheduling/task-switching operations: **run, resume,** and **suspend.** The **run** operation makes a *ready* task into a *running* task (and at the same time makes the previously-running task *ready*), **resume** makes a *waiting* task *ready* (and possibly *running*, if it has higher priority than the currently-running task and if preemption is allowed), and **suspend** makes a *running* or *ready* task into a *waiting* task. **Suspend** usually involves specifying the event which the task is waiting for.

A scheduling decision has to be made whenever a *waiting* task is resumed (whether to run it or simply make it ready), and whenever a running task is suspended (which ready task to run).

The Ready Queue.   The *ready* tasks waiting for the CPU are usually kept on a queue, sorted according to priority. If there are only a small number of priority levels, there may actually be a separate queue header for each priority, which saves searching when a task is made ready.

An alternative structure is a list of all tasks, with the *ready* tasks marked. This, of course, takes time to search. It is possible to avoid searching when resuming a task; simply compare its priority with that of the current task. A search is unavoidable when the current task is suspended, but we can cut it

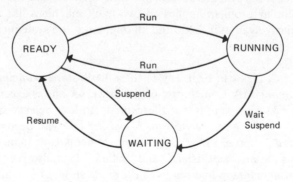

Figure 8.2. Task state transition diagram.

short by starting with the current task, since we know that there is no task of *higher* priority ready to run. Also, if an interrupt arrives during the search and resumes a task of higher priority than the task currently being examined, we can abandon the search and run the new task. (This is slightly tricky to implement—there are mutual exclusion problems.)

Scheduling Operations. Simplified versions of the basic scheduling operations are presented here. Note particularly that **resume** assumes that all it needs to do is delete the task from whatever queue it is on. In some systems, the task control block may have to contain information about what else to do, if it is possible for a task to be waiting for one thing, and resumed for some other reason.

We also present declarations for the current task pointer and the *ready* queue, and an external declaration for the routine that does the work of actually switching CPU states. Note that **run** has no parameters—it runs the highest-priority ready task.

```
/*****************************************
** t_switch(old, new)
**      switch tasks.
**      Must be written in assembler.
*****************************************/
extern t_switch();

/*****************************************
** Variables:
**      cur_task -- currently-running task
**      ready_q  -- the ready queue
*****************************************/
struct task    *cur_task;
struct q_node  ready_q;

/*****************************************
** run()    -- run highest-priority task
*****************************************/
run()
{
    struct task *t;

    /*
     * Look for highest-priority task.
     *    (Since the queue links are at the
     *     front of the task structure, we
     *     can simply type-cast a queue link
     *     instead of computing an address.)
     */
```

```
            if (cur_task == (struct task *)ready_q.next) {
                /*
                 * highest-priority task already running.
                 * -- nothing to do
                 */
                return;
            } else {
                /*
                 * Switch tasks.
                 */
                t = cur_task;
                cur_task = (struct task *)ready_q.next;
                t_switch(t, cur_task);
            }
    }


    /*****************************************
    ** suspend(task, queue)
    **      suspend a task on a queue
    *****************************************/
    suspend(t, q)
    struct task *t;
    struct q_node *q;
    {
        /*
         * Remove task from ready queue.
         * Insert on the given queue,
         *  (if there is one).
         */
        n_delete(&t->t_queue);
        if (q != NULL)
            q_insert(q, &t->t_queue);
        /*
         * If we just suspended the current task,
         *  run the next one.
         */
        run();
    }


    /*****************************************
    ** resume(task)
    **      resume a task
    *****************************************/
    resume(t)
    struct task *t;
    {
```

```
        struct task *temp;
        /*
         * Remove t from queue it is waiting on.
         */
        n_delete(&t->t_queue);
        /*
         * Search ready queue and insert t.
         *    Includes check for empty queue.
         */
        temp = (struct task *)ready_q.next;
        while (&temp->t_queue != &ready_q
              && temp->t_priority > t->t_priority)
            temp = (struct task *)temp->t_queue.next;

        q_insert(&temp->t_queue, &t->t_queue);
}
```

Multiple Waits.   The **suspend** and **resume** operations, and their associated data structures in the TCB, are more complicated if a task can be waiting for more than one event (for example, a semaphore or a timeout). One approach is to separate the queue node from the task, and to allocate nodes from a free list whenever one is required. Allocating a data structure, unfortunately, is usually expensive, and there is always the danger of running out of free nodes.

A better approach is to determine *when a task is compiled* (or linked, or whatever) what will be the maximum number of queues that the task will need to wait on at any one time, and to allocate that many queue nodes in the task control block or some associated area. The queue nodes can then be referenced as an array instead of having to be linked together with the task.

The Real-Time Clock

The real-time clock, with its regular ticking, is the heart of the real-time system. It schedules events, allocates the processor's time among tasks, times delays and timeouts. There are real-time systems that don't need a clock (and are driven entirely by external events), but not many.

Types of Real-Time Clock.   There are two general ways of implementing a real-time clock. The most common uses a device that interrupts the CPU at regular intervals (*ticks*). A less common form, requiring more elaborate hardware, lets the processor specify the interval to the next interruption.

Regular Intervals.   A clock that interrupts at regular intervals is simple, and keeps good time. Usually the interrupt service routine (*clock server*) maintains a time of day, or time since startup, along with its other duties. The tick interval is usually between one and 100 milliseconds, with the most common interval being about 17 mS ($\frac{1}{60}$th of a second, derived from the US power-line frequency). One millisecond is too fast for most microcomputers; the trouble with a regular-interval clock is that the clock server eats up CPU time even if nothing is scheduled to happen for a long time. At least, it eats up a relatively *constant* fraction of the CPU, and predictability can be helpful.

The regular-interval clock is the best method to use if something has to be done at short, regular intervals anyway, such as refreshing a display. (On the TOPS-10 timesharing system for the PDP-10, there is a system call to attach a piece of code to the real-time clock, to be run every N ticks. The code was said to be running in "spacewar mode," after the early video game that was the first application for this feature.)

Specified Intervals. As we have mentioned, frequent clock interrupts can use up lots of time. The solution is for the CPU to compute the interval to the next event, and instruct a timer to wake it up after that amount of time. With the variety of counter-timer chips available, this is almost as simple as the regular-interval clock.

There are two problems. One is that most counter-timers keep only an eight-bit count, which doesn't last long, so that long intervals have to be split up. The other is that it is hard to maintain an accurate time of day, because there is no good way to either control or measure the interval between the time the interrupt occurs, and the time the timer is reset (in other words, the response time).

In many applications, however, only intervals matter, and an accurate time of day is not required (or can be kept independently). Because the resolution of the timer is limited only by the system clock frequency and not by the number of interrupts the CPU can respond to, intervals can be specified very accurately with this method.

Clock Servers. Along with the two kinds of clock, there are two ways of servicing it: either all clock operations can be done at interrupt level, or the interrupt can simply signal a semaphore when something has to be done, and a *task* can do the rest. The former is much more common—clock operations occur frequently in real-time systems, and task-switching is expensive.

Scheduling. The basic function of the clock is scheduling: making sure that things happen at particular times. One major factor that distinguishes the various scheduling techniques is exactly *what* things are being scheduled. There are several possibilities.

Task Scheduling. The simplest kind of thing to schedule is a task which is waiting for either a particular time or day, or a specified interval. Given a wakeup-time field in the task control block, the waiting tasks can simply be queued in time order on a *clock queue*. The only problem with wakeup times is keeping enough bits in the time to accommodate the maximum time the system will be running (or else taking the limited precision of the time field into account).

One solution is to keep, not a wakeup *time*, but an *interval* (sleep time) in the task block. This is natural for an interval timer, and pretty simple for a regular-interrupt clock. Now, inserting a task on the clock queue requires searching through the queue, subtracting wakeup intervals, until the result is less than the delay for the next task in the queue. The new task is then inserted at that point, and the wakeup interval of the next task is adjusted. The program is then

```
/***********************************************
** clk_sched(task, delay)
**        suspend the task at the appropriate
**        point on clk_queue.
***********************************************/
clk_sched(t, d)
struct task *t;
unsigned    d;
{
    struct task *p;        /* position on queue */
    /*
     * Search for place to put task t.
     */
    p = (struct task *)clk_queue.next;
    while ((p != (struct task *)&clk_queue
           && p->t_delay <= d))
    {
            d -= p->t_delay;
            p = (struct task *)p->t_queue.next;
    }
    /*
     * Insert t before p.
     * If p is not the queue header,
     * adjust its delay.
     */
    if (p != (struct task *)&clk_queue)
            p->t_delay -= d;
    t->t_delay = d;
    suspend(t, &p->t_queue);
}
```

Event Scheduling.   Not only tasks can be scheduled, but more general kinds of events as well. This kind of scheduling requires special-event nodes on the clock queue, and since allocating special-purpose nodes is expensive, this kind of scheduling is less common than task scheduling (which can be used to simulate it).

The kind of event that can be scheduled includes not only the usual kind of "event" which is related to the semaphore, but more general operations. In the most general case, the clock-event node could include a pointer to a subroutine and a list of parameters, permitting any kind of operation to be scheduled. But this is almost the same as creating a task, and scheduling *it*! The main difference is that the operation would be done by the clock server, at *its* (usually high) priority level, or even at interrupt level.

Time-Slicing.   One variant on scheduling is *time-slicing*, or *round-robin scheduling*—sharing the CPU among several ready tasks with the same priority. Each task has associated with it a *quantum* of time. When it has run for this amount of time, it is reshuffled to a point on the ready queue *after* any other tasks with the same priority. By assigning different quanta to different tasks, it is possible to adjust the relative amount of CPU time each will receive.

Time-slicing is the basic operation of a time-sharing system's scheduler; these usually have tricky ways of adjusting a task's quantum and priority according to whether it seems to be interactive, disk I/O-intensive, or compute-intensive. This kind of trickiness does not come cheap—some timesharing systems spend an amazing amount of time in their schedulers, which is another good reason why timesharing systems are poor for real-time.

Delays and Timeouts.   Another variant on scheduling is the *delay*: suspending a task for a specified interval. A close relative of the delay is the *timeout*, which amounts to suspending a task for a specified interval, or until some hoped-for event happens, whichever comes first. (In Ada, a task can wait for any of several events, one of which can be a delay. This shows the relationship between the two operations very clearly.)

Timeouts are tricky. There are two problems with waiting for more than one event: data structures (a single queue node for each task is not enough), and the fact that when one event happens, the task has to be removed from the other queues it was waiting on.

Time of Day.   As we have seen, a clock can keep the "time of day." This is sometimes called *wall* time, from the "clock on the wall," as opposed to the one in the computer. There are two problems involved with letting the system's scheduling clock keep the time of day: the system's clock is often not accurate enough (especially if it is an interval timer or is derived from the CPU's clock oscillator instead of from the power line); and when the system is not running (either because the power is off, or because the system has "crashed" in some way) the time is lost.

This leads to the obnoxious necessity in many microcomputer systems of telling the system what time it is (and often what date it is, as well) whenever the system is reset. The solution is obvious, and becoming more common: get an independent, battery-powered clock that can be read by the computer. There are now several clock chips that are designed to be interfaced to a computer rather than a display. Another possibility is a simple CMOS counter that keeps time in microseconds (or whatever); this is slightly less convenient to use, and no cheaper. Clock chips are mass-market items.

Signalling Between Tasks

Given a multiplicity of tasks attempting to co-operate on performing some function, it is necessary to pass information from one task to another. (This is in contrast to most timesharing systems, in which the main function of the operating system is to *prevent* interactions between the tasks.) Some of this information being exchanged is in the form of messages, which we will consider in the next section. Some information, however, consists of simple signals—"it's time to wake up" . . . "the data is ready" . . . "this resource is now in use."

Semaphores.   The basic structure for signaling between tasks is the *semaphore*, which we have already met descriptively in Chapter 3, and in a restricted form, for communicating with interrupts, in Chapter 7. A semaphore consists of a counter for signals that have not been received, and a queue for tasks that are waiting to receive signals.

Here we present a possible structure for semaphores, and the full implementation of the **wait** and **signal** operations:

```
struct semaphore {
        int             counter;
        struct q_node sem_queue;
}

/*****************************************
** sem_wait(semaphore)
*****************************************/
sem_wait(s)
struct semaphore *s;
{
```

```
        if (s->counter == 0)
                suspend(cur_task, &s->sem_queue);
        else
                s->counter--;
}


/*****************************************
** sem_signal(semaphore)
***************************************/
sem_signal(s)
struct semaphore *s;
{
    if (s->sem_queue.next == s->sem_queue.last)
        s->counter++;    /* queue empty */
    else
        resume(s->sem_queue.next);
}
```

Notice that **resume** removes its task from any queue it might be waiting on, so we don't have to worry about that in **sem_signal.** These operations have to be atomic, i.e. surrounded by lock-unlock pairs.

It is also possible to let the semaphore's counter go negative, in which case it counts the number of tasks waiting. The disadvantage of this is that, as usual, if a task is removed out of sequence the counter would have to be updated, requiring more information to be stored in the task-control block.

A semaphore's counter may be restricted to the values zero and one, in which case it is called *binary* semaphore.

Events. A close relative of the semaphore is the *event*. It differs from the semaphore in that if any tasks are waiting for an event, they are all resumed; and if none are waiting, the event is not recorded. Events are only useful for signaling, not mutual exclusion. (Some operating systems have events but not semaphores; they are afflicted with "race conditions," in which a task starts up an operation which will eventually signal its completion, and the completion event occurs before the task gets around to waiting.)

Notice that since events do not need to be remembered if no tasks are waiting for them, an event structure is simply a queue.

```
/*****************************************
** await(event)
***************************************/
await(event)
struct q_node *event;
{
    suspend(cur_task, event);
}
```

```
/******************************************
** cause(event)
******************************************/
cause(event)
struct q_node *event;
{
     while(event->next != event)
            resume(event->next);
}
```

The main attraction of events is their simplicity.

Uses of Signals. Semaphores and events are used for synchronization, mutual exclusion, and resource allocation. These tend to overlap to some extent: synchronization signals concern time, mutual exclusion signals concern control, and resource allocation signals concern objects; but there is a common thread of program structure among the three.

Synchronization. The use of semaphores for synchronization can be seen in the interaction between a clock (or other) interrupt and a server task. The interrupt routine's job is simply to wake up the task whenever an interrupt needs to be processed.

```
struct semaphore sem = {0, {&sem.sem_queue,
                             &sem.sem_queue}};

interrupt()
{
    sem_signal(&sem);
}

task()
{
    while (TRUE) {
        sem_wait(&sem);
        process_interrupt();
    }
}
```

Notice that the semaphore is initialized with a zero count, so that the task must wait until the first interrupt arrives. (Notice also the way the semaphore's empty queue is initialized.) If the interrupt arrives first, however, or if another interrupt arrives while the first is being processed, the task will simply proceed.

Notice that if an event had been used, extra interrupts would be *lost* in either of these situations. If the interrupt is a clock, for example, this would be a mistake—the task would keep bad time. With semaphores, it would have a chance to "catch up." On the other hand, if the interrupt is due to, say, the completion of some output operation, it may be acceptable to ignore the fact if no task is waiting for its completion.

Events can also be useful if they are associated with some other counter or queue that is going to be tested anyway.

Mutual Exclusion.   The "classical" use of semaphores is for controlling access to some data structure, such as a buffer or queue. If a data structure such as a queue is shared between two tasks, it can become corrupted if one task attempts to modify it while it is also being modified by the other. (Think what would happen to a queue if the operations of two instances of **insert** were interleaved!)

It is sometimes possible to design a data structure that is immune to such corruption. The ring buffer, for example, can tolerate a single writer and a single reader without corruption, *if* you are cautious about the order in which things are done, and if increment and decrement are atomic operations which return a condition code. In general this kind of design depends on tricky details of the instruction set, and can result in more trouble than it is worth. This is where semaphores come in.

The section of code that modifies a shared data structure is called a *critical section*. Each critical section begins with a **wait** on a semaphore (which is almost always called **mutex** in example programs in the literature), and ends with a **signal**. Thus,

```
struct semaphore mutex = {1, {&mutex.sem_queue,
                                &mutex.sem_queue}};


    /* start critical section */
    sem_wait(&mutex);
        /* critical section code */
    sem_signal(&mutex);
```

Notice that the semaphore is initialized with a count of one, indicating that no tasks are initially in the critical section. Here, **mutex** is a binary semaphore.

Getting the pairing of waits and signals right is something that should have help from the programming language. Semaphores, like "goto" statements, are a low-level primitive operation, and need to be used in a controlled manner. In C, they can be tamed by defining a few macros, like the following:

```
#define CSEC(s)      struct semaphore s = {1, {&s.sem_queue, \
                                               &s.sem_queue}}

#define CBEGIN(s)    wait(&s)
#define CEND(s)      signal(&s)
```

These are not perfect, but at least you can look for "begin ... end" pairs and be reasonably certain that you are doing the right thing. A simple checking program could make even more certain. *Monitors* are an essentially syntactic structure for declaring data structures with critical sections.

Resource Allocation. A critical section, or the data associated with it, can be considered as a kind of shared resource. The more general case has a pool of several identical resources (buffers, for instance) for which several tasks are competing. Once again a semaphore is used, this time with its count initialized to the number of resources available.

Tasks can then wait on the semaphore for a resource to become available, and signal the semaphore when releasing a resource. We will see this in action later when we look at messages.

Some systems provide a semaphore operation that lets a task wait for a specified number of signals before being resumed, and a complementary operation that generates a given number of signals. These are more efficient when a task has to accumulate several copies of the resource before proceeding—without them the task would sit in a loop waking up every time a resource became available, then go back to sleep to wait for the next. The extended operations will then save $2n$ task switches, where n is the number of resources required.

As an example of resource allocation using semaphores, let's re-do the ring buffer of the last chapter using semaphores to count the number of characters in the buffer, and the number of empty spaces remaining.

```
/***********************************************
** buffer data structure
***********************************************/
#define BUFSIZE 100
struct buffer {
    struct semaphore full;        /* full slots */
    struct semaphore empty;       /* empty slots */
    int size;                     /* total slots */
    int readp;                    /* read pointer */
    int writep;                   /* write pointer */
    char data[BUFSIZE];           /* the data itself */
};

struct buffer a_buffer = {        /* initialization*/
    {0, {NULL, NULL}},            /* full sem. */
    {BUFSIZE, {NULL, NULL}},      /* empty sem. */
    BUFSIZE,                      /* size */
    0,                            /* readp */
    0,                            /* writep */
    0,                            /* data */
};
```

```
/*********************************************
** write(item, buf)
**        Wait for an empty slot,
**        then write an item into the buffer.
*********************************************/
write(item, buf)
char item;
struct buffer *buf;
{
    sem_wait(&buf->empty);
    buf->data[buf->writep++] = item;
    if (buf->writep == buf->size) buf->writep = 0;
    sem_signal(&buf->full);
}


/*********************************************
** char read(buf)
**        Wait for a character to arrive,
**        then return it.
*********************************************/
char read(buf)
struct buffer *buf;
{
    char item;

    sem_wait(&buf->full);
    item = buf->data[buf->readp++];
    if (buf->readp == buf->size) buf->readp = 0;
    sem_signal(&buf->empty);
    return(item);
}
```

Deadlocks. A problem for any operating system in which tasks can wait is the *deadlock*, or *deadly embrace*. This occurs when two tasks are each waiting for the other to finish with something. This can occur whenever two or more resources are being shared. For example, task A has acquired the line printer (by waiting for a semaphore that indicates its availability), and is now waiting for task B to send it some data. But task B also wants to print the data before sending, and is now waiting for the line printer.

Avoiding Deadlocks. One simple way of avoiding deadlocks is to follow these rules:

1. Each task that needs a set of resources for some operation must acquire them all before starting the operation, and not release any of them until the operation is complete.

2. Resources must be allocated in the same order by all tasks, and released in the reverse order.

It is easy to see that following these rules will prevent the situation of the previous paragraph. This is not the only way of avoiding deadlocks, but it is by far the simplest. Unfortunately it only applies to resources that are manipulated within critical sections.

(Note that the program just presented for a ring buffer is not covered under this simple set of rules, because there are actually two sets of resources involved: empty spaces, and characters. Moreover, these resources are never *reserved*, in the sense of critical sections.)

Another way to deal with deadlocks is *not* to try to avoid them, but simply to provide a method of detecting and breaking them. This is usually done with *timeouts*—placing limits on the time that a task will wait for a resource. (This gets complicated, of course, since the task then has to deal with the error condition. Better to avoid the problem in the first place.)

Timeouts have another function, of course, which is preventing the system from hanging up while waiting for an *external* event, which may not happen. In other words, a resource may fail to signal its availability not because some other task is using it, but because it has been turned off, unplugged, jammed, or damaged. Obviously this kind of thing can *not* be prevented, and must either be suffered or allowed for. Deadlocks can thus be considered as one of several different kinds of error conditions that you are already checking for.

Communication Between Tasks

Now that we have considered the transmission of signals between tasks, it is time to consider the transmission of data. The most general kind of communication mechanism is the *message*.

Messages. A message is a piece of data being sent from one task (the *sender*) to another (the *receiver*). Usually messages are queued up on objects called *mailboxes* or *exchanges*, rather than on queues directly associated with tasks. This lets any of several co-operating tasks process a message. In multi-processor systems based on networks, messages are usually called *packets*. (See Fig. 8.3.)

There are as many different message-passing schemes as there are operating systems that use them (maybe more). Implementations can vary wildly. Depending on their efficiency, messages may be used to only a limited extent, or for every function in an operating system. It is fairly easy, for example, to view a semaphore as a mailbox for zero-length messages.

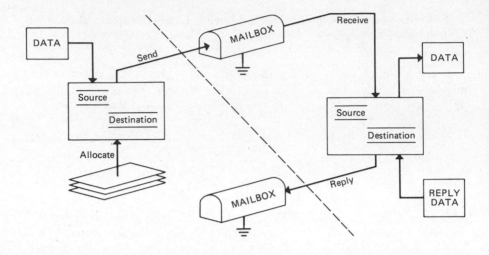

Message Structures.   A message is logically divided into two parts: a buffer for the data, and a *header* which contains queue links and other housekeeping information. One of the parameters of message-passing is whether the data have to be copied into a buffer, or whether the header simply contains a pointer to the data. Another possibility (becoming more common) is for the data to take the form of a pointer to a system-maintained *object*. Intel's iAPX 432, with its object-oriented architecture, supports this form of message-passing very well—objects are maintained and protected by the system.

Message Buffers.   One advantage to copying data into a message buffer is that the data can be sent between tasks in different address spaces. Since the buffer is separate from both the sending and receiving tasks, this works especially well for systems in which tasks can be swapped on and off of disk—it is not necessary for both tasks to be in main memory at the same time. (In many simple swapping systems, it may not be possible.)

Message buffers can be of fixed or variable size. Fixed-size buffers are often small (16 bytes or so), making them a rather low-bandwidth communication path. An alternative is to make them the size of a disk sector or memory-allocation page, somewhere between 128 and several thousand bytes. This may or may not include a header. Not only is allocation simplified, but page-sized messages can be transferred from one memory space to another just by changing the system's memory map.

Allocation.   Message headers and buffers have to be allocated somehow. The questions are *when*, and *by whom*. They can be allocated in advance of their use, or as part of the send operation, by either the system or the sender. "When" and "by whom" are obviously related; if the structure is allocated as part of the send operation it is necessarily done by the system. The converse is not always true, however—the sender may have to request a message structure from the system before sending it.

Fixed-size structures are easier and faster to allocate, so it is not surprising that most system-allocated message structures either have fixed-length buffers, or are mere headers with pointers into the sender's memory.

One excellent way of allocating message headers is to construct a large number of them and send them to some mailbox. Whenever a task needs to send a message, it first waits at this mailbox for an empty one. The mailbox is, of course, simply a free list in another guise.

Another allocation technique is for the sender to construct the message header and data somewhere in its own memory, either statically or dynamically. The system then "borrows" the structure, and the sender must refrain from changing it until the receiver is done with it. This, of course, requires that sender and receiver be in the same address space. Because it places the burden on the application programmer, this technique is popular in small systems, such as Intel's iRMX-80. It is also fast, since the entire structure—header, data, and all—can be created at compile time.

Message Operations. The basic operations on messages are **send** and **receive.** Each comes with several variants. For example, **receive** may either wait for a message if none is present, or return a null or an error code. The **send** operation may proceed immediately after queuing the message, wait for the message to be received, or even wait for a reply. If **send** waits, the message-passing operation is said to by *synchronous*; otherwise it is *asynchronous*. (We will examine synchronous communication later.)

There are other variations. The **send** operation normally takes two or three parameters: a message, a destination mailbox, and sometimes a "source" mailbox to which a reply can be sent. One obvious variant is **reply,** which sends a message back to its source. (It helps if the message header contains pointers to its source and destination.) Another variant is **forward,** which passes a message on to a further destination, without changing its source.

Variations on **receive** include the possibility for timeouts, and the ability to wait for a message from more than one mailbox. Like all forms of multiple waiting, this is tricky, and less efficient than the simple form. In systems that lack the feature, it can be simulated using forwarding tasks, one for each mailbox being waited on. Each forwarder passes messages on to a single mailbox that the ultimate destination task is waiting on.

Message Types. Sometimes messages can have types attached to them, and tasks can receive only the types they request. It is not clear that this has any advantage over setting up separate mailboxes for different types of message—certainly **receive** becomes slower, since it has to search through all the messages on the queue. Similarly messages can have priorities, and be received in priority order; this has a similar effect on **send.**

Message Implementation. One possible, simplified implementation for message-passing is presented here. The data portion of the message is here represented by an integer; it could just as well be a pointer or a buffer. No assumptions are made about how messages are allocated, or about how the data are put into the message. Messages include an optional reply field.

```
/*********************************************
** Mailbox and Message data structures.
*********************************************/
struct mailbox {
    struct q_node    x_queue;
    struct semaphore x_sem;
};
struct message {
    struct q_node    m_queue;
    struct mailbox  *m_reply;
    int              m_data;
};


/*********************************************
** send(message, mailbox, reply)
*********************************************/
send(msg, mbox, reply)
struct message *msg;
struct mailbox *mbox, *reply;
{
    msg->m_reply = reply;
    q_insert(msg, &mbox->x_queue);
    sem_signal(&mbox->x_sem);
}


/*********************************************
** struct message *receive(mailbox)
**        Receive a message.
**        Wait if no message present.
*********************************************/
struct message *receive(mbox)
struct mailbox *mbox;
{
    sem_wait(&mbox->x_sem);
    return((struct message *)q_delete(&mbox->x_queue));
}
```

```
/*************************************************
** int reply(msg)
**        Reply to a message.
**        Returns 0 if the message has no reply field,
**        1 otherwise.
*************************************************/
int reply(msg)
struct message *msg;
{
    if (msg->m_reply) {
            send(msg, msg->m_reply, NULL);
            return(1);
    } else {
            return(0);
    }
}
```

Messages for I/O. There is a clear similarity between message headers and buffers, and the buffer headers and block buffers used for logical I/O. Indeed there is no reason why logical I/O cannot be implemented using messages, and every reason it should be. One thing is lacking: a simple way to shuttle a message back and forth between two tasks (a device driver and a client task). The solution is a modified version of *reply*:

```
/*************************************************
** int shuttle(msg, mbox)
**        Shuttle a message back to its own reply
**        mailbox, and give the recipient a new
**        reply mailbox to shuttle back to.
**
**        Returns 0 if the message has no reply field,
**        1 otherwise.
*************************************************/
int shuttle(msg, mbox)
struct message  *msg;
struct mailbox  *mbox;
{
    if (msg->m_reply) {
            send(msg, msg->m_reply, mbox);
            return(1);
    } else {
            return(0);
    }
}
```

Pipes. Another form of intertask communication is the *pipe*, or *pipeline*. This is a Unix concept (indeed, pipes are one of the main attractions of Unix). A pipe is a connection between a pair of tasks which behaves like a pair of logical

I/O devices. One task writes characters into the pipe, and the other reads them out. The pipe in between is usually a ring or block buffer.

The big attraction of pipes is that they behave just like I/O. Especially in Unix, where files and devices are simple streams of characters, this means that programs that read a file from their "standard input" (the terminal, by default) and, after making some transformation on it, write their results on the "standard output," can be connected together like pieces of pipe. Such programs are called *filters*.

Pipes are exceedingly useful for building utilities and as a user interface device; they may have fewer uses in real-time systems, although the applications for (low-bandwidth) digital filtering, data-logging, and so on should be obvious.

Synchronous Communication.   Synchronous communication has the advantage that messages do not need to be buffered. Since the sender is waiting for the message to be received, there is no danger that the data in the sender's memory can be modified before the receiver gets around to looking at it. (Of course, it may be useful to buffer the data anyway if it is possible for the receiver to get swapped out while it is waiting.)

Monitors.   Instead of sending data to tasks, it is possible for the tasks to come to the data. A *monitor* is a shared data structure which contains a semaphore. It can only be operated on by a set of subroutines, each of which is a critical section. In other words, it is a sharable object which can only be operated on by one task at a time, and so it is always self-consistent.

Monitors have been used as the basis of complete operating systems, but their usefulness is limited. Since the monitor's data structure has to be shared, it cannot be used by tasks in separate address spaces, such as are found on some of the newer 16-bit machines with segmented address spaces. Another problem is that nested monitors and operations on two monitors at a time can easily lead to deadlocks.

Also, the monitor is really nothing more than a form of syntactic support for critical sections; no special programming is required to make use of them— only a compiler that lets you declare them.

Rendezvous.   The Ada language includes multitasking, and uses a form of synchronous communication called the *rendezvous*. This has the syntactic form, and much of the semantics, of a procedure call—the difference is that the called procedure is in a task environment different from the caller. Parameters can be passed by reference as well as by value, the implication being that the two tasks share the same address space. Obviously, the "message buffer" is the caller's stack frame, where the parameters are placed.

On the calling end of things, the rendezvous looks just like a procedure call. On the receiving end things are a little more complicated—an *entry* statement looks rather like a procedure *declaration*, except that a task can wait on more than one entry. Timeouts are also provided. Entry statements present all the usual problems associated with waits for more than one condition.

It is worth noting that at the time of writing, very few complete implementations of Ada's multitasking exist. The complicated semantics of the entry statement make it likely that implementations will tend to be inefficient.

Smalltalk Classes. The Smalltalk language is based on a construct called "message-passing" which is really a form of procedure call—there is no actual multitasking. Relatives of Smalltalk, however, *do* include multitasking with a similar form of message-passing. Briefly, all operations in Smalltalk are done by sending a "message" to an object.

A Smalltalk message is essentially a subroutine parameter list, as in Ada. The difference is that the object that receives the message is not a complete task, just a data structure. Also, and more important, the first parameter in the message is the name of the operation to be performed; this is then looked up in a table associated with the object's *class* (another object, that describes the structure and behavior of the first object). The result of this look-up is a *method*—a procedure for performing the operation, which is then called.

It is fairly simple to generalize such objects as either monitors, which would let multiple tasks operate on them, or as full tasks, in which case the method table would become a list of mailboxes or an Ada *select* statement. The idea of treating messages as requests for service to tasks or objects is a powerful one. By selecting the method for doing the operation at run time, it becomes easy to substitute one module for another with similar behavior.

Interaction with Interrupts

A multitasking system can deal with interrupts in one or more of three ways: switch tasks whenever they occur, treat them as part of the operating system, or treat them as a special kind of foreground task.

Interrupts as Task Switches. Switching tasks on every interrupts is "clean," in the sense that it is simple to implement. Whenever an interrupt occurs, a server task attached to that interrupt is resumed, or possibly a semaphore attached to the interrupt is signaled. All further processing is done in the interrupt.

The difficulty of this approach is that task-switching is usually much more expensive than simply saving context for an interrupt. (Of course, this is not *always* true. In systems with only one address space and little other context for each task, there may be little difference between a task switch and an interrupt. This may be especially true on working-register-in-memory machines like the TI 9900 and Zilog Z8, and on machines like the 6800 family that save all the registers on the stack when an interrupt occurs.)

Because of its nice theoretical properties, this approach to interrupts is often seen in operating systems developed in research environments such as universities.

Interrupts as Kernel Calls. The second way of looking at interrupts is as unexpected system calls (just as, in a foreground-background system, they are treated as unexpected subroutine calls). This is a natural view when all system calls share a common system-mode stack pointer, and tasks always run in normal mode. In this case, interrupts cannot issue system calls, but instead have access to all of the internal subroutines used by the kernel for operating on system data structures. This method works best when the kernel operations are done with interrupts turned off.

As usual, this technique has a price. In this case, it becomes difficult to nest interrupts. Worse, because interrupts become part of the kernel, the interrupt service routines usually have to be linked in with the kernel instead of being separately loadable. And worst of all, if users (as opposed to operating system implementors) are allowed to write interrupt service routines, all of the necessary kernel subroutines have to be documented and their interfaces frozen.

This approach to interrupts is seen in many "monolithic" operating systems, especially timesharing systems, in which user tasks are isolated from the "real world," and all I/O is done by the kernel. This is not a realistic view for real-time work.

Interrupts as Foreground Task. The last way of dealing with interrupts is to treat them as a special kind of foreground task. This is a natural way of working in systems where every task has its own system-mode stack (or in which there is only one stack pointer), and in which kernel operations are interruptable. The performance advantages are obvious: interrupts are rarely disabled, and no task switch is required when one occurs, so response time is short.

The price here is complexity: subtle problems arise in the interaction between interrupts, ordinary tasks, and the kernel. For example, there are three different cases that have to be considered, depending on whether an interrupt has happened during a task, a system call, or another interrupt. Also, although interrupts have most of the properties of tasks, they usually operate in the system's address space, and other parts of their context (such as their stack pointer and priority) are "borrowed" from whatever task was interrupted. The gains in performance are usually worth the price, however, and this view is taken by most real-time systems.

In this kind of system, interrupts can execute a limited subset of the system calls available to tasks. In particular, an interrupt routine usually cannot do anything that might cause a task to wait (such as waiting on a semaphore or receiving a message), because there is no way of knowing what task is actually executing. On the other hand, interrupts **signal** semaphores and **send** messages (sometimes using specially modified operations that use a different mutual-exclusion mechanism, in case a semaphore or message operation is in progress when the interrupt occurrs). To make up for the lack of wait operations, interrupts are given "test" operations, which return a failure code if a wait could occur.

Another odd aspect of interrupts is that task-switching operations such as **signal** or **resume** have to be deferred until just before control returns to the interrupted process. Otherwise, if a task switch occurs in the middle of an interrupt routine, anything done after the task switch will wait until *whatever task was interrupted* gets around to executing again. This delay can be enforced by "saving up" task switches until the end of the interrupt routine, or by forcing the programmer to save any task-switching operations until the last moment. Sometimes **lock** and **unlock** routines can be used to advantage here, to surround a section of code inside an interrupt routine that might cause a task switch.

Avoiding Task-Switching. Because task-switching is expensive, it is important to avoid it wherever possible. This is best done by treating interrupt service routines as if they were a kind of DMA hardware device. Data and commands are left in some shared data structure, and thereafter the interrupt routine can function independently. Eventually, when all of the data has been processed, the *last* interrupt can signal a semaphore or send a message to inform the task that the operation is complete.

In spite of the ring-buffer example above, signaling a semaphore every time a character goes in or out of a buffer is a *bad* idea unless it simply cannot be avoided. (For example, an interactive task like a display-oriented editor may really need to wake up for every character coming from a terminal. More often, however, a task can afford to wait for a complete line. The interrupt routine can handle the details of echoing and intra-line editing with backspacing.

This view of interrupts also provides a natural transition to multi-processor systems.

APPLICATION PROGRAMMING TECHNIQUES

Now that we have examined the foundations, as it were, of a multitasking system, it is time to turn our attention to the superstructure—the application program and the tasks that compose it.

Partitioning the Application

The first problem that faces the designer of a multitasking application is that of partitioning the application into tasks, and determining the interfaces between them. (We will assume that a multitasking operating system or kernel either already exists, or is being designed along with the tasks. In the first case, the services it provides determine the mechanisms by which the tasks must interact; in the second, it is just the opposite.)

Objects and Tasks. In most cases, the best way to proceed is with object-oriented design—identify the "real-world" objects and the operations to be performed on them, and then assign them computational counterparts. In many cases, real-world objects (such as limit switches) will correspond to operating-system objects (such as semaphores). In other cases, new objects will have to be defined.

Tasks Vs. Structures. One major decision is when to represent a real-world object as a task, and when a data structure is sufficient. A rule-of-thumb is to use a task whenever an ongoing process in the real-world is under computer control, and data structures for inert "things." Thus, a controller for a robot arm might use a task to control each motor, and a data structure to represent whatever the hand is carrying. When the ongoing process is fast, an interrupt server may be necessary instead of a task.

There will still be a data structure (though possibly a simple one) associated with each task, and the task will be performing operations on it. The task's job is feedback—keeping the data structure and the real-world object it represents up to date and mutually consistent. (Even with open-loop control, as for stepper motors, the task's job is to step the motors at the right time.) Any *other* task which needs to operate on the object will have to do so by sending a message to the managing task.

Of course, it is always possible for a task to manage several objects (as in a uniprocessing system). One reason for doing this is efficiency—task switches are expensive. Presumably the objects operated on by a task are either similar (making the task a manager for a particular data type), or different but causally related (making the task an overseer for a particular set of processes).

Object Managers. Tasks *can* be assigned to physical objects (object managers) as well as controlled processes (process managers). For example, when physical objects are being transformed (say, a block of metal in a milling machine) it may be useful to assign a task to maintain the computer's view of the state of the object.

Merely *following* the state of an object is rarely necessary unless the state of the object is not entirely determined by the processes being done on it by the machine. Another way of looking at an object-manager task, though, is that the object is giving *directions* to the process-manager tasks. Thus in the milling-machine example, the object-manager task is really in control: it knows what the finished part is supposed to look like, and guides the tools in order to get there.

A very special case of object managing occurs when the "object" is a human being issuing commands! In this case a user-interface task is almost certainly necessary.

Static Vs. Dynamic Creation. It is rarely desirable to create tasks dynamically, that is, while the system is running. Task creation requires storage allocation for the task control block, at least, and possibly access to mass storage to load the task's code. This should be done rarely if at all.

There are exceptions, of course. Tasks can be spawned to execute commands issued by an interactive user, as in a timesharing system. Object-manager tasks can also be created and destroyed as objects enter and leave the system, provided this does not happen very often (the milling machine is still a good example).

Possibly the best reason for creating and destroying tasks is to change the behavior of the system, or to reflect a change in its configuration. A good example is a communications controller in which protocols are handled by tasks. Changing the network interface from, say, Ethernet to X.25 doesn't happen very often, and can be easily accomplished by downloading a new set of protocol tasks. Another example might be a robot changing the tool on the end of its arm (for example, putting down a screwdriver and picking up a drill).

Coupling Between Tasks. Tasks can be coupled either *tightly*, by shared memory, or *loosely*, by messages or some other controlled communication channel. The difference is mainly one of bandwidth, but is reflected in other aspects of the system. Essentially, interaction bandwidth can be traded off against the degree of security provided.

Tight Coupling. Tightly-coupled tasks interact by means of data structures in shared memory. The bandwidth available is high—data generated by one task are instantly available to the other. On the other hand there is also considerable danger: what keeps one task from "clobbering" data private to the other (protection), or simultaneously modifying it (integrity)?

Compilers can provide much of the necessary data protection, since if the tasks are compiled separately each can have local variables inaccessible to the other. Compilers that "know about" critical sections, monitors, or rendezvous can also control data integrity by automatically enforcing mutual exclusion. Languages such as Ada, Modula-2, and Concurrent Pascal all help here.

In the absence of help from the compiler (and languages like C and Fortran provide little or no help), it is up to the programmer to use operating system aids like semaphores in a disciplined manner. On systems with memory management hardware, it is also possible to protect shared structures by placing them in a special section of memory accessible to both tasks, while also giving each task some private memory. Mutual exclusion can be accomplished in part by granting only one task access to the shared memory at any one time.

Loose Coupling.   There is a continuum from tight to loose coupling; moving a segment of memory between tasks in a controlled way is roughly in the middle. Loosely-coupled tasks communicate by some kind of asynchronous message-passing. Protection is easy, since the tasks can be in separate memory spaces. Data integrity is also easy to provide, since no data structures are shared (except structures maintained by the system, such as message headers, and we can assume that the system will take good care of them).

Loose coupling is both theoretically clean, and very practical. It has the further advantage of providing a nice transition to a multi-processor system if your single CPU runs out of capacity. And by swapping large memory segments, it can even be made efficient. Its main disadvantage is that most real-time operating systems don't support it well. Even those with efficient message-passing usually *allow* tight coupling (as indeed they should—sometimes you really *do* need it), giving lazy programmers an opportunity to "cheat."

Protection.   Regardless of whether coupling between tasks is tight or loose there are ways of controlling, if not preventing, undesirable access to shared data. ("Undesirable" in this context covers mainly access due to program bugs, rather than deliberate attempts to "break" the system. Hardly anyone attempts to break into the software of a voltmeter or milling machine.)

Software protection is provided by a compiler, and is limited at best. Since most compilers do not produce code to check array bounds or stack limits, it is always possible for a program to make accesses outside its own data areas. C, with its uncontrolled use of pointers, is especially prone to this problem.

Hardware protection is much more reliable, if you can afford it. Most 16-bit processors have optional memory-mapping chips which let you make chunks of memory read-only, execute-only, or completely inaccessible. This can be costly; there is the cost of the hardware itself, and also the cost in time of switching memory maps every time you switch tasks. (As usual, there is a trade-off: you can sometimes switch memory-management chips when you switch tasks. This only works if you have at least as many chips as you have tasks.)

CPU's with segmented address spaces, like the 8086 and Z8001, give you a certain amount of protection even without extra hardware, by running different tasks in different segments. The task-switching overhead is low, too. The 8086 has only four segment registers; the Z8001 has only one if you run tasks in "non-segmented" mode, in which they can access only 64K of memory. (The single segment pointer is part of the program counter. Of course, you need a 64K segment for each task.)

The Uses of Device Drivers

In many operating systems the only place to put direct I/O instructions, interrupt service routines, and so on, is in a device driver. This is especially true on those 16-bit machines which distinguish "system" and "user" modes. Since most real-time systems have strange I/O devices, you are likely to find that your application includes special-purpose device drivers.

Even if your operating system lets you put I/O instructions into tasks, it is a good idea to isolate the code that deals with each device into a separate task or subroutine package, thus giving you what amounts to a device driver. If nothing else, sending messages to a device-driver task ensures that the system's idea of the device's state stays consistent. Also messages, as we have seen, provide a good way of managing buffers. (You have to balance the convenience and simplicity of this scheme with the extra overhead of task-switching and message-passing.)

Operating systems that *do* have device drivers usually have a collection of subroutines and other aids for constructing them, making your job much easier. Device drivers have a standard interface to the operating system, and usually the code to implement this interface will be available, either as a "skeleton" with the actual I/O missing, or in the form of a sample driver for some existing device. Filling in the blanks is usually straightforward.

Designing the User Interface

The Command Interpreter.   There are two main approaches to a user interface (if your application has one—many embedded applications do not). The first is to have a task which interprets and executes user commands, either as subroutines or as overlays (programs loaded on top of the command processors, but called as subroutines). This is the approach taken with simple operating systems such as CP/M. Most of these are uniprocessing systems, and so have no choice in the matter.

In a multitasking system, there is another choice: to execute each command by spawning a new task. This allows commands to be pipelined, as in Unix, or to execute in the background while the user interface continues to accept commands. Note that it is not necessary to have dynamic task creation and loading in order to do this, although it helps. All of the command-processing tasks can be resident in main memory all the time, to be activated on demand.

In both cases, you have the option of using whatever command interpretor comes with your operating system, or building one tailored to your particular needs. Since executing a command may be as simple as calling a subroutine or scheduling a task, there is really no reason not to write your own. If your application does not have a standard keyboard as its user interface, you will have to write your own interface anyway.

Command Parameters.   There are also two ways to handle command parameters. One is for the command interpretor to obtain and perhaps partially decode the parameters before starting the task or subroutine that executes the command. The other is for each command processor to interpret its own parameters. The advantage of the first approach is uniformity: command parameters are always handled the same way. The advantage of the second is versatility: each command can have a unique syntax especially designed for it. Usually it is more desirable to have command syntax as uniform as possible.

In most C programming environments, the command processor (shell) takes the command line and breaks it up into words, passing the command two parameters: the number of words, and an array of pointers to the words. Each word is terminated with a null. This kind of processing is simple, and saves some duplication of effort in the command programs. It is not enough to ensure uniformity, however, since what each command does with its list of words is rather arbitrary.

One additional bit of pre-processing done by the Unix shell and some other command processors is to expand "wildcard" characters in command parameters that represent file names. Thus, the parameter **foo*** would be replaced by a list of all filenames that start with **foo**. A similar form of expansion could be applied in systems where command parameters were not file names but the names of some other kind of entity (such as sensors, recorded waveforms, dated reminders, or what have you).

Some systems go further: parameters are obtained interactively, usually by prompting the user for each one. Sometimes default values are displayed, and the user is allowed to edit them or accept them as given. On a display-oriented system this can get quite fancy, presenting the user with a "fill-in-the-blanks" form. One difficulty of menus and forms is that filling them in may require more keystrokes than simply typing a list of parameters, which makes the interactive techniques better for new or casual users than for experts.

Dealing with the Operating System

Finding a Kernel. This section was going to be called "Picking a Kernel," until I realized that there is rarely much choice involved. Indeed, as seen by the average programmer, the process of finding a real-time kernel is more like turning over the nearest rock and being bitten by whatever is lurking under it, than like leaving no stone unturned. Rarely do you have complete freedom of choice.

Selecting a CPU, and possibly an OEM board line, automatically limits your choices for operating systems. There are three basic sources: get the OS from the chip or board manufacturer, get it from some independent vendor (for example, Hunter and Ready, which sells its VRTX kernel for several 16-bit CPU's), or build one yourself. An intermediate possibility is to transport an existing operating system already written in a high-level language, but there are few portable real-time systems available for porting. There is a positive side to this—the field is small enough for you to examine most of the possible choices.

Language can also have an influence. Languages designed for multitasking, such as Ada, already come with their own kernel. Other languages, like C, are almost completely independent from the operating system (I/O libraries have obvious system dependencies, but if you're not doing logical I/O you don't have to use them). Languages like Pascal, Fortran, or (shudder!) Basic may limit your options by making it difficult to construct the data structures required to communicate with some kernels. This problem can be avoided, of course, with assembly-language interfaces.

If possible, code up the most time-critical part of your application and benchmark it on as many systems as possible. This may eliminate some candidates immediately. The rest of the choice will probably depend on how well the inter-task communication mechanisms of each system fit the way you intend to organize your tasks.

Customizing a System. Most real-time operating systems require some customizing, if only to add device drivers and command processors. The simple kernels, like Hunter and Ready's VRTX, Intel's RMX series, and Zilog's ZRTS, need more than this—a complete set of descriptors for tasks, memory, interrupts, device drivers, and other parts of the kernel's run-time environment needs to be set up.

Operating systems that require this kind of customizing sometimes include a "system generator" or "sysgen" program to set up the data structures required to initialize a system. Other systems simply let the user build the necessary structures using an assembler, sometimes with the help of a macro library. This approach is probably better; the system generator will want to run on a specific operating system.

Adding a File System.   Many commercially-available real-time kernels lack a file system; it is possible to use one of these kernels and still avoid having to write your own file system. The method is to obtain a customizable *single-user* operating system (such as CP/M, an excellent choice for most small, single-user applications), and run it as a task under the real-time kernel. This also gets you a user interface and a way of loading tasks. The simplest way of dealing with memory is to give each task, including the operating system, its own partition of memory to use.

Real-time tasks that need to do I/O communicate with a *server* program that runs as a user program under the single-user operating system. This unfortunately means that user programs cannot be run in the background, at least not without considerable extra work. It is also possible to take a multitasking operating system such as MP/M or Unix, and rewrite its kernel using a real-time scheduler. Several companies have done this with Unix already.

A Few Hints

Don't expect a multitasking application to out-perform one built as a uniprocessing or foreground-background system. It won't—task switching takes time. Don't expect it to make debugging any easier, either. Bugs in multitasking system run the full range among bizarre, subtle, and labyrinthine, and the higher the level at which you are programming, the poorer the debugging tools will be (a logic analyzer or emulator is of little use in a high-level language environment, and even less use on a timesharing system).

The main reason for using multitasking is to make the jobs of design, programming, and maintenance easier. Applications split up into tasks are *much* easier to build, and later to modify. The trick is to *avoid* bugs by designing carefully and by programming defensively. Check for unusual conditions. Use macros, pre-processors, or anything else you can to make sure you are using semaphores correctly. Use messages where possible, instead of shared data structures that might get corrupted.

Make sure your kernel is reliable. If necessary, protect yourself by writing a few simple test programs. There are few things worse than chasing a bug for several weeks, only to find that it was actually in the kernel and not your program. (In fact, the only worse things are finding it in the compiler, or in the chip itself. Fortunately these two are unlikely unless you work for a chip manufacturer.)

9
Multi-Processor Systems

INTRODUCTION

Definition

A *multi-processor* system is one in which several CPU's are operating simultaneously and co-operatively. Multiprocessing systems are sometimes called *de-centralized* or *distributed*. (The semantic quibbler might well ask what a *central* processing unit is doing in a *de-centralized* system. Jargon has its little quirks.)

Multi-processor systems differ from multitasking systems in that in a given system some tasks are actually running simultaneously on different processors, instead of merely appearing to do so. It is not unusual, however, for each processor in a multiprocessing system to be sharing its time among multiple tasks as well.

Taxonomy

The main division in multi-processor structures is between tightly-coupled systems, in which the processors share at least some of their memory space, and loosely-coupled systems, in which communication is by means of some kind of I/O mechanism. This corresponds to a similar distinction among multitasking systems. A third category might be distinguished of very-tightly-coupled, or *co-processor*, systems, in which two or more processors share parts of a single instruction stream (Fig. 9.1). This category includes both floating-point co-processors (such as Intel's 8087 working with the 8086 microprocessor), and some rather unusual memory management and task switching schemes. (Purists might be justified in excluding this category from the area of multi-processor systems, but it will be discussed in this chapter nevertheless.)

Symmetry. It is also possible to divide multi-processor systems according to their degree of symmetry. A highly symmetrical system has a number of identical processors with identical capabilities; in a system like this it doesn't matter where a task is run, because each processor is equally capable of running it. A

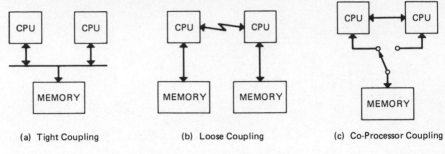

(a) Tight Coupling   (b) Loose Coupling   (c) Co-Processor Coupling

Figure 9.1. Processor-coupling.

less symmetrical arrangement is a hierarchy of processors, with one processor "in control" of the others.

Further down the chain, we find systems in which the processors become more specialized, with different memory and I/O configurations. Different processors are dedicated to different tasks. This kind of system includes those with "smart" I/O controllers. Finally, even the types of CPU can be different in the various processors.

Topology. Finally, multi-processor systems can be classified by the topological structure of their interconnections. Possible topologies include the bus, ring, star, and tree connections familiar to network designers, cellular automata (regular arrays of processors), and totally-connected systems. (Fig. 9.2)

Performance

The performance advantages of multi-processor systems are obvious—having several processors means that several things can be going on at once. There is a limit, however, to the improvement that can be gained by adding processors—for exactly the same reason that adding more people to a project does not produce a proportional increase in the amount of work done: communication. The processors must communicate in order to co-operate, and at some point the extra overhead of communication exceeds the benefit of the extra processors.

The trick, then, is in knowing when to stop, in dividing the problem at hand into the "right" number of tasks, and in allocating these to processors in a reasonable way. Multi-processing systems are quite prone to "anomalous" behavior—the possibility of getting slower when another processor is added, for example. Fortunately, most real-time applications have a "natural" breakdown into tasks, with clear lines of communication between them, and the job of allocating tasks to processors can usually be done simply and accurately.

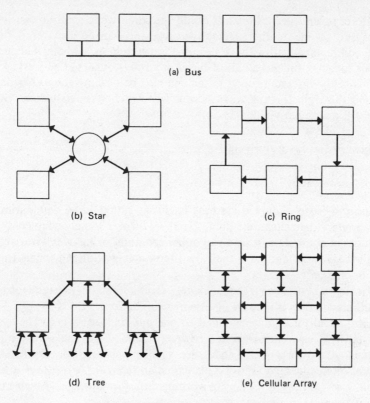

Figure 9.2. Multi-processor topologies.

Applications

The low cost of microprocessors makes it easy to solve the problems of limited compute power by throwing processors at them. Multi-processor systems can be applied anywhere a problem can be broken down into multiple tasks, but a single CPU is insufficient for the job. The robotics area is one example—many robots use a separate computer to control each joint motor.

Another good application for multi-processor systems is a system distributed over a wide geographical area. In this case it is often simplest to spread out the computer power as well, and to put computers wherever they are needed. (One is reminded of the dinosaur which had a "second brain" at the base of its spine to control its tail.) Systems with "smart terminals" are of this type. This kind of system is what goes by the currently-fashionable title of *distributed computing*.

Yet a third application for multi-processor systems is the high-reliability area. Here, several processors are doing the same work simultaneously, and checking up on one another. Defective processors can be discovered, disconnected, and replaced, all without stopping the system as a whole. This usually implies a topology such as a pair of buses or a fully-connected network, so that problems in the interconnection paths can also be circumvented. Needless to say, doing this right is not easy, as anyone who watched the first Space Shuttle launch will remember vividly.

LOOSELY-COUPLED SYSTEMS

A Bit of Terminology

The world of loosely-coupled systems itself has rather loose boundaries: any two computers that exchange data somehow form a loosely-coupled system. Collections of computers in separate boxes communicating over wires are usually called *networks* and have their own terminology, difficult for us to avoid in this discussion.

The main piece of new jargon is *packet*, which refers to a message formatted for transmission over a network. Networks can be *local* (LAN = Local Area Network), usually meaning confined to one building, or larger. The systems connected by a network are called *nodes* (a node is not necessarily a single processor). A network whose nodes are smaller networks, or alternatively a system of interconnected networks, is called an *internet*. A *protocol* is the set of (mainly software) conventions governing data formatting and transmission for the network.

Now that the jargon is out of the way, we can proceed.

The ISO Network Model

The International Standards Organization (ISO) standard DIS7498 specifies a seven-layer architecture which is commonly used as a reference model for networks, even if not followed exactly. Each layer provides a virtual connection used by the layer above.

Note that it is rare for all layers of the ISO model to be represented as separate layers in an actual implementation of a multi-processor system—the model is really designed for large networks. In a smaller system, the physical and data-link layers might be handled by some interface chips, and the higher layers lumped together in a few small subroutines.

Layer 1: Physical. The first layer defines the electrical and mechanical aspects of the connection: connectors, signals, and handshakes. This layer is covered by such standards as the EIA's RS-232C and the CCITT's standard X.21.

Layer 2: Data-Link. The data-link layer defines message formats, addressing techniques, and the data structures used for detecting and correcting errors (such as checksums). The ISO's SDLC format (see Fig. 2.19) is an example of a standard covering this layer. The IEEE 802 network standard covers both the physical and data-link layers.

The data-link layer is often implemented in peripheral chips, especially the synchronous serial interface chips, which also handle the handshake signals of the physical layer. (The electrical aspects of the physical layer are handled by *line-driver* and *line-receiver* chips, such as the Motorola 1488 and 1489 RS-232 driver and receiver chips.)

Layer 3: Network. In a larger network, the third layer defines the procedures necessary for transferring data packets between nodes. This layer provides routing, buffering, and forwarding operations, so that higher-level layers can use the network as a simple, direct connection. CCITT standard X.25 covers this layer.

Layer 4: Transport. The transport layer includes operations to transfer data and control information efficiently. It includes protocols for transferring complete files and obtaining services.

Layer 5: Session. The session layer provides the network equivalent of a *job* on a timesharing system: a way of starting and organizing an ongoing dialog between a user and the resources of the network.

Layer 6: Presentation. The presentation layer covers the transformation and translation of dialogs, including character set, terminal control, and graphics representation translation. Some of the recent Teletext standards, such as the North American Presentation Level Protocol Syntax (NAPLPS), are efforts in this direction.

Layer 7: Application. The highest layer, finally, contains the user and the application programs being used.

Hardware Configurations

The way in which the processors of a loosely-coupled system actually communicate matters very little to the software, or to the system as a whole, except for the overall effect of bandwidth. The main influence of the hardware is on the physical structure of the system (in other words, how far apart you can put the processors), and its price. (The *topology* of the interconnection has a large effect, but we will get to that later.)

Connections between a pair of nodes are called *point-to-point* connections; a single set of wires connecting several nodes is called a *multi-drop* connection. Note that a network can be either a single multi-drop connection, or made up of several point-to-point connections. The main practical distinction is whether data have to be buffered when passing through an intermediate point on the network: if the network is made of point-to-point connections, each intermediate node has to receive and retransmit the data, whereas in a multi-drop connection the source and destination are directly connected.

Parallel Interfaces. The largest bandwidth with the least cost is obtained with a parallel interface over a short distance. Usually the width of the parallel connection is 8 bits, although with the coming of the 16-bit microprocessors we can expect a few 16-bit connections to make their appearance. Over long distances the cost of cable and the electronics to signals and receive signals starts to become important, and parallel interfaces lose their advantage.

I/O Ports. Over short distances (a few inches to a few feet), parallel connections are inexpensive because the interface to each processor is a simple parallel I/O port—possibly as simple as an addressable latch at each end. The simplest connection is usually between parallel I/O chips, since these have strobe lines that pulse when a byte is written, and ready lines that generate interrupts when a byte is available to be read. Most such chips have two eight-bit ports, so a pair of them makes a nice, simple bidirectional connection between two processors.

Buses. A parallel interface is not limited to connecting a pair of processors. Add some address lines, and you get a bus that can connect several processors. Such an interface can be almost exactly like a memory bus, and can even be accessed as a special block of memory, with each word corresponding to a processor's communication register. (Taken somewhat farther, processors can share *blocks* of memory—then you have a tightly-coupled system.)

Another parallel bus is the IEEE 488 bus, which was designed by Hewlett-Packard to connect smart instruments. This is a 16-line bus with 8 address/data lines and 8 handshake and control lines. This bus is also used by some computer manufacturers to communicate with intelligent peripherals; this feature has made Commodore's PET personal computer very popular in laboratories. (See Chapter 2 for a description.)

Serial Interfaces. For longer distances, the prices of cable and drivers start to become important and the serial interface, with a single wire in each direction, starts to look attractive. Now that serial interface chips have become common and cheap, parallel interfaces have no price advantages even for short distances—their advantage lies solely in bandwidth.

Another place where serial interfaces are starting to show up is on backplanes, as an auxiliary message-passing channel to supplement a standard backplane memory bus. Motorola's Versabus and VME buses use this technique.

The problem with serial interfaces is simply that sending information one bit at a time takes longer than sending it all at once. Unless DMA is used, though, this is not much of a problem; serial I/O chips run at up to several hundred thousand bits per second. (And the new generation of network interface chips run even faster—10 MHz, or over a megabyte per second.) Using interrupts, most processors are in trouble at more than 40 Kbits (5 Kbytes) per second.

The hardware used in serial interconnections is discussed more fully in Chapter 2.

Improving Transmission Speed. The simplest way of transmitting data packets over a serial or parallel interconnection is programmed I/O to send each byte or word, with the interface device generating interrupts whenever it is ready for another. If the transmission medium can keep up with a tight loop or block I/O instruction without forcing the processor to wait, it is possible to avoid most of the overhead by interrupting only at the start of a packet, and transferring the rest all at once.

A similar procedure can be used at the receiving end, but here small differences in timing between sending and receiving processors may result in data being lost unless the device can make the processor wait, or unless the processor has time to poll the device to see whether a byte is ready. In either case, some time is wasted. In addition, if an interrupt occurs in the middle of a packet, the remainder of the packet will be lost unless there is a handshake that lets the transmitter wait until the receiver is ready.

DMA's. Most of these problems can be solved by using a DMA (Direct Memory Access) controller. This will take care of moving the actual data, and will generate an interrupt when all the data have been transferred.

DMA has its own problems: most DMA chips are extremely complicated, and the software to initialize them is lengthy. Moreover, DMA chips usually have strange quirks—this register has to be initialized before that register, otherwise you get an unexpected interrupt, or a byte might get transferred before you tell the chip where to find it. It often takes a lot of trial and error to get the initialization sequence right, and the data book is usually not of much help.

Another problem with DMA is that both processors have to agree in advance on how many bytes are going to be transferred, so that they can program their DMA's. This is fine if you are dealing with fixed-size messages; it is no help at all with random-length ones. And DMA is worse than useless with very short messages—the overhead of starting up the DMA swamps any advantage you might get. Probably the practical lower bound on the size of a DMA message is 128 bytes.

FIFO's. An alternative to DMA is to put a FIFO buffer between the parallel ports instead. This is especially good if the communicating CPU's have block-move instructions, which can move data almost as fast as DMA. With variable-length messages, the first byte sent can be the size of the message.

Zilog has a chip called the FIO which does it all—it's a 128-byte FIFO between two parallel ports, one for each processor. (In an unusual move for a chip manufacturer, they even laid out the pins well, with one port on each side of the package!) There is also a pair of communication registers for sending single-byte messages independent of the FIFO. (This is useful, because the two processors have to agree on which direction data are being sent.)

Networks. Networks are larger collections of loosely-coupled processors; they can be either local area networks (LAN's), or large networks. The difference is essentially that LAN's are confined to a single installation, and so can use any type of interconnection (usually coaxial cable), while large networks require the use of common carriers (such as the telephone system or microwave links) for data transmission.

Networks require both hardware and software (protocol) standards. A complete discussion of these is beyond the scope of this book, but some of the hardware standards are mentioned in Chapter 2, and some of the protocols used will be discussed in the next section. Networks are almost invariably serial connections, although a few local, high-speed networks use parallel connections.

Low-Level Software

Loosely-coupled systems are in many ways the easiest to deal with in software; message-passing is a good way of keeping tasks well-separated. From a reliability standpoint, this means that a task in one processor cannot interact with a task in another processor except by permission—a message is a request for service, and can be denied. There is no way a task can clobber another's data structures, either accidentally or deliberately (the last being a problem only in multi-user systems). This also helps in debugging, by avoiding a whole class of hard-to-find bugs.

A second advantage for debugging is that since all interactions between tasks are in the form of messages, a trace of those messages will be a complete record of those interactions. In other words, to find the criminal, all you have to do is read its mail.

There is also a major advantage for development and maintenance: since the interface to a task is entirely specified by its response to messages, it is possible to completely re-implement a task without having to change anything else. This is object- oriented design at its best.

Messages. In a loosely-coupled system, messages are *everything*. There is actually little difference between message-passing in a multi-processor system, and in a multitasking system. Indeed, most multi-processor systems also do multitasking in the individual processors, and it is usual for the same message formats to be used between tasks in the same processor.

Ideally, it should not matter to a task sending a message whether the recipient is in another processor or not. The only differences are how fast the message travels, and the probability of its getting lost or scrambled. In practice, it is often a good idea to allow tasks in the same processor the privilege of communicating by other, more efficient means.

Usually, each processor has a special task whose duty is to forward messages to and from other processors. It is this task that knows about message formats and transmission techniques. At some cost in cleanliness and a corresponding gain in efficiency, the job can also be done as an interrupt process. In smaller, dedicated systems, it is perfectly feasible to have only a single task in each processor.

What Can Be Sent.   Since tasks in different processors cannot share memory, any objects being transmitted have to be sent by value. It is, therefore, impractical for tasks to share access to arrays and data structures. Files and I/O devices generally *can* be shared, since I/O is closely related to message-passing. Indeed, one of the main justifications for local networks is to allow shared access to data bases and expensive devices. Multi-processor systems are also common in the form of a central processor with intelligent peripherals.

The content of messages is not limited to "raw data." Messages can also carry commands, or requests for service. This sort of message is usually short, and it is sometimes useful to have different formats for data and command messages. A related third kind of message is used for controlling the communication process itself. This kind includes routing information, error checking, and acknowledgements. Such control messages are often "piggybacked" on top of data messages for efficiency.

Formatting.   Data and commands can be sent in the form of text strings or data structures. Text is easier to trace or hand-generate for debugging, and can be formatted using ordinary formatted I/O routines in high-level languages. Text is something of a "universal language." On the other hand, numeric data have to be converted from binary to text by the sender, and back into binary by the receiver, leading to a considerable loss of efficiency both in time and volume.

The use of binary data structures is limited by the fact that most operating systems use ASCII control characters for control, and many also strip off the high-order "parity" bit from characters coming in, or supply a parity bit on characters being sent. Thus, systems that were not originally designed for multi- processor linkages usually have to communicate via text.

Efficiency. As suggested above, simply sending data in binary rather than text can save a great deal of time (though the convenience of text is then lost), both by reducing the amount of data to be sent (with a corresponding reduction in bandwidth or transmission time), and by completely eliminating the encoding and decoding processes.

Another factor influencing efficiency is traffic *volume*—the total amount of data being sent between processors in a network. Systems connected by a bus or other shared structure (such as a central message switch in a star configuration) are limited by its bandwidth, and so tend to "saturate." In such systems, there comes a point when increasing the number of processors actually reduces overall performance by using up bandwidth. The effect is similar to the limitation imposed by task-switching overhead in multitasking systems.

Finally, within a single processor, handling messages takes time and memory. It is possible for an individual processor in a system to spend so much time sending or receiving messages that it can't get any work done. A solution for this kind of problem is to redistribute the functions of the processor in question, to put them where they are needed and avoid message-passing altogether. Notice that this may require turning some shared tasks into library subroutines, which is not always possible.

Some of the worst problems in networks occur when I/O-bound tasks are using remote data. For example, consider what happens when a task in one processor tries to sort or search a large file in a disk attached to another processor. The entire file will get transferred, piecewise, and as fast as possible because hardly any computation is being done on its contents. A better solution is to add "sort" and "search" commands to the repertoire of the processor that owns the file. (In other words, to turn the processor from a simple file server into a data-base server.)

Addressing and Routing. A major concern in larger collections of processors is making sure that a message gets to the right place. This requires, first of all, an *address* to designate the destination, and secondly, proper *routing* to find a path to it. Addresses are usually structured in some way; in a completely general address there may be a field to identify a network, a processor on that network, and a task within that processor. This is an *absolute* address; there are other kinds.

The problem with absolute addresses is that they contain no routing information. If source and destination are on different processors or networks, there is no way to tell what intermediate places a message may have to visit. There are ways of dealing with this problem, involving making maps of some sort and keeping them up to date, usually by the periodic exchange of messages saying "I'm over here!" or some electronic equivalent.

The other solution is to use *pathnames* instead of addresses. Here, the route *is* the address. This is really a much worse situation, since it simply means that every task that sends a message has to know the route to every other task it intends to communicate with. This solution *does* work, however, for small networks that don't change much.

Of course, in small systems with bus, ring, star, or fully-connected topology, the problem of routing does not arise at the processor level: there is only one way of getting a message from one place on the network to another. Since these are the kinds of structure most common in real-time systems, it is sufficient for us to take note of the problem and then ignore it.

Naming.   A problem closely related to addressing is naming, or somehow finding out the address of a task that performs a particular function. Again, in small systems this is rarely a problem—if you don't know which CPU controls the motor on the elbow, you're in trouble. In systems of this kind, where all the programming can be kept under central control, it is sufficient to have an **include** file with numerical definitions for processor names.

In larger systems, and also in systems that are changing dynamically, this doesn't work. Here it is necessary to have one or more *name servers*: tasks (with known addresses!) that maintain a directory for the system. Another possibility (which, by the way, can cope with pathnames as well as absolute addresses) is to send out a *broadcast* message with a name in it, asking "Where are you?" Obviously, this only works if it isn't done very often, and if the network isn't very large. It works especially well if the network is simple. (Pathnames are derived by having every node that forwards a message add its name to the message's return address. When the message arrives, the return address is not only the path to the sender, but the reverse of the path to the recipient.)

Error Recovery.   One of the problems with loosely-coupled systems is that data transmission media are unreliable, especially over long distances. Hard-wired RS-232C links might have an error rate of a few parts per billion; the error rate of a 1200-bit/second telephone link might be several parts per million, if you are unlucky. (A page of text is about 2000 bytes, or 20,000 bits counting the start and stop bits, so one error per million bits is one every 50 pages.)

In the next section, we will see some techniques for dealing with errors. The necessary tools include a timeout mechanism (in case a message, or part of it, never arrives), and checksums or CRC words.

Higher-Level Protocols.

Reliable Transmission.   One of the more basic services provided at the network layer is reliable transmission of data. Packets, as we have seen, can become lost or scrambled, so a mechanism is needed for acknowledging their correct receipt, or requesting a retransmission. In larger networks, it is also possible for packets to arrive several times by different routes, so duplicates must also be removed.

In a small system, as opposed to a network, it is not necessary to go to much trouble. A message header with a byte count, and a trailer with a checksum or CRC, are sufficient for checking, along with a (preferably short) timeout in case a byte is lost. An identifiable starting character-sequence for the header is a good idea in case extra bytes are inserted, and an end-marker, although not a substitute for a timeout, helps.

Acknowledgement can be a single ACK or NAK (negative acknowledgement) character, which the ASCII character set thoughtfully provides for the purpose. Another refinement is to ensure that the character sequence that starts a packet cannot appear inside one. If the data are ASCII text and the start character a SOH (Start Of Header), this is guaranteed. The EOT (End Of Transmission) character is used to end a message; the STX (Start of TeXt) and ETX (End of TeXt) characters can be used to separate the actual data from the header (address, count, and so on) and trailer (including checksum).

Transmitting Binary Data. If the data are arbitrary eight-bit bytes, it is a good idea to precede control characters with an escape character such as DLE (Data-Link Escape). Another possibility (especially with off-the-shelf operating systems that distort control characters) is to convert binary data to hexadecimal, or to pack six bits of data into an eight-bit character, using the six-bit subset of ASCII. The latter course is more efficient, but requires more effort from the software. Since the transmission speed is probably limited by the media more than by the software, the effort should be worthwhile.

Transport-Level Protocols. Given reliable transmission of messages, other protocols can be constructed for dealing with specific types of interactions. These include access to remote files, operating systems, and programs.

Remote I/O. There are two kinds of access to remote files and I/O devices: sequential access (file transfer), and random access. Sequential access is simpler: the whole file is split into packets and copied from one system to another. Random I/O is more complicated, and much less efficient. Not only must data be transferred, but its location in the file as well. Since the location is not known ahead of time, it takes a complete round-trip time for each operation, whereas with sequential access a stream of packets can be sent, with the network serving as a big FIFO buffer.

Another problem that arises with random access is simultaneous access by several tasks. Somehow, things have to be co-ordinated to prevent corruption or loss of data. This is usually done by means of *transactions*: a part of the file (or parts of several files) can be locked until the whole transaction is complete, and all the changes done at once. Care has to be taken to ensure that if the requestor or the network crashes in the middle of a transaction, *nothing* is done. Ways of doing this, beyond the scope of this book, are an active subject of research.

A related topic is reliable data storage in a system with distributed control and data. It would be nice if one could keep local copies of various files, but elaborate measures are required to make sure that the various local copies are up to date, and that transactions are done on all or none of the copies.

Remote Terminal Interaction. Another form of interaction over networks is remote use of an operating system, as if the remote task (usually simply an agent for an actual user at a terminal) were a local user. Things get even more interesting in a Unix or similar situation where tasks can be connected by pipelines: What if some of the tasks are executing on different systems?

Remote Program Execution. Finally, it is necessary to use remote programs. This is the situation most likely to interest the real-time system-builder. Obviously one way of doing this is to pretend to be a user at a terminal. This results in a system in which messages are encoded as text: easy to build and debug, but inefficient. In most cases this quick-and-easy approach is sufficient.

The two alternatives are remote server tasks, and remote procedure calls. Remote server tasks are the more common: asynchronous tasks that take requests, in the form of encoded blocks of data, forwarded over a network. These work just like tasks on a single processor interacting via messages.

Remote procedure calls are a little more elaborate. Here, the requestor executes what appears to be a simple procedure call, and waits for a result. The procedure's arguments are formatted into a message (which can be large if data structures are to be sent), and shipped over the network to another machine, where a task is *created* to execute the procedure body. Eventually it sends a result. This method makes it easy to write programs (you can use perfectly usual uniprocessing programming techniques), but takes its toll in inefficiency. It *is* a good way to make use of remote or shared resources while keeping the program that uses them simple.

Applications

Loosely-coupled systems with a small number of small processors are the easiest systems to write applications for. Networks, which have many processors and many tasks on each process, are harder but fortunately much less common in real-time situations.

Allocating Tasks to Processors. The problem of allocating tasks to processors is similar to the problem of partitioning an application into tasks in the first place: the object is to position the interfaces so as to reduce the amount of communication. This is especially important in a loosely-coupled system, in which everything is shoved through a knothole.

The allocation task is much harder when the functions of the various processors are not well-defined, or in other words if the processors are equal in their capabilities. It is much simpler if there are good, obvious reasons for allocating tasks to processors, such as the presence of unique I/O devices, or differences in memory or CPU's.

For example, if there is a processor controlling each motor on a robot arm, it is pretty obvious which tasks belong in each processor. The question in this case is only *how much* of each task to allocate to each processor: Can the motor-control processors store a whole trajectory, or should the central processor send more detailed commands?

Network Elements. Sometimes a real-time product is not a complete network, but something designed to be part of one. Examples include single-chip and single-board controllers of various kinds (for example, stepping-motor controllers), and smart instruments (such as those that interface to the IEEE 488 bus). Although complete systems in themselves, their position as components in a larger network has to be considered in their design.

Larger Networks. Larger networks are not usually involved in real-time systems, except peripherally as shared resources with comparatively loose response-time requirements. One exception is the transmission of real-time data such as voice over a local network; another is transmission of control information from a master to its slaves. In the latter case the situation is simplified by the fact that the master usually has full control of the traffic.

Using any kind of general-purpose network in a real-time situation requires some way of controlling bandwidth and traffic. Some forms of network, such as broadband cable, ring networks, and token-passing buses, are able to guarantee a minimum level of service to each node; these are preferable to collision-detection schemes where the guarantee is a statistical expectation instead of an absolute minimum.

Topology. Closely related to the allocation problem is the topology of the system. The most common organization in real-time systems is a star, with a processor in the middle. In control applications, the central processor is usually the master, sending commands or requests for information to its slaves.

Sometimes, however, the peripheral processors are all "masters," sharing a common data base, communication facility, and perhaps other resources. On-line transaction-processing systems are of this type (i.e. real-time systems in the older sense), but so are other systems in which the central processor is simply a data-collection and file storage point. The machine shop, as usual, provides a good example: computer-controlled tools sharing a common database for program storage and inventory control.

Build or Buy?   As with real-time operating systems, a major question is whether to build a network in-house, or to buy it. The answer is the same: buy it, if possible. If building a custom operating system is a can of worms, building custom network software is a pit-full of snakes. Don't try it unless you have plenty of time and money. (Of course, if your real-time product is a communications controller, you're probably stuck with building it. Don't overlook the possibility of buying the programs, however, or of getting them free from some research institution that has already written them using public funds.)

Small systems with limited objectives are a different matter. As a general rule, they can't be bought; on the other hand they are actually pretty easy to build. Just be sure to build in plenty of hooks for debugging, and try to use text as opposed to binary for messages, at least in the prototype. The robot or machine-tool controller is the typical case in point: the system is small, and each processor has an obvious and well-defined function in it.

TIGHTLY-COUPLED SYSTEMS

Hardware Configurations

Shared Memory.   Tightly-coupled systems, by (our) definition, are those in which processors communicate by means of shared memory. There are several ways to accomplish this: a shared memory bus, memory accessible from each of several buses (multi-port memory), and more elaborate variations on these themes.

Arbitration.   A requirement common to all tightly-coupled systems is the need for an arbitrator to allocate the shared memory resources among the processors. Such arbitrators can be either symmetrical or asymmetrical (prioritized), with the symmetrical ones being generally more complex. An exception is the round- robin arbitrator, which gives access to each processor in turn. This gains its simplicity by being slow.

Another complication is clock synchronization. Things are made *much* simpler if all of the processors in a system run off the same clock (they may run at different rates provided all of the rates are sub-multiples of the same master clock). Asynchronous systems are subject to the well-known problem of metastable states: the arbitrator can get into a state in which it may take an arbitrarily long time to make a decision (in typical systems it may take several microseconds to stabilize). Asynchronous systems are still possible: it is possible to design an arbitrator which can reduce the probability of a meta-stable condition to a vanishingly small amount.

Shared Buses.   The simplest (and most limited) way of sharing memory is for all processors in the system to share a single memory bus (Fig. 9.3a). In this case, the system is limited by the bandwidths of the bus and (more important) the memory attached to it. An arbitration mechanism is needed to allocate the bus among the processors.

The 6800 and 6500 families of microprocessors, with their two-phase clocks, allow a particularly simple round-robin arbitration scheme for two processors: simply run them 180 degrees out of phase.

Multiple Buses.   The next level of complexity comes with multiple buses and multi-port memory. In this arrangement, each block of memory is accessible from either of two or more buses, or *ports*, and contains its own arbitrator. The bandwidth of the system is increased because accesses to different blocks of memory can proceed simultaneously, with arbitration only happening when two processors try to access the same block of memory.

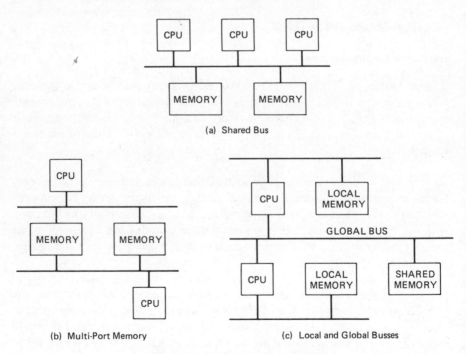

(a) Shared Bus

(b) Multi-Port Memory

(c) Local and Global Busses

Figure 9.3. Ways of sharing memory.

There are two main variations on the multiple-bus configuration. In one, there are N buses for an N-processor system, and all memory is accessible from all buses (Fig. 9.3b). This has the highest complexity, since each block of memory has N ports.

In the other variation, there are $N+1$ buses in an N-processor system, and each block of memory is shared between only two buses. One bus, the *global* bus, is shared by all processors; the others are each *local* to a single processor (Fig. 9.3c).

The local-global system is by far the most popular. It is easily expandable, since the number of buses remains constant no matter how many processors are in the system. All of the arbitrators are two-way, which makes things simple. Since the global bus is only used for communication and for access to shared I/O devices (if any), the demands on it are usually low. It is not unusual for the global bus to have lower bandwidth than the local buses, which can sometimes be confined to a single board.

It is worth noting that dual-port memory is not at all uncommon: CRT controllers, some other DMA devices, and refresh generators for dynamic memory all are frequently implemented this way.

Message Buses.   It is possible to get the advantages of multi-port memory without multiple buses. Consider the problem: multiple buses are used because a memory read ties up the bus from the time the address appears, until the time the data appear in response. Writes can be made to use less bus time by latching the data on the memory board, and doing the actual write operation later. (This only speeds things up, of course, if there are many memory units that can be completing their writes simultaneously.)

Reads can be similarly sped up by splitting them into two bus transactions: sending the address to the memory along with a "processor address," and sending the data to the processor after the memory has completed its read. In this kind of bus (which is still largely experimental), memories and processors are essentially independent entities sending messages to one another. This can obviously be generalized to allow processors to communicate directly.

Hardware Mutual Exclusion.   There is another hardware aspect to tightly-coupled systems besides the physical organization of their memory systems: it is necessary to provide some method of mutual exclusion on which to base the software synchronization primitives. It is possible to use the basic bus arbitrator for this purpose, and build primitives using nothing but the fact that load and store are indivisible. It is much easier, though, if the hardware provides an indivisible "test-and-set" or similar read-modify-write or read-write transaction.

What is needed is a way for one processor to reserve or *lock* the bus for more than one transaction. Most 16-bit processors now have this capability in one form or another. The 8086 has it in a fairly general form: a prefix instruction causes the bus to be locked until the next instruction, which may be an increment or an exchange, is completed. Other processors such as the Z8000 and 68000 provide a single "test-and-set" instruction, which sets a word to ones, and returns the *previous* value of its high-order bit. The test-and-set is completed in a single read-modify-write bus transaction, or with a pair of transactions between which the processor will refuse to give up the bus.

Software

Software in tightly-coupled systems presents problems not found in loosely-coupled systems, especially those having to do with synchronization of access to the shared memory. Although it is possible to organize a tightly-coupled system using messages for inter-task communication, sending the messages still involves access to shared memory, and therefore synchronization.

Synchronization. Synchronization in a tightly-coupled system requires the use of some kind of operation which cannot be interrupted by another processor. It is always guaranteed that LOAD and STORE (to a given memory operation) are uninterruptable, and it is possible to implement a binary semaphore using only those operations. This, however is inefficient, and there are other alternatives.

Test-and-Set. Here are the programs for the *wait* and *signal* operations using a test-and-set operation. We assume that **test__and__set** sets a flag to a nonzero value, and returns zero only if the previous value was zero. (This curious phrasing is intended to cover most of the existing implementations of this operation, including an uninterruptable exchange operation.) The programs themselves are trivial.

```
/**************************************
** mp_wait(semaphore)
**      multi-processor (busy) wait
**      using test-and-set
***************************************/
mp_wait(sem)
int *sem;
{
    while (test_and_set(sem)) /* spin wait */ ;
}

/**************************************
** mp_signal(semaphore)
**      multi-processor signal
```

```
*****************************************/
mp_signal(sem)
int *sem;
{
    *sem = 0;
}
```

Note that if the processors in the system lack a test-and-set instruction, it is possible to implement the necessary bus-locking mechanism using external hardware (for example, writing to an I/O port to reserve the global bus for the next instruction). Little hardware is required.

Interrupts.   Lacking a test-and-set instruction, it is also possible to use interrupts for synchronization. This is actually closest to a loosely-coupled organization. It does require special hardware that allows one processor to interrupt another. This can be simply a pair of I/O ports.

The use of interrupts for synchronization is common in systems where one of the processors is functioning as a smart I/O controller. It works best where a master-slave relationship exists, or in other systems where the traffic to any one processor is infrequent; otherwise interrupt-handling overhead becomes excessive.

Other Methods.   The interrupt method of synchronization can be generalized to include the exchange of a simple message, usually a single word. This can be done using paired parallel interface chips, or an auxiliary serial bus (which several backplane buses provide for this purpose). Obviously, the message exchanged can be either a simple signal, or a pointer to a data structure being sent from one processor to the other. With the use of this technique, a tightly-coupled system is transformed into a loosely-coupled system with a very fast data-transport mechanism.

It is worth noting that Zilog's Z8000 microprocessor has a "multi-micro" interface, consisting of a pair of pins (input and output), and a set of instructions (MRES, which resets the output line, MSET, which sets it, MBIT, which tests the input, and MREQ, which performs a handshake with timeout). It is also worth noting that no Z8000 systems known to the author make use of it.

Task Assignment.   Tightly-coupled systems present another problem to the system designer: assigning tasks to processors. The problem is not so much how to do it, as whether to do it once (statically), or each time a task is run (dynamically). With shared memory, it is possible to build a system in which a task can be run on *any* free processor, rather than being permanently assigned to a single processor.

In systems with local and global buses, dynamic allocation is usually a bad idea: it ties up the global bus with instruction fetches. Consequently it is restricted to systems with multi-port memory. It is further restricted to systems whose processors have similar capabilities.

Asymmetrical tightly-coupled systems are more common; each processor in the system is given a specific set of tasks. These systems usually take on a "master-slave" structure—one processor is "in charge," and the others are slaves (for example, I/O controllers with DMA), a much simpler organization.

Dynamic allocation of tasks to processors permits the first N tasks on the ready queue to be run, and requires multi-processor synchronization for access to the queue. Static allocation allows a separate ready queue for each processor, and no synchronization is required, so that the time required to switch tasks is correspondingly reduced.

I/O Assignment.   Without special hardware, it is necessary for a given interrupt line to be connected to only a single processor. This simplifies the problem of assigning I/O routines to processors, by forcing it to be done statically. Even in otherwise symmetrical systems, such a configuration tends to lead to systems in which one or more processors are specialized for I/O.

The effect of this on application programs is minimal. Operating systems, however, can reap large benefits by moving their I/O drivers into slave processors. There are two advantages: driver code and buffers no longer take up space in the main processor, and performance is also improved by the ability to overlap computation with I/O.

Further advantages come when parts of the file system are moved into the I/O processor. This is especially true in multi-terminal systems when low-level character processing and line editing (echoing, backspace processing, etc.) are handled in another processor. One of the major bottlenecks in many systems (especially Unix systems) is interrupt processing for terminals. Huge improvements are possible with little change to the system.

A further extension of this is to start move interactive programs such as editors into the I/O processors. The ultimate move in this direction is to give each user or small group of users a whole peripheral processor, with the former "master" CPU becoming a shared disk I/O processor. This kind of system can achieve very high performance, since its computing capacity rises proportionally to the number of users. (The bottleneck is disk I/O. Compare this to a similarly-organized loosely-coupled system, in which the bottleneck is the network bandwidth.)

(The tendency to migrate computational functions to I/O subprocessors, and the subsequent temptation to add sub-subprocessors to these to handle their I/O, was first noticed in interactive graphics systems, where it was called "Wheel of Reincarnation." [1])

Applications

There are three main tightly-coupled multiprocessing system configurations of interest for real-time applications: master-slave with intelligent I/O processors, symmetrical, and multi-master with shared I/O processors. From an application standpoint, they are all essentially the same as single-processor multitasking systems. The difference is mainly in performance and expansion capability, although symmetrical systems also have a reliability advantage.

Reliable Operation.   One advantage of symmetrical multi-processor systems is that if one processor is broken the others can take over its functions. The operating-system and even hardware implications of this are profound, however: data-base transactions have to be done reliably, processors have to check one another's work, and it must be possible to switch I/O devices between processors. Even the communication paths have to be redundant, which affects the system's topology.

Tandem is the pioneer in this field, and a few companies are now venturing into it with microcomputer-based systems. The investment required to develop a highly-reliable system is considerable.

Make or Buy?   This leads to the next topic: where do you find an operating system suitable for multi-processor operation? If ultra-reliable operation is the goal, the best answer is to buy the hardware and operating system from one of the increasing number of vendors in the field. Some vendor-supplied real-time operating systems (e.g. Intel's iRMX-86) support multiple processors, and can be used for symmetrical systems where the goal is simply load-sharing and not redundancy. Systems in which the goal is redundancy without load-sharing can sometimes be treated as single-processor systems, with the redundancy handled purely in hardware (as in the co-processor systems discussed in the next section).

Systems in which each task is confined to a single processor, such as master-slave and multi-master systems, are much simpler. Each processor can run its own multitasking operating system, with inter-processor communication treated as I/O and confined to a low- level device driver. This you can write yourself. The MP/M operating system from Digital Research, a multi-processor version of CP/M, is worth noting—it provides for file-sharing among multiple processors. As with CP/M, all the OEM has to do is supply the low-level drivers.

CO-PROCESSOR SYSTEMS

There is another form of multi-processor system, in which the processors share not only memory, but also a single instruction stream. In the current terminology, these are SIMD (Single-Instruction, Multiple-Data) systems, as opposed to the MIMD (Multiple-Instruction, Multiple-Data) systems we have discussed so far.

Vector Co-Processors

The "classical" SIMD system is a set of identical processors executing identical instruction streams in parallel, operating on different data. This is a "super-computer" organization, designed for massive number-crunching. It is easy to see that decision- making is difficult in such a system: with a single instruction stream you can't have different processors taking different paths at a conditional jump.

With inexpensive memory, it is hard to see the usefulness of vector co-processing in the microprocessor world. The one place where it *is* useful is in signal processing (digital filtering or image analysis, for example), in which it is actually *desirable* for several identical operations to proceed in lock-step on different data.

Redundancy Co-Processors

A close relative of the vector co-processor systems is the kind of system in which multiple processors are used for redundancy. This is actually a SISD (Single-Instruction, Single-Data) system: the multiple processors are executing the same instructions *on the same data*, and their results are compared using some kind of voting logic. A processor which disagrees is switched out of the system. (This is best done with *four* processors; if one dies, there are still three left so that a second fault can be corrected later.)

Since all of the processors are operating on the same instructions and data, they can share the same memory bus. Redundancy in memory is best handled with an error-correcting encoding; it may be desirable to have three parallel buses, however. (It is also possible to use completely separate systems, each with its own memory as well as its own processor.)

This is an expensive way to get reliable operation, but it has the advantage of simplifying the software: all of the redundancy-checking is done in hardware; no multitasking or multi-processor synchronization is required. Since simplicity in software greatly improves reliability, this is a good way to go. (The Space Shuttle goes a step further: it not only has four redundant main computers running the same software, but it also has a fifth computer running a totally different software implementation of the system just in case a software bug should appear, which would disable all four of the main computers. The bug which delayed the first launch of the Shuttle had to do with synchronizing the two software systems.)

Instruction-Set Expansion Co-Processors

The term "co-processor" has been introduced rather recently in the industry in connection with chips that extend the instruction set of a microprocessor in some way, usually by adding floating-point instructions. Although early floating-point chips were accessed as special I/O devices, more recently co-processors have been designed to work more closely with a specific CPU. These co-processors work by watching their host's instruction stream for a floating-point instruction. The host generates memory addresses, if necessary, while the co-processor reads or writes data. The co-processor has its own set of registers and instructions.

The effect of this is to add a set of floating-point registers and instructions to a microprocessor in a very clean way, almost as if they were part of the original chip. Obviously, the microprocessor and its co-processor have to be designed together—you can't "mix-and-match" manufacturers here! Most of the 16-bit microprocessors have floating-point co-processors. Intel has recently announced a co-processor intended for text processing.

(Some co-processors, like Intel's text co-processor, actually execute their own instructions rather than watching the host's instruction stream. They are still very tightly coupled to the host, however, usually sharing the same bus and interacting via special instructions.)

Memory Management Co-Processors

In order to support virtual memory schemes, in which a reference to a non-existent block of memory causes it to be swapped in from disk, a processor has to be able to recover from such a "page fault" by saving enough information to permit "un-doing" an instruction which has accessed such nonexistent memory. Most early 16-bit processors and all 8-bit processors were unable to do this, but the 16-bit processors have been followed by later versions, such as the Z8003 for the Z8001 and the 68020 for the 68000, which *do* support virtual memory.

In the meantime, a new form of co-processor has been developed. In this scheme, when a page fault occurs, the main processor is simply wait-stated, as if it was accessing very slow memory. A second processor, sharing the same bus, is then started up to bring the required page into memory. This doesn't allow other tasks to proceed during the I/O, as virtual memory on a single processor would, so it is unsuitable for multi-user systems. It *does* permit very large tasks to run on a single-user system with limited memory.

Multitasking Co-Processors

One of the problems with multitasking systems is the time it takes to save and restore the state of a task. This problem is getting worse with the 16-bit processors, which have more registers than their 8-bit ancestors, and thus more state to save. One radical solution is to switch processors! After all, processors are cheap.

In systems with a small number of tightly-coupled tasks, processor-switching makes a great deal of sense. (Notice that this is simply an extension of the previous scheme, in which one of the tasks is the page-swapper.) Notice that not all tasks have to have their own processors, only the ones that need fast response.

A variation on this is the kind of system in which several processors with different instruction sets share the same bus. This is something of a kludge, developed so that personal computers could run software intended for machines with a different CPU. The first version was Microsoft's "Softcard," developed so that their Z-80 software could run on a 6502-based Apple computer.

Another variation uses one CPU for computation and another for I/O. This is really a poor substitute for a tightly-coupled multi-processor, although it does solve the synchronization problem. The often-forgotten ancestor of this scheme is DEC's LINC-8, a combination of MIT's LINC (Laboratory Instrumentation Computer) and a PDP-8, in which the PDP-8 did I/O for the LINC.

REFERENCES

1. Meyer, T. H. and Southerland, I. E. On the Design of Display Processors. *Comm. ACM* 11(6):410 (June 1968).

10
Special Techniques

Apart from the general techniques of program design and the more specific techniques of the various system organizations, there are a few special techniques that are especially useful for real-time applications. These include finite-state machines and state-transition diagrams, timing utilities, digital filtering, and digital control.

Each of these techniques could easily fill a book by itself, and in fact there are many such books. Here we will confine ourselves to an overview.

FINITE-STATE MACHINES

Possibly the most useful technique for the design of real-time systems is the *finite-state machine* (FSM), or *state-transition diagram*. A FSM is an "abstract machine," meaning that it is a theoretical construct that models many kinds of real systems. The FSM consists of a controller whose input and output are streams of symbols (which may represent actual symbols, but are more likely to represent control signals or other conditions). The controller can be in any one of a finite number of *states* (hence the name). Depending on the machine's current state and its input, it will make a *transition* to another state, possibly produce an output, and obtain another input symbol. Sometimes outputs are associated with states rather than with state/symbol combinations (Fig. 10.1).

The name *finite-state* implies that the machine must be in one of a finite number of discrete states—a digital system rather than analog, and with a limited amount of memory.

(The FSM is one of the fundamental concepts of the theory of computation, and is the basis for many other abstract machines. For example, if the FSM's input and output, instead of being separate streams, are a "tape" that can be read, written, and moved in either direction, it becomes a *Turing Machine*, which can model any known computing device. Such is the power of adding infinite memory.)

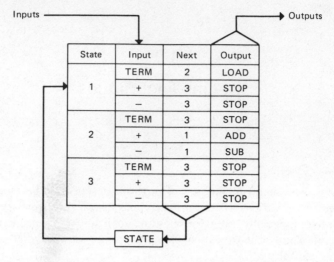

Figure 10.1. A finite-state machine to interpret simple arithmetic expressions.

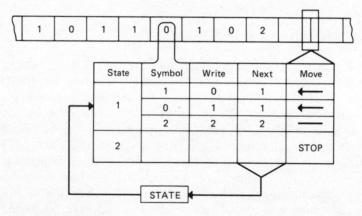

Figure 10.2. A Turing Machine. This machine inverts binary numbers (strings of 1's and 0's), stopping when it reaches a 2.

State-Transition Diagrams

A finite-state machine is easily described by a diagram, usually with circles representing states, and lines labeled with inputs representing the transitions (Fig. 10.3). Equivalently, it can be represented as a table of quadruples: current state, output, input, new state. This form, naturally, corresponds closely to the internal representation in a computer.

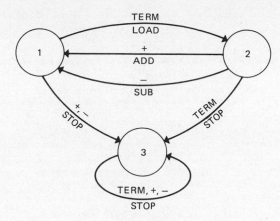

Figure 10.3. A state-transition diagram for the machine of Fig. 10.1.

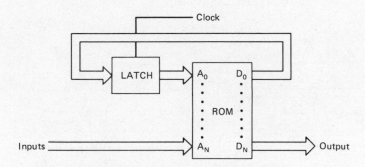

Figure 10.4. A finite-state machine in hardware.

Hardware Implementation

FSM's are good for describing the action of simple controllers, and are easy to implement either in hardware or software. A finite-state controller can be implemented in hardware using only a PROM to hold the state table, and a latch for the current state (Fig. 10.4). They are also good for describing the action of simple sequential circuits, and are usually a familiar and comfortable idiom for hardware designers.

Software Implementations

FSM's are also easy to implement in software, either using conditionals or by interpreting a table. The table interpreter is slower, but easier to change. It is also usually more compact, an advantage in small control applications.

```
/***********************************************
** A finite-state machine
**       Implementation using direct tests
***********************************************/
fsml()
{
    extern int in();    /* get next input symbol*/
    extern     out();   /* send output          */
    int        state;   /* current state        */

    state = 1;
    while (1) {          /* loop forever         */
        switch (state) {
          case 1:
            switch (in()) {
              case TERM:
                out(LOAD);     state = 2;
                break;
              case PLUS:
              case MINUS:
                out(STOP);     state = 3;
            } break;
          case 2:
            switch (in()) {
              case TERM:
                out(STOP);     state = 3;
                break;
              case PLUS:
                out(ADD);      state = 1;
                break;
              case MINUS:
                out(SUB);      state = 1;
                break;
            }
            break;
          case 3:
            in();          /* ignore inputs        */
            out(STOP);     /* and stay in state 3  */
            break;
        }
    }
}
```

```
/*************************************************
** A finite-state machine
**      Implementation using table interpreter
*************************************************/
static struct {          /* table entry          */
        int    this;     /*      this state       */
        int    sym;      /*      symbol           */
        int    next;     /*      next state       */
        int    output;   /*      output           */
} table[] = {
        {1,    TERM,    2,      LOAD},
        {1,    PLUS,    3,      STOP},
        {1,    MINUS,   3,      STOP},
        {2,    TERM,    3,      STOP},
        {2,    PLUS,    1,      ADD },
        {2,    MINUS,   1,      SUB },
        {3,    TERM,    3,      STOP},
        {3,    PLUS,    3,      STOP},
        {3,    MINUS,   3,      STOP},
};

fsm2()              /* the interpreter           */
{
    extern int in();    /* get next symbol        */
    extern     out();   /* send output            */

    int        state;   /* current state          */
    int        sym;     /* current symbol         */
    int        i;       /* temporary              */

    state = 1;
    while (1) {          /* loop forever          */
        sym = in();      /*    get next symbol     */
        for (i = 0;      /*    search table        */
            state != table[i].this &&
            sym != table[i].sym;
            i++);
        state = table[i].next;
        out(table[i].output);
    }
}
```

The search in the table interpreter can be eliminated if the values of the symbols and state-numbers permit a doubly-indexed array.

It is also possible to implement a FSM by encoding the state in the machine's program counter. This may lead to the use of GOTO's, which are sometimes considered improper, but their use in this case is well-controlled.

```
/***********************************************
** A finite-state machine
**        Implementation using program location
**        to encode state.
**********************************************/
fsm3()
{
    extern int in();      /* get next input symbol*/
    extern     out();     /* send output          */

  state1:
    switch (in()) {
     case TERM:
         out(LOAD);        goto state2;
     case PLUS:
     case MINUS:
         out(STOP);        goto state3;
    }
  state2:
    switch (in()) {
     case TERM:
         out(STOP);        goto state3;
     case PLUS:
         out(ADD);         goto state1;
     case MINUS:
         out(SUB);         goto state1;
    }
  state3:
    in();          /* ignore inputs */
    out(STOP);             goto state3;
}
```

Regular Expression Languages

FSM's are important in the theory of computation, in which they are related to a family of languages called *regular expressions*. Regular expression languages are simple, and often useful as command languages for interactive systems. To every regular expression language there corresponds a FSM which *recognizes* it by reaching a state which outputs a "recognized" output whenever the machine is presented with a sequence of input symbols which form an expression in the language.

Regular expressions are described using a *meta-language* consisting of the symbols of the language (*terminal* symbols), and the following meta-symbols:

| read as "or," separating two alternative expressions;
* meaning "zero or more of" the preceding expression;
? meaning "zero or one of" the preceding expression;
+ meaning "one or more of" the preceding expression;
(. . .) for grouping.

Thus, "a b c" is a simple regular expression, which describes the single sequence of symbols "abc." "a b* c" is more interesting, since it describes any string consisting of "a" and "c" separated by any number (including zero) of "b"'s. Thus, it includes "ac," "abc," "abbc," and so on.

The regular expression "a | b" describes either "a" or "b." Finally, "a (b | c) d" describes a string consisting of "a" and "d," separated by any number of either "b"'s or "c"'s.

Strictly speaking, "?" and "+" are not necessary, since they can be expressed by combinations of the others. Thus, "a b?" is the same as "a | a b," and "a+" is the same as "a a*." They are useful because they simplify expressions.

The regular expression corresponding to the finite-state machine in Figure 10.1 is, of course, "(term (+ | −) term)*," an expression consisting of any number of terms separated by "+" or "−." Regular-expression notation is a familiar idiom to most programmers, who are used to reading descriptions of programming languages in this or a similar form.

FSM Applications

Many simple controllers are usefully described as finite-state machines. Anything with discrete states, and discrete (digital) inputs and outputs is a possible application. Examples include traffic lights, safety interlocks, and so on. A digital combination lock is easily described as a FSM that recognizes an expression which happens to be the right combination.

FSM's are also good for describing simple user interactions such as the control panels of smart appliances. They are easy to describe in a "First you do this, then you do this" style. (A good rule to follow is that anything that is hard to document or describe is probably too complicated.)

Regular expressions are particularly useful for describing the *tokens* that make up programming and command languages: numbers, names, keywords, and so on. Scanners for such languages are often implemented as finite-state machines.

Recursive FSM's

Many interesting and useful languages are too complicated to be recognized by a finite-state machine. In particular, any language that includes balanced parentheses or other nested constructions cannot be recognized. (This is easy to demonstrate: if parentheses can be nested to any depth, at some point a machine with only a finite number of states must "lose track" of how many parentheses have been seen.)

Consider a machine consisting of a FSM and a pushdown stack which can be used to remember states. This means that some states of the FSM can be "subroutine calls." This machine is called a *recursive* FSM, and can recognize a much larger class of languages (including arithmetic expressions with nested parentheses).

A common notation for describing such languages is by a set of regular expressions, in which some symbols, instead of being input (or *terminal*) symbols, are the names of other regular expressions *(non-terminal* symbols). For example, these equations describe ordinary arithmetic expressions:

$$
\begin{aligned}
\text{expression} &::= \text{term} ((\text{``}+\text{''} \mid \text{``}-\text{''}) \text{ term })* \\
\text{term} &::= \text{factor} ((\text{``}*\text{''} \mid \text{``}/\text{''}) \text{ factor })* \\
\text{factor} &::= \text{number} \mid \text{``(``} \text{ expression } \text{``)''} \\
\text{number} &::= \text{digit digit}* \\
\text{digit} &::= \text{``0''} \mid \text{``1''} \mid \text{``3''} \mid \text{``4''} \mid \text{``5''} \\
&\quad \mid \text{``6''} \mid \text{``7''} \mid \text{``8''} \mid \text{``9''}
\end{aligned}
$$

Notice the use of ":: =" (sometimes written ":" or "=") *to define a non-terminal symbol.*

BNF.   There are many variations on this notation, all called "modified BNF," after the Backus-Naur Form used to describe the language Algol 60 (in a document, *Report on the Algorithmic Language Algol 60*, which remains one of the clearest descriptions of a programming language ever written). The original BNF used only ":: =" and "|"; the other constructs of regular expressions were built by adding more non-terminals. Non-terminals were enclosed in brackets "⟨ ... ⟩," rather than quoting terminal symbols.

This was slightly awkward, as can be seen from the preceding example rewritten in "original" BNF:

$$
\begin{aligned}
&<\text{expression}> ::= <\text{term}> \mid <\text{term}> <\text{addop}> <\text{expression}> \\
&<\text{addop}> \quad\quad ::= + \mid -
\end{aligned}
$$

\<term\>	:: =	\<factor\> | \<factor\> \<multop\> \<term\>
\<multop\>	:: =	* | /
\<factor\>	:: =	\<number\> | (\<expression\>)
\<number\>	:: =	\<digit\> | \<digit\> \<number\>
\<digit\>	:: =	0 | 1 | 2 | 3 | 4 | 5 | 6 | 7 | 8 | 9

Railroad Diagrams.   Sometimes languages are also described by state-transition diagrams, sometimes called "railroad diagrams" from their resemblance to railroad layouts (Fig. 10.5). The *Pascal User Manual and Report* [1] uses this technique.

Parsers.   A recognizer for such a language can be constructed by replacing each non-terminal symbol by a subroutine which uses finite-state machine techniques to recognize the right-hand side of the definition. Usually such a recognizer also does something with the expression it recognizes. For example, a recognizer for the language above might be used as a calculator, and would return the value of the expression it recognizes.

This kind of recognizer, built using subroutines, is called a *top-down parser* (*parser* being the general name for language recognizers). Parsers can be constructed in other ways, too; the top-down method is merely one of the easiest.

For more detail on parsing and language-processing techniques, see any good book on compiler theory and construction, such as Aho and Ullman.[2] Research papers in the field have largely gone beyond the point of usefulness; they are more concerned with theoretical points such as the speed of parsing algorithms than with any potential usefulness for actually writing language processors.

If you have access to a parser-generator, such as *yacc* on Unix, consider using it if you have to write a parser. Otherwise, a top-down parser is probably the fastest way to get one. (A "bottom-up" table-driven parser, such as a precedence or LR(1) parser, will *run* faster but, without a parser-generator, will be much more difficult to construct.)

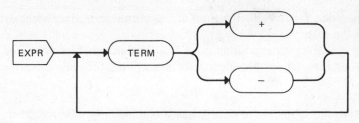

Figure 10.5. A Railroad diagram.

TIMING UTILITIES

Real-time programming is largely concerned with *time*, so it is not surprising that a collection of utility programs for dealing with time is a useful thing to have. In this section, we will define a minimal set of timing utilities.

There are two basic kinds of timing utility: those concerned with relative intervals, and those concerned with absolute time (sometimes called "real time," "clock time," or "wall time").

Most of the following operations are provided in some form by real-time operating systems.

Operations on Absolute Time

There are comparatively few operations on absolute time. Not all systems provide them, either, since they require the presence of a clock which runs continuously, at least while the system is turned on.

Clocks.   The simplest kind of "real-time" clock is something that generates an interrupt once every time unit. The associated interrupt routine increments a counter whose value is equal to the number of time-units since system initialization. For many purposes, this is sufficient.

Many computer systems keep track of the actual ("wall") time and date, and many still have the annoying habit of asking for them when the system is powered up. This can be avoided by adding a peripheral consisting of a clock chip or timer with a battery to provide power when the system is turned off. With the availability of wrist-watch chips modified for computer interfacing, these clocks are becoming more common.

Present Time.   The most obvious operation on absolute time is to get its current value. This could be stored in a variable which is continuously updated by an interrupt routine, or it might be necessary to read from an input port. In any case, we will assume that

```
Present_Time()
```

is an operation that returns the time in basic time-units since some arbitrary point in the past.

Many operating systems either provide a time already formatted into hours, minutes, and seconds, or provide the obvious utilities for conversion from basic units.

Clock Setting.   Even if the system has a continuously powered clock, it will sometimes be necessary to set it. The simplest possible operation of this sort is

```
Set_Time(time_in_units)
```

which initializes the running count returned by **Present__Time**. Again, some systems give the ability to set the time in natural units.

Wait Until.   Once there is a clock, an obvious operation is the alarm-clock function

```
Wait_Until(time)
```

which waits until the present time is equal to the given time. It should also return immediately if the requested time has already passed. An obvious (and inefficient) implementation is

```
Wait_Until(time)
int     time;
{
        while (Present_Time() < time) /* loop */;
}
```

A real-time operating system would implement this function by putting the requesting task on a queue of tasks waiting to be awakened at particular times.

Synchronize.   Given an external clock "ticking" at regular intervals, a simple operation is

```
Synchronize()
```

which waits until the next "tick" occurs. The simple implementation is

```
Synchronize()
{
        extern int Sync_Signal;

        while (!Sync_Signal) ;
        Sync_Signal = 0;
}
```

where **Sync__Signal** is a variable which is set by an interrupt routine on every tick (and reset by **Synchronize**). Something like this is often used in single-chip controllers and clocks to wait for the next zero-crossing of the 60 Hz power line. This is usually a good time to turn devices on or off to avoid power-line spikes.

Operations on Intervals

Wait.   The most common operations in real-time programming involve time intervals, and the most common such operation is **Wait**. This usually takes the form:

Wait(interval)

where the interval is given in seconds, clock- ticks, or some other convenient unit. A common but poor implementation is a simple loop:

```
Wait(time_units)
int time_units;
{
        int t;

        for (t = 0; t < time_units; t++)
                Wait_One_Unit();
}
```

The very worst form of this has the **Wait__One__Unit** function implemented as another loop, counting down from a constant equal to the number of machine cycles in a time unit divided by the number of machine cycles in the loop. This is bad because if the program is transported to another machine with a different clock speed, or a different CPU, the constant will have to be recomputed. The accuracy is also affected by such things as DMA, interrupts, and memory refreshing.

A better way is to wait for some external event that occurs once every time-unit. (In other words, **Wait__One__Unit** is the same as **Synchronize**, above.) Since the event occurs asynchronously with the program, the wait for the first one may be anything from zero to one time-unit, a considerable error if the time-unit is large. This problem is shared by the obvious implementation in terms of absolute-time routines:

```
Wait(time_units)
int time_units;
{
        Wait_Until(Present_Time() + time_units);
}
```

If a counter-timer peripheral is available, the best implementation of Wait is to program the peripheral to generate an interrupt or other signal after the required amount of time. This gives a resolution equal to the system clock.

Timeouts. Operating systems sometimes allow a task performing a wait operation to specify a time interval, called a *timeout*, after which the wait is aborted and returns an error indication. Such an operation might be called

```
Set_Time_Out(interval)
```

Alternatively, a timeout parameter might be added to the wait operation.

DIGITAL SIGNAL PROCESSING

Digital signal processing is the attempt to perform useful operations, such as averaging, rectification, differentiation, and so on, on a sequence of numbers that represent samples of some analog signal. As such, discussions of the field tend to become very mathematical, often losing sight of the initial objective, which is to do something useful with a signal.

Rather than go deeply into the mathematics of digital signal processing, this section will instead attempt to introduce the necessary concepts. It is, in other words, a sort of road map and traveller's guide to the jungle of digital signal processing. On the other hand, there is no information here on how to *design* digital signal-processing systems. Designs, and design techniques, are readily available; the main problem is learning enough of the jargon to dig them out.

Why Process Signals?

This may seem like a foolish question, but why *should* you process signals, and especially why should you do it digitally? (Many times, a cold look at this question will convince you that you *shouldn't* do it digitally: op-amps, active filters, and the like will do a lot of signal processing very easily.) The answer comes in two parts: the kinds of operations that need to be done on signals, and the advantages of doing them digitally.

Signal-Processing Operations. Suppose that your real-time system is connected to some measuring device, and that its task is simply to display the current value of some quantity. The first problem is that the quantity being measured is, in general, not the quantity you want to display. For example, you may be measuring a voltage (and usually are), but this really represents a temperature, and so some kind of scaling has to be done on each value. This usually means multiplying by a scale factor and adding an offset.

A further problem arises if the quantity being measured is, say, a position, and you need a velocity (or vice versa). Here you have to perform a differentiation (or integration). Now you can no longer operate on each input value individually, but have to operate on two or more successive values.

Finally, suppose that your input signal has some kind of noise in it (real signals usually do). Assuming that the noise is varying quickly and the signal slowly, what you need is a *low-pass filter*, which takes out the high frequencies and leaves the low ones. This can be done by some kind of averaging process.

Advantages of Digital Processing.　Now, all of these operations can be done using analog circuitry. For example, a pretty good differentiator, integrator, or filter can be made out of a resistor and a capacitor. Why use a computer?

Precision.　One advantage of digital signal processing is precision: a 16-bit sample represents a dynamic range of about 35 dB. (For the programmers in the audience, 10 dB is a *ratio* of 10/1. The abbreviation "dB" stands for decibel, $\frac{1}{10}$ of a "Bel," which nobody uses. A ratio x/y can be expressed in dB as $10 \log(x/y)$. The *dynamic range* of a signal is the ratio of the largest to the smallest possible values.) Floating-point numbers can represent even larger dynamic ranges.

Moreover, analog devices are only approximations to ideal devices; they have non-linearities and other peculiarities. It is also impossible to get devices in exactly the values you want: 1% precision is pretty good; 0.1% is excellent (and expensive). Digital computations can be done as precisely as they need to be— just add more bits to your numbers.

Stability.　Another advantage of digital signal processing is stability. The values of analog components can drift, due to aging, temperature, and other effects. Numbers stored digitally don't change. This, by the way, is the main advantage of the new digital audio recordings; no matter how many times the recording is played, it doesn't wear out.

Expediency.　The final advantage of digital signal processing in a real-time system is expediency: if there is a computer in the system already, you may as well use it. This, of course, cannot justify the computer in the first place, but there may be other advantages to using a computer, such as being able to do calculations with measurements. ("Smart" instruments are in this category; the computer is there to add versatility. Any signal processing it can do is an added advantage.)

Disadvantages of Digital Processing.　Some disadvantages of digital signal processing have to be mentioned. It is expensive, and it is slow. The two are related, in that the processing can be sped up by throwing money at it. Things are getting better in this respect; 16-bit machines have at least twice the bandwidth of 8-bit ones, and multiply and divide instructions are becoming common.

There are also more specialized solutions: special-purpose signal-processing computers, and discrete registers, adders, and multipliers. These are, of course, expensive.

Theory of Digital Signal Processing

The theory of digital signal processing is essentially the theory of what happens when a continuous function (an analog signal) is approximated by means of samples taken at finite time intervals. This is primarily the theory of difference, as opposed to differential, equations. The two fields are closely related, and many of the same analytical techniques are used.

The Sampling Theorem. The fundamental sampling theorem states that if you are taking f samples per second, you can reproduce a signal whose highest frequency component is at most $f/2$. The frequency $f/2$ is called the *Nyquist frequency* of the sampled system.

If frequencies greater than the Nyquist frequency are present in the signal being sampled, a phenomenon called *aliasing* occurs: a lower-frequency signal appears in the sampled output (Fig. 10.6). It is impossible to distinguish the results of sampling the higher-frequency waveform, and the lower-frequency one.

From this we can see that it is important to ensure that any inputs being sampled do not contain frequencies higher than the Nyquist frequency (and a generous margin for error helps). Analog filtering of the input to a D/A converter is usually necessary to prevent aliasing.

Difference Equations. Consider a sequence of samples $x(0)$, $x(1)$, ..., $x(k)$. Consider also some process that produces a sequence of corresponding output samples $y(0)$, $y(1)$, ..., $y(k)$. If the process is linear* and depends only on a finite number of its inputs, it must take the form:

$$y(k) = a(0)x(k) + a(n)x(k-1) + \cdots + a(n)x(k-n) \quad (10.1)$$

---

*For the non-mathematicians, a function $f(x)$ is linear if and only if $f(x+y) = f(x) + f(y)$, and $f(ax) = af(x)$. Linear functions are easy to analyze, and can be computed using only sums, and products with constants. Many well-behaved things in the world are linear.

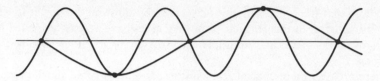

Figure 10.6. Sampled signal with aliasing.

where the $a(i)$ are constant coefficients. This operation is essentially a weighted, moving average. (It is a simple $n+1$-point moving average if all of the a's are equal to $1/(n+1)$.)

If we further allow the output of the process to depend on some of the previous outputs, introducing feedback into the process, we get

$$
\begin{aligned}
y(k) = \ & a(0)x(k) + \cdots + a(n)x(k - n) \\
& + b(1)y(k - 1) + \cdots + b(m)y(k - m)
\end{aligned} \qquad (10.2)
$$

Such equations are called *linear difference equations,* or *linear recurrence equations.* Using feedback can often reduce the number of terms needed for a given effect, and also allows us to do operations like integration. (It also introduces the possibility of instability, as we will see.)

Many filtering-type operations can be done using linear difference equations, and the tools for analyzing their behavior are well-developed. Difference equations, in the world of sampled functions, are closely related to differential equations in the world of continuous functions.

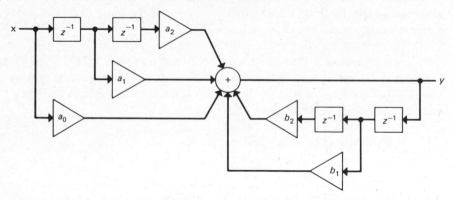

Figure 10.7. Data flow for the difference equation $y(n) = a(0)x(n) + a(1)x(n-1) + a(2)x(n-2) + b(1)y(n-1) + b(2)y(n-2)$.

Computing Linear Difference Equations. If we were to construct a machine to compute such a function, it would look like Fig. 10.7 (several alternative forms are possible). Such a diagram can be turned directly into a circuit diagram for a machine composed of constant multipliers, adders, and registers, or it can also be turned into a computer program.

There are several possible ways of turning the difference equations into a computer program, mainly depending on whether the values $x(0), \ldots, x(k)$ are all available in an array, or whether they are arriving in a stream and values have to be computed on the fly. The program we present for the latter case is rather inefficient; many forms of tricky coding are possible.

```
/************************************************
** filter an array
**        Assume that x[-n] ... x[-1] = 0,
**                    y[-m] ... y[-1] = 0.
************************************************/
filter_array(a, n, b, m, x, y, k)
float *a, *b;          /* coefficient arrays    */
int    n, m;           /* ... and their sizes   */
float *x, *y;          /* input and output arrays */
int    k;              /* ... and their sizes   */
{
    int i, j;

    for (i = 0; i < k; i++) {
        y[i] = 0;
        for (j = 0; j <= n && j <= i; j++) {
            y[i] += a[j] * x[k-j];
        }
        for (j = 1; j <= m && j <= i; j++) {
            y[i] += b[j] * y[k-j];
        }
    }
}


/************************************************
** filter next element of a stream
**        The past inputs and outputs are saved
**        in the static arrays x and y.
**
**        The coefficients and history-storage
**        arrays are declared as externals, and
**        have to be long enough.
************************************************/
```

```
float filter_stream(xk)
float xk;
{
    extern float x[], y[];      /* history buffers  */
    extern float a[], b[];      /* coefficients     */
    extern int    n,   m;

    float yk;
    int j;

    /* Compute yk, the next output              */
    /*    Simultaneously, shift the saved inputs */
    /*    and outputs by one position.           */

    yk = a[0] * xk;
    for (j = 1; j <= n; j++) {
        yk += a[j] * x[n-j];
        x[n-j] = x[(n-j)-1];
    }
    x[0] = xk;
    for (j = 1; j <= m; j++) {
        yk += b[j] * y[n-j];
        y[n-j] = y[(n-j)-1];
    }
    y[0] = yk;

    /* return next value */

    return(yk);
}
```

Note that these programs would probably be less transparent but more efficient if we used pointers rather than array subscripting. Also, if the *a* and *b* coefficient arrays are the same size, we can combine the two loops.

Note to the Practical Reader.

The rest of this chapter is purely theoretical. It sets forth the mathematical basis of digital signal processing and control, but contains no design techniques of practical value. The reader who does not intend to wrestle with the literature of the subject might wish to read the section on least-squares filters (which has some usable filtering coefficients in it), skim the introduction to feedback and control, and skip the rest.

A good non-theoretical introduction to some of the basic concepts can be found in Foster[3], but there are no general design techniques there.

The Z-Transform. Assuming that we want to implement some kind of signal-processing function using a linear difference equation, we need some way of determining the a and b coefficients. Alternatively, given a set of coefficients, we need some way of analyzing what they will do to a signal. The main tool for doing this is the *z-transform*.

Books and articles about digital filtering usually introduce the z-transform with much fanfare and little explanation. I will attempt to provide some justification.

Consider a unit pulse ($x(k) = 1$ if $k = 0$; 0 otherwise), and put it through the difference equation:

$$y(k) = ax(k) + by(k - 1) \qquad (10.3)$$

The result is the sequence a, ab, ab^2, ab^3, ..., ab^k, etc. We begin to suspect that difference equations and infinite series of the form $y(n) = x^n$ or $y(n) = x-n$ might have a useful relationship, and we may even be reminded of a power series.

Let us transform a series of $x(k)$'s into a function of a complex variable z by means of the following sum:

$$X(z) = \sum_{k=-\infty}^{\infty} x(k)z^{-k}$$

(We assume that we can find a range of values for the magnitude of z for which this series will converge.) This is called the z-transform of the series. It is closely related to the Laplace transform of a function, which is used to solve differential equations.

What does this get us? Well, first consider the unit pulse, $x(0)=1$, $x(n \neq 0)=0$. Its z-transform is obviously 1. Now consider the unit pulse delayed by one period: $x(1)=1$, $x(n \neq 0)=0$. *Its* transform is $z-1$. We immediately suspect that $z-1$ is the z-transform of a unit delay ($y(k) = x(k-1)$), which indeed it is.

Now consider the difference equation (10.3) above. We would like to express the z-transform of its output in terms of the z-transform of its input. We want

$$
\begin{aligned}
Y(z) = \Sigma y(k)z^{-k} &= \Sigma(ax(k) + by(k - 1))z^{-k} \\
&= \Sigma ax(k)z^{-k} + \Sigma by(k - 1)z^{-k} \\
&= \Sigma ax(k)z^{-k} + bz^{-1}\Sigma y(k)z^{-k} \\
&= aX(z) + bz^{-1}Y(z) \\
&= \frac{aX(z)}{1 - bz^{-1}} = \frac{az}{z - b}X(z)
\end{aligned}
$$

The quantity $az/(z-b)$, the ratio of the transform of the output to the transform of the input, is called the *transfer function* of the function defined by the difference equation (10.3).

More generally, the transfer function of the general linear difference equation (10.2) is

$$\frac{a(0) + a(1)z^{-1} + \cdots + a(n)z^{-n}}{1 - b(1)z^{-1} - \cdots - b(m)z^{-m}}$$

If $m > n$, we can write this as the ratio of polynomials in z:

$$\frac{a(0)z^m + a(1)z^{m-1} + \cdots + a(n)z^{m-n}}{z^n - b(1)z^{n-1} - \cdots - b(m)}$$

Properties of Transfer Functions. Suppose we have a system, described by a difference equation, whose transfer function is $H(z)$. We already know that the z-transform $U(z)$ of the unit pulse at zero is 1, so $Y(z) = H(z)U(z) = H(z)$. In other words, the transfer function of a system is the z-transform of its response to a unit pulse. (This corresponds to the fact that the Laplace transform of a differential equation is its response to a unit impulse, the Dirac delta function.)

One might wish that the inverse transform were simple, so that knowing the transfer function of a system, one could determine its response to an impulse after a given amount of time. Unfortunately, the inverse transform is *not* simple; it's a complex contour integral, and not at all trivial to apply.

We can, however, discover a great deal about a system from its z-transform. In particular, consider the *poles* of the transfer function, the places in the complex z-plane where the denominator of the transfer function becomes zero. These turn out to be intimately related to the *stability* of the system.

We already know that the z-transform of the series $y(k) = ab^k$ is $az/(z-b)$, which has a pole at b. This series diverges (grows without limit) if $b > 1$, converges (decays to zero) if $b < 1$, and is constant if $b = 1$. This suggests the more general rule that a system is stable if its poles are inside the unit circle on the complex plane. Moreover, the impulse response of a system will decay faster the closer the poles are to the origin.

Now let's look at a periodic signal, say $y(k) = \cos(\omega k)$. This can be resolved into the sum of two complex exponentials,

$$y(k) = \frac{e^{i\omega k} + e^{-i\omega k}}{2}$$

which we can transform separately and add afterwards because the z-transform is linear. (In the electronics field you will more often see i, the square root of -1, represented as j to prevent confusion with a current, abbreviated by i. Here, however, we are sufficiently far from electronics to prefer clarity to custom.) Taking $\exp(i\omega k)$ first, since $\exp(i\omega k) = \exp(i\omega)\exp(k)$, its z-transform must be $z/(z-\exp(i\omega))$. Thus the z-transform of $\cos(\omega k)$ is

$$\frac{1}{2}\left(\frac{z}{z - \exp(i\omega)} + \frac{z}{z - \exp(-i\omega)} = \frac{z(z - \cos\omega)}{z^2 - 2(\cos\omega)z + 1}\right)$$

This has a pair of poles on the unit circle, at angles $\pm\omega$ from the positive real axis (Fig. 10.8).

The number of samples per cycle of the function is equal to $2\pi/\omega$ (with ω in radians).

It is also worth noting that a function without feedback has no poles in its transform, and so is guaranteed stable. Such a function is also called a *finite impulse response* filter; its response to a unit pulse goes to zero after a finite number of delays. In fact, if the function is $y(k) = a(0)x(k) + a(1)x(k-1) + \ldots + a(n)x(k-n)$, then its impulse response will be $a(0), a(1), \ldots a(n), 0, 0, \ldots$

Convolution. Consider the sequences $f(k)$ and $g(k)$. The sum

$$f * g(k) = \sum_{j=-\infty}^{\infty} f(j)g(k - j)$$

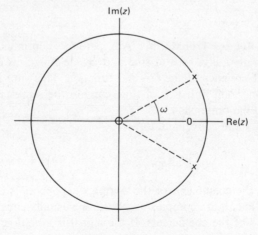

is called the *convolution* of f and g.

By taking the z-transform of both sides, we find that

$$\sum_k f * g(k)z^{-k} = \sum_k z^{-k} \sum_j f(k)g(k - j)$$

Exchanging the two summations gives:

$$\sum_j f(j) \sum_k z^{-k} g(k - j)$$

And by letting $i = k - j$ we get

$$\begin{aligned} F * G(z) &= \sum_j f(j) \sum_i z^{-(i + j)}g(i) \\ &= \sum_j f(j) \sum_i z^{-i}z^{-j}g(i) \\ &= \sum_j f(j)z^{-j}\sum_i z^{-i}g(i) \\ &= F(z)G(z). \end{aligned}$$

In other words, the z-transform of the convolution of two series is the product of their z-transforms. We conclude that if f is the impulse response of a system, and g is an input sequence, then $f*g$ is the resulting output sequence from the system.

If the output of a system depends only on its inputs, so that it has the form of (Eq. 10.1), there are only a finite number of terms in the convolution sum for each output. This gives us our old friend the weighted moving average in another form.

The Discrete Fourier Transform. Any periodic, continuous function of time can be represented as a sum of sine and cosine functions of multiples of the fundamental frequency of the original function. This sum is called a *Fourier series*. A non-periodic function of time can also be represented as an integral of sine and cosine functions.

It is usually more convenient to use

$$\exp(i\omega) = \cos \omega - i \sin \omega$$

and to obtain the coefficients of the complex exponentials directly. (Since the resulting coefficients are complex numbers, one usually ends up using the magnitude squared of the coefficients. If the signal is a voltage (for example), its magnitude squared is proportional to the *power* delivered into a fixed load.)

The *Fourier Transform* of a continuous function $f(t)$ is

$$g(i\omega) = \int_{-\infty}^{\infty} f(t)e^{-i\omega t} \, dt$$

If $f(t)$ is being sampled at discrete points $t = nT$ (where T is the sampling interval), then the integral above can be reduced to the summation

$$F(i\omega) = \sum_{k=-\infty}^{\infty} f(kT)e^{-i\omega kT} \qquad (10.4)$$

which is simply the z-transform of $f(n)$ with $\exp(-i\omega)$ substituted for z.

Usually only a finite number of samples (say for $0 \ldots n-1$) are available, so the sum becomes

$$F(i\omega) = \sum_{k=0}^{n-1} f(kT)e^{-i\omega kT}$$

It is then usual to compute $F(i\omega)$ for the n discrete frequencies $\omega = 2\pi k/nT$ ($k = 0, \ldots, n-1$). This transform is called the *Discrete Fourier Transform* (DFT). It is clear that computing $f(i\omega)$ for n values of ω and n samples requires computing n^2 complex product terms, which is not practical in real time.

The Fast Fourier Transform (FFT). If n is a power of two, however, there is a fast way of computing the DFT: the Cooley-Tukey[4] algorithm, published in 1965. This algorithm, now called the FFT for Fast Fourier Transform, takes advantage of redundancies in the computation, so that some of the product terms only have to be computed once. This is done by splitting the signal to be transformed into two signals, consisting either of odd and even samples respectively (decimation in time), or of the first $n/2$ and the last $n/2$ points (decimation in frequency). The decimation process is then applied again to each sub-transform. The n^2 complex multiplications are reduced to $(n/2)\log_2 n$.

Programs for computing FFT's can be found in Gold[5] and many other places, including the ACM's *Collected Algorithms*.

The FFT algorithm is still not fast enough for real-time signal processing, in the sense that analyzing a set of samples will generally take longer than collecting them, unless the computer is very fast or the signal very slow. The FFT is nevertheless used in real-time applications, especially in smart instruments such as digital oscilloscopes or spectrum analyzers; a set of samples is collected in real-time, then analyzed off-line.

Digital Filtering

This book is not going to tell you how to *design* a digital filter. Lots of good designs for digital filters exist; this section is mainly concerned with helping you to understand their descriptions.

Most of the digital filters you will meet are based on the linear difference equations that we have already studied.

Digital Filter Taxonomy. In most cases, a digital filter is a process applied to a sampled, digital signal with the intent of modifying its frequency spectrum. In general, we want to pass some of the frequencies present in the original signal, and to reject others. Filters thus fall into the natural categories of *low-pass* filters, which pass low frequencies, *high-pass*, which pass high ones, *band-pass*, which pass a band of frequencies, and *band-reject* or *band-stop*, which pass everything outside of a band (Fig. 10.9).

The frequency at which the amplitude of a signal going through a high-pass or low-pass filter is reduced by a factor of the square root of two (meaning that the *power* output is cut in half) is called the *cut-off* frequency of the filter.

Why Filter? There are two main reasons why one would want to filter a signal: to *smooth* it (that is, reduce noise, or random variations), or to separate out unwanted frequency components (for example, to remove an interfering signal). Smoothing is generally a low-pass operation, since noise usually has a high frequency compared to the signal. Separating unwanted signals might involve any of the filter types.

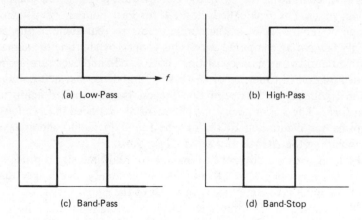

(a) Low-Pass   (b) High-Pass

(c) Band-Pass   (d) Band-Stop

Figure 10.9. Ideal filter frequency responses.

Frequency Response. Suppose we have a filter whose difference equation is

$$y(k) = \sum_{i=0}^{n} a(i)x(k - i) + \sum_{i=1}^{m} b(i)y(k - i)$$

We can see from its transfer function that its frequency response to signals of angular frequency ω is

$$Y(i\omega) = \frac{a(0) + a(1)e^{-i\omega} + \cdots + a(n)e^{-ni\omega}}{1 - b(1)e^{-i\omega} + \cdots + b(m)e^{-mi\omega}}$$

where $\omega = 2\pi fT$ where f is in cycles per second and T is the time between samples in seconds (ω is in radians).

Mapping $z = \exp(i\omega)$ for real values of ω in the z-plane (Fig. 10.8), we can see that the frequency of a frequency maps onto the unit circle, with $z = 1$ corresponding to all integral multiples of the sampling frequency, and $z = -1$ to the Nyquist frequency of half the sampling frequency. If our digital filter has only real coefficients in its difference equations, the magnitude of its z-transform must be symmetrical about the real axis ($|Y(a+ib)| = |Y(a-ib)|$), so that its frequency response is symmetrical about the Nyquist frequency.

Relations Among Filter Types. Most books about digital filtering spend almost all of their time on low-pass filters, barely mentioning the other types (if at all). This is because the other filter types can be derived from low-pass filters. However easy it may be, the relations are often hard to find, so here they are.

Suppose we have a low-pass filter $l(x)$, with z-transform $L(z)$. Taking advantage of the fact that a filter's frequency response is symmetrical about the Nyquist frequency, we can derive a high-pass filter by letting $H(z) = L(-z)$. This has the effect of changing the sign of the coefficients of odd powers of z.

A band-pass filter can be obtained by following a high-pass filter with a low-pass filter, or vice versa. Thus, its transform looks like $H(z)L(z)$. A band-stop filter can be obtained by putting a high-pass and a low-pass filter in parallel; its transform looks like $H(z) + L(z)$.

Non-Recursive Filters. Non-recursive filters enjoy the advantage of unconditional stability: their impulse response always goes to zero after a finite number of delays. For this reason they are sometimes called *finite impulse response* filters. The price of this stability is that it usually takes more terms in the difference equation, and consequently more time, to produce the same amount of filtering as a similar recursive filter.

Another advantage of non-recursive filters is that they are easy to understand. Because a non-recursive filtering operation is equivalent to convoluting the signal with a finite impulse response (the filter coefficients), its frequency and phase responses are easy to determine (or to specify).

When we deal with non-recursive filters, it will simplify things if we renumber the filtering coefficients, and make their indices symmetrical about zero. Then we have

$$y(k) = a(-n)x(k-n) + \cdots + a(0)x(0)$$
$$+ \cdots + a(n)x(k+n). \quad (10.5)$$

This appears to mean that $y(k)$ depends on future values of x, a difficulty which is resolved when we realize that its appearance is simply delayed by n sample-times.

Phase Response. It is easy to see that if $a(k) = a(-k)$, the filter will have no phase-shift in its output; a unit pulse at time $k=0$ will always transform into something symmetrical about zero. This is usually desirable. Since the output of the filter is actually delayed by n samples from its input, the true phase response is linear in frequency, which is usually acceptable.

(It is worth noting at this point that since $a(k) = a(-k)$ for most filters of interest, a filter using $2n+1$ coefficients only requires $n+1$ multiplications per point to compute. Its data-flow diagram is shown in Fig. 10.10.

Frequency Response. Since the impulse response of the filter is simply the sequence of $a(k)$'s, its frequency response is simply the Discrete Fourier Transform of the sequence of $a(k)$'s.

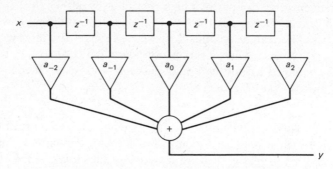

Figure 10.10. Data-flow diagram for the symmetric, nonrecursive filter $y(n) = a(-2)x(n-2) + a(-1)x(n-1) + a(0)x(n) + a(1)x(n+1) + a(2)x(n+2)$.

This might lead to the temptation of designing an ideal filter by running the process backwards, and taking the inverse DFT of desired response. Unfortunately, this inverse transform has an infinite number of components. Cutting them off after a finite number of components gives an actual response shown in Fig. 10.11.

Better results can be obtained by not insisting on such a sharp transition. The transition itself is low-pass filtered by convoluting the coefficients with a *window function*, of which several different varieties exist.

Least-Squares Filters. Suppose we have a signal which contains some noise, and which can be locally approximated by a polynomial. The noise can be reduced by fitting a polynomial to the data such that the sum of the squares of the differences between the polynomial and the data points are minimized. It turns out that this process can be performed using an appropriate non-recursive filter. (These filters are popular in the field of spectrometry, where they are known as Savitzky-Golay filters after the article by A. Savitzky and M. Golay[6] which popularized them in 1964.)

It can be shown that a least-squares filter based on polynomials of degree $2M$ preserves exactly every polynomial signal of degree $2M+1$ or less. They are also low-pass filters having a maximally-flat passband.

The filter coefficients for $(2n+1)$-point least-squares linear, and cubic filters are[7]

$$a_1(\pm k) = \frac{1}{2n + 1}$$

$$a_3(\pm k) = \frac{3((3n^2 + 3n - 1) - 5k^2)}{(2n - 1)(2n + 1)(2n + 3)}$$

(Tables of coefficients, and derivations for the general case, can be found in Savitzky-Golay[8] with corrections in Steinier[9].)

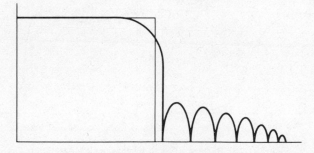

Figure 10.11. Ideal and actual frequency responses for a sharp-cutoff filter.

It is worth noting that other operations can be performed at the same time as filtering. In particular, differentiation (which is closely related to high-pass filtering) is easy to do.

Recursive Filters.   Recursive filters include, among other things, the digital counterparts of analog filters built using capacitors, inductors, resistors, and op-amps. Because recursive filters have poles in their transfer functions, it is possible for them to become unstable, producing either an exponentially-growing output, or an unwanted oscillation (just like their analog counterparts). Especially when the poles are close to the unit circle, it is possible for round-off error to cause instability.

The most common recursive filter designs are those based on the Butterworth and Chebyshev polynomials. Butterworth filters have a maximally-flat passband (frequency response), while Chebyshev filters trade a slight ripple in the frequency response for a sharper cut-off (Fig. 10.12).

It is possible to derive recursive filters either from corresponding analog filter designs by mapping their poles and zeros from the Laplace transform S-plane to the z-plane, or by any of several direct methods.

Other Signal-Processing Techniques

Averaging.   If the signal being sampled is periodic, or can be made to repeat in some way, it is possible to smooth it by averaging samples from successive repetitions. Since the signal is constant and any noise present is random, the noise will tend to cancel itself out. Noise reduction varies as the square root of the number of points averaged, so an improvement of a factor of 10 in the signal-to-noise ratio will require averaging 100 repetitions of the signal.

Naturally, this method is of no use at all if the signal cannot be made to repeat.

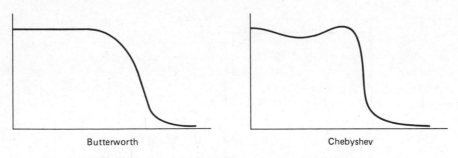

Butterworth   Chebyshev

Figure 10.12. Butterworth and Chebyshev low-pass filters.

Image Processing. Filtering can be applied to a two-dimentional array of points, as well as a one-dimentional sequence. This kind of filtering is a subset of the more general field of *image processing*, since most of the two-dimentional arrays one might want to filter are digitized pictures. High-pass filtering, for example, tends to enhance edges in the image, and low-pass filtering tends to remove noise.

Signal Generation. It is sometimes useful to consider a system without inputs: a *signal generator*. Clearly, a digital computer can generate any computable function to any required precision (though not necessarily quickly). Obvious benefits in applications such as test equipment, musical instruments (music synthesizers), and so on include precision, low distortion, and repeatability.

Direct Signal Generation. Some types of signal are easy to generate by direct computation: square-waves, triangles, and ramps are obvious. Sine and cosine functions can be generated using the pair of simultaneous difference equations:

$$x(n + 1) = Ax(n) - By(n)$$
$$y(n + 1) = Bx(n) + Ay(n)$$

with $A = \cos(bT)$ and $B = \sin(bT)$, $x(0) = 1$, $y(0) = 0$, which produce $x(n) = \cos(nbT)$ and $y(n) = \sin(nbT)$ where T is the sampling interval. (These equations can be derived in many equivalent ways: from z-transforms, the equations for the sine and cosine of the sum of two angles, and the equations for rotation of coordinate axes.)

One problem of this technique is that round-off and other errors tend to accumulate. This can sometimes be dealt with by applying a correction after some reasonable number of cycles. For example, if the period of the sine and cosine signals being generated is an exact multiple N of the sampling interval, then after every N cycles x and y can be reset to 1 and 0 respectively.

Table-Driven Signal Generation. It is also clear that any periodic function can be generated by stepping a pointer through a table of values with a sampling interval $T = t/n$ where t is the period of the signal and n is the number of points in the table. It is less obvious that the same thing can be accomplished with a constant sampling interval!

This is done by making the index into the table at time kT be the closest integer to knT/t, which obviously reduces to the previous case if t is an exact multiple of T. It works best if n is a power of two; then the index can be obtained by rounding and shifting. On a byte-oriented computer with a table size of 256, things are even simpler: just use the high-order byte. Multiple-precision integer arithmetic can be used to compute the index to any desired precision, giving precise frequency control. A typical program is

```
/***********************************************
** next_sample(table, interval, index)
**
**       return the next sample and update index.
**
**       Table size is 256.
**       interval = 256*T/t where T is the sample
**       interval and t is the period of the signal.
**
**       index is passed by reference so that
**       it can be updated.
***********************************************/

int next_sample(table, interval, index)
int table[], interval, *index;
{
    *index += interval;
    return(table[((*index + 128) / 256) & 255]);
    /* adding size/2 does true rounding
     * instead of truncation
     */
}
```

which simply illustrates that this is easier to do than to describe. The table must not contain frequency components higher than the Nyquist frequency, or aliasing will result.

FEEDBACK AND CONTROL

Usually the purpose of a real-time system is not simply to analyze, transform, or generate some signal, but to control a physical or electronic system. Many of the concepts of signal processing still apply, but there are obviously complications.

As with digital filtering, this section is not going to tell you how to design control systems; it is simply a guide to the thornier parts of the literature. Also as with filtering, Caxton Foster's book[10] provides a lucid introduction without going into theory.

Closed-Loop Control

Sometimes it is possible to control a system by sending out a signal and assuming that the system will do what you told it to. This is especially true of systems involving stepping motors or other digital devices (traffic lights, for instance). Often, however, the system is less co-operative; it may have errors, noise, or other deviations that keep it from doing exactly what you want.

In this case it is necessary to observe what the system is doing, and to change the orders accordingly. The process of generating control signals based on the deviation of a system from its intended behavior is called *feedback*, or *closed-loop control*. (Control without feedback, obviously, is called *open-loop control*.)

The basic block diagram of a closed-loop system is shown in Fig. 10.13. There are three main components: the system being controlled, usually called the *plant* in the literature; a *sensor* monitoring its outputs; and a *controller*, which is attempting to keep the outputs equal to the *reference* inputs that represent the outputs desired from the system.

The intermediate quantities are the error signal $e(t)$ and the control signals $u(t)$. It is possible to treat noise and sensor errors as separate inputs, along with disturbances to the plant.

Strictly speaking, the closed-loop system described above is a servomechanism. It is characterized by the fact that the input to the controller is the error, which is the difference between the reference input and the system output. A more general kind of closed-loop system is shown in Fig. 10.14. Here, a command input is given directly to the controller. In this kind of system, a really clever controller could attempt to "second-guess" the command inputs, and so apply early corrections to the system. This sort of system is rarely seen in the literature—it's not simple enough.

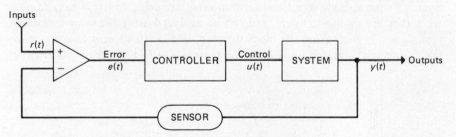

Figure 10.13. A closed-loop servomechanism.

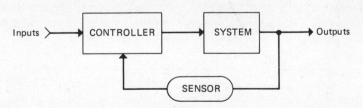

Figure 10.14. A more general closed-loop controller.

System Specifications.   We are going to move rapidly away from reality and into the realms of abstract mathematics, so it is important before we go to list the reasons for the trip. The important specifications for a control system are *steady-state accuracy, transient response, disturbance rejection, control effort,* and sensitivity to parameter changes.

Steady-state accuracy is the requirement that, after a change in the inputs to the system, the error $e(t)$ eventually becomes acceptably small. Transient response is the behavior of the system immediately after a change in the reference input. Components of transient response include rise time, overshoot, and settling time (Fig. 10.15). These are usually specified in terms of the response to a step input. The settling time may include either a smooth, monotonic transition, or a damped oscillation called "ringing."

Disturbance rejection is the response to a disturbance (unwanted) input, and includes both steady-state and transient components. Control effort is related to the size of the inputs that have to be presented in order to achieve the desired response; it may be specified in terms of maximum value (voltage, current, etc.) or in terms of energy.

Sensitivity to parameter changes includes sensitivity to changes in the plant parameters, which can be treated as a form of disturbance, and to changes in the controller. This area also may include analysis of errors (such as round-off and sampling) in the controller and sensors.

Single-Variable Systems

Systems with a single input and output value are comparatively easy to deal with: they are similar to filters, and can be analyzed using the same transform techniques. In fact, using the block diagram of Fig. 10.13, it is easy to derive the z-transform transfer function of the system. Let $G(z)$ be the transfer func-

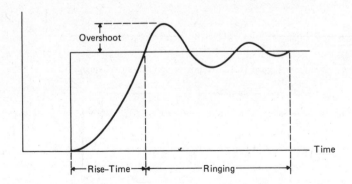

Figure 10.15. Dynamic response of a system, showing rise time, overshoot, and ringing.

tion of the controller, and $H(z)$ the transfer function of the plant. Then the transfer function of the system as a whole is

$$\frac{G(z)H(z)}{1 + G(z)H(z)}$$

and the usual methods of pole-zero analysis can be used to obtain the response characteristics of the system, or to design G so as to make the total system response meet its specifications.

Notice that a certain amount of sleight-of-hand has been involved here: the plant is *not*, in general, a discrete system but a continuous one. However, the slightly larger system consisting of an A/D converter sampling the output of the plant, and a D/A converter at its input, *is* a discrete system. If the plant is described by a Laplace transform, we can derive its z-transform by letting $z = \exp(sT)$ where s is the Laplace-transform variable and T the sampling time.

State Space

The *state* of a system is the set of variables which are necessary to predict its future behavior. It is usually represented as a vector variable **x** or, since the state changes with time, a vector function $x(t)$. Most systems of interest (at least, the ones that are easy to analyze!) are described by sets of linear differential equations, so that the elements of the state vector are variables that describe the present condition of the system, and their derivatives.

You will often see diagrams in which the behavior of a system is represented as a *trajectory* in *state space*. Usually the x axis is some variable in the system's state, and the y axis is its first derivative, in which case they are also called *phase-plane* diagrams. These are a convenient way of representing the behavior of the system over time. For example, Fig. 10.16 shows the trajectory of a simple system in both space-time and state space.

Matrix Description of System Behavior.   Representing the state of a system as a vector makes it possible to describe the system's behavior using the following matrix equations:

$$\dot{\mathbf{x}} = \mathbf{Fx} + \mathbf{Gu} \tag{10.6}$$
$$\mathbf{y} = \mathbf{Hx}$$

where **u** is the vector of inputs to the system, **y** the outputs, and **x** the state.

Non-linear systems can be represented as time- varying linear systems: systems in which the **F**, **G**, and **H** matrices vary with time. This works if the changes are not too rapid. Many systems have this form, for example, systems

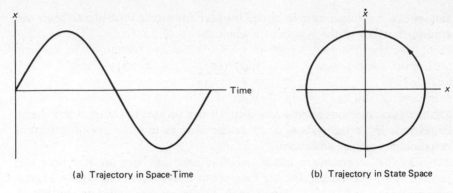

(a) Trajectory in Space-Time   (b) Trajectory in State Space

Figure 10.16. A simple harmonic oscillator: $\ddot{x} = -\omega x^2$.

which are basically linear, but in which the values of some of the parameters gradually drift.

In the case of a sampled system, Eq. 10.6 turns into

$$x(k) = F'x(k - 1) + G'u(k - 1)$$
$$y(k) = Hx(k)$$

The advantage of state-space analysis is that multi-variable systems are as easy to represent as single-variable ones.

Controlling the System

It is usual to design the controller for a system in two parts. The first part, the *control law*, is obtained assuming that all of the states of the system are available for feedback; the inputs can then be expressed as linear combinations of the states. The resulting matrix is called the *gain* of the system. The system at this point is described by the matrix equations

$$\dot{x} = Gx + Hu$$
$$u = -Kx + Nr$$

where **r** is the reference input; if it is zero the system is called a *regulator*.

The second part of the process reflects the fact that we do not have direct access to all the states of the system, only the outputs. Moreover, even if we could measure all the state variables (i.e. positions, velocities, and accelerations), the cost of the necessary sensors might be prohibitive. As a result we need an *estimator*, a function which computes the state vector from the past values of the outputs and inputs of the system.

Estimators. An estimator is essentially a model of the system's behavior. If we had an exact model, which is to say knew the **F** matrix exactly, we could simply use the values of the inputs and our previous estimate of the state to predict the current state. This is called an *open-loop* estimator, and is essentially useless.

In practice, we can't model the system's behavior exactly, and even if we could our measurements are limited in precision. Thus, we have to feed back the outputs of the system to verify our estimates. Such a *closed-loop* estimator looks like Fig. 10.17, and has the equation

$$\mathbf{x}_e(k + 1) = \mathbf{F}'\mathbf{x}_e(k) + \mathbf{G}'\mathbf{u}(k) + \mathbf{L}(\mathbf{y}(k) - \mathbf{H}\mathbf{x}_e(k))$$

where $\mathbf{x}_e$ is the estimated state vector.

This kind of estimator is called a *prediction estimator*, because the estimate is based on the measurements from the previous sampling period. It is also possible to construct a *current estimator*, whose equations look like:

$$\mathbf{x}_p(k + 1) = \mathbf{F}'\mathbf{x}_e(k) + \mathbf{G}'\mathbf{u}(k)$$
$$\mathbf{x}_e(k + 1) = \mathbf{x}_p(k + 1) + \mathbf{L}(\mathbf{y}(k + 1) - \mathbf{H}\mathbf{x}_p(k + 1))$$

Here, a prediction $\mathbf{x}_p$ is made using the past estimate and inputs, then updated using the *present* outputs. This works if the calculations required for the correction step can be done quickly enough (within one sampling period).

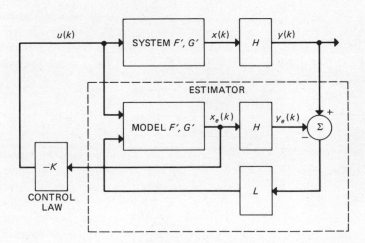

Figure 10.17. Servosystem with closed-loop estimator.

REFERENCES

1. Jensen, Kathleen and Wirth, Niklaus. *Pascal User Manual and Report*. Second Ed. New York: Springer-Verlag, 1975.
2. Aho, Alfred V and Ullman, Jeffrey D. *Principles of Compiler Design*. Reading, MA: Addison-Wesley, 1977.
3. Foster, Caxton C. *Real Time Programming: Neglected Topics*. Reading, MA: Addison-Wesley, 1981.
4. Cooley, J. W. and Tukey, J. W. An Algorithm for the Machine Computation of Complex Fourier Series. *Mathematics of Computing*, 19:297-301 (April, 1965).
5. Gold, Bernard and Rader, Charles M. *Digital Processing of Signals*. New York: McGraw-Hill, 1969.
6. Savitzky, Abraham and Golay, Marcel J. E. Smoothing and Differentiation of Data by Simplified Least Squares Procedures. *Analytical Chemistry* 36(8):1627- 39 (July 1964).
7. Bromba, M. U. A. and Ziegler, Horst. Efficient Computation of Polynomial Smoothing Digital Filters. *Analytical Chemistry* 51(11):1760-2 (Sept. 1979).
8. Savitzky and Golay *op. cit.*
9. Steinier, Jean; Tremonia, Yves; Deltour, Jules. Comments on Smoothing and Differentiation of Data by Simplified Least Square Procedure. *Analytical Chemistry* 44(11):1906-9 (Sept. 1972)
10. Foster *op. cit.*

Appendices

A
Glossary

absolute encoder A *shaft** or *position encoder* that produces a unique number for each resolvable position. See *incremental encoder*.

abstract machine A theoretical computing device used for the mathematical analysis of algorithms.

AC Alternating Current.

acceptance testing Testing of a product by its end user to determine suitability, before accepting delivery and paying the vendor.

accumulator A register in a computer which is the destination for arithmetic operations.

accuracy A measure of the difference between the theoretical and actual outputs of a process.

ACK Acknowledgement Control Character (ASCII).

ACM Association for Computing Machinery. A professional society for people in the computer field.

Ada The DOD's new programming language for embedded computer applications. (From Ada Augusta Byron, Countess of Lovelace, an associate of Charles Babbage and the first programmer.)

ADC See Analog-to-Digital Converter.

address A location in a computer's memory.

address space Any of one or more separate regions of memory, for example separate program and data spaces.

address stop Hardware which stops or interrupts a computer when a specified address is accessed. A debugging tool.

addressing mode A method of generating an effective address for an instruction.

Algol The International Algorithmic Language: the programming language Algol 60 or one of its dialects.

algorithm A computational method for solving a problem. A program, abstracted from its representation in a specific language. More precisely, a program which always halts after computing a correct result.

aliasing The situation whereby a frequency higher than the Nyquist frequency of a signal being sampled appears as a lower frequency in the sampled data.

all-pass filter A filter which passes signals of all frequencies (but may perform some operation other than rejecting certain frequencies).

alpha-site testing Testing by the manufacturer of a product. See *beta-site testing*.

+ Italicized terms are defined in the Glossary.

ALU See Arithmetic and Logic Unit.

AMD American Micro Devices, Inc.

AMI American Microsystems, Inc.

analog Continuously-varying quantities represented by a proportional voltage or other signal. See *digital*.

Analog-to-Digital Converter (ADC) A device which converts analog quantities to a digital (numeric) representation.

and A logical operation which produces a true (1) output if and only if all of its inputs are true.

ANSI American National Standards Institute.

APL *A Programming Language* specialized for array manipulation, with very compact notation.

application program A program which accomplishes some desired result for the end user of a computer system. See *system program*.

application-oriented language A programming language specialized toward a particular class of applications.

applicative language A programming language without the assignment operator. Variables are bound as the arguments of function calls, and cannot be changed.

architecture The structure and instruction set of a computer.

Arithmetic and Logic Unit (ALU) The portion of a computer which performs arithmetic and logical operations.

array A *data structure* consisting of many elements of the same *data type*, accessible by number (*index*).

ASCII American Standard Code for Information Interchange.

assembler A program which converts *assembly language* to *machine language*.

assembly language A programming language in which statements correspond more or less directly to machine instructions or data elements. See *machine language*.

asynchronous Not synchronized with respect to a given clock or timing signal.

ATE Automatic Test Equipment.

attributes Information associated with a data structure (memory *segment*, file, etc.) including protection, ownership and accounting information.

auto-decrement An addressing mode in which the register or memory location containing the address is decremented before or after use.

auto-increment An addressing mode in which the register or memory location containing the address is incremented before or after use.

automatic variable In C, a variable for which storage is allocated automatically whenever the procedure in which it is declared is called. See *static variable*.

background The main program in a computer system with *interrupts*. See *foreground*.

Backus-Naur Form (BNF) The method for describing the syntax of programming languages developed by John Backus and Peter Naur for the Algol 60 report. Loosely applied to any of several variations.

band-pass filter A filter which passes only those frequencies above a lower cut-off frequency and below an upper cut-off frequency.

band-reject filter A filter which passes only those frequencies below a lower cut-off frequency and above an upper cut-off frequency.

band-stop filter A band-reject filter.

bandwidth The difference between the lowest and highest frequency components in a signal. The throughput of a computer or the capacity of a transmission medium expressed in bits or events per second.

bank switching A method of *memory mapping* in which several blocks of memory share the same fixed address, but only one is enabled at any one time.

base register A register which holds the address portion of a *based addressing* calculation. See *based addressing*.

base-bound registers A method of *memory mapping* in which registers define the lower limit (base) and upper limit (bound) of a memory *segment*.

baseband network A *network* in which digital signals are present directly on the transmission medium, rather than modulating a high-frequency carrier. See *broadband network*.

based addressing An addressing mode in which the *effective address* is the sum of an address contained in a register (*base register*) and an offset contained in an instruction. See *indexed addressing*.

BASIC Beginner's All-purpose Symbolic Instruction Code. A programming language, usually interpreted, originally developed at Dartmouth.

baud One signal change ("flux transition") per second. Sometimes erroneously applied to the bit rate (bits per second) of a serial signal.

BAZ A nonsense name, commonly used in example programs. (From FOOBAR.)

BCD Binary Coded Decimal.

benchmark A test program intended to measure the performance of a computer system.

beta-site testing Testing a product on the premises of a favored customer prior to the general availability of the product. See *alpha-site testing*.

bit A binary digit (one or zero). The unit of information.

bit rate A *data rate* expressed in bits per second.

bit-slice An IC containing some registers, an ALU, and the associated data path of a microprogrammed computer.

black box Any system considered in terms of its inputs and outputs without regard to its internal structure.

block A set of contiguous memory locations or data items. See *array, stream*.

BNF See *Backus-Naur Form*.

Boolean Having to do with the set of values {1, 0} or {true, false}. From George Boole. See *logical operation*.

boot (v.) To load a program (usually an operating system) into a newly reset or initialized computer system. See *bootstrap loader*.

bootstrap loader A program, usually contained in ROM, which loads an operating system or other program from disk or other mass-storage device.

bottom-up parser A *parser* which operates by processing its input stream from left to right, based on its current state, the current token, and possibly the next several tokens. See *top-down parser*.

bottom-up programming Programming by writing the lower-level subroutines before writing the routines that call them. See *top-down programming*.

boundary value testing Testing a program by giving it values that are the maximum or minimum acceptable, or the minimum or maximum unacceptable.

breadboarding socket A breadboarding device which permits connections to be made by plugging devices and wires into sockets.

breadboarding Prototyping electronic hardware. From the wooden boards once used as supports for early prototypes.

breakpoint A location at which program execution is to be stopped or interrupted for debugging purposes. See *address stop*. A breakpoint is likely to be implemented using software, while an address stop is usually implemented in hardware.

broadband network A *network* in which digital signals are used to modulate high-frequency carrier signals. See *baseband network*.

broadcast message A *message* sent to all *nodes* on a *network*.

BSR A manufacturer of wireless home appliance controllers.

buffer A data structure or hardware device which is used to hold data temporarily while the data are being sent between two tasks or devices.

bug A defect in a program or piece of hardware. See *glitch*.

burn in To run equipment with power applied, sometimes at an elevated temperature, in hopes that, if it does fail, it will do so before being used.

bus A data transmission medium (usually a set of parallel wires) shared by several computers or other devices.

bus acknowledge line A signal on a bus which indicates that the device originating a *bus request* has permission to transmit information.

bus analyzer A *logic analyzer* specialized for examining the signals on some particular type of bus.

bus request line A signal on a bus which indicates that the device originating the signal wants to transmit information.

busy wait A program synchronization technique in which the program loops, testing some condition.

byte A small group of bits, usually eight. A character.

C A programming language developed at Bell Labs by Dennis Ritchie. The successor to B, a variant of BCPL.

CAD Computer-Aided Design

CAM Computer-Aided Manufacturing.

canonization Putting something into a "canonical" (standard) state. Sometimes used for *intra-line editing* of terminal input.

capability A reference to some *object* which carries with it the permission to perform some operation on the object.

carrier current Transmitting information using a high-frequency signal imposed on the household power lines.

CCITT Consultative Committee on International Telephony and Telegraphy.

Central Processing Unit (CPU) The part of a computer which processes instructions. Consists of an *arithmetic logic unit*, a *program counter*, and an instruction decoder.

chaining (1) Connecting two DMA controllers so that one is fetching addresses, counts, and control information for the other. (2) An arrangement whereby a program causes another program to be loaded on top of it and begin executing, to continue a computation.

change review board An organization whose function is to approve changes in a product being manufactured.

channel (1) An I/O device, especially a DMA device capable of fetching its own control information. (2) A *mailbox*.

character The unit of textual information. Sometimes used interchangeably with *byte*.

characterization Testing a device to determine the limits under which it will function, and the variation in its parameters with time, and from one device to another.

checksum A number derived from a sequence of bytes, usually their sum or exclusive-or, used to verify correct transmission. See *CRC*.

chip An *integrated circuit*, so called from its implementation as a small rectangle of silicon.

CIO Counter and parallel I/O chip (Zilog Z8036).

circuit simulator A *simulator* which models the operation of an electronic circuit by modeling the electrical characteristics of its components (transistors, resistors, capacitors, inductors, etc.).

circular buffer A *buffer* in which a read pointer and write pointer are incremented modulo the buffer size when removing and inserting data.

class In *Smalltalk*, a collection of *objects* having the same structure and behavior, or by extension the object which describes this class.

closed-loop control Control of a system in which the current state or output of the system is compared with the intended state or output. See *regulator*, *servomechanism*.

CMOS Complimentary *MOS*.

co-processor A device very tightly coupled to the central processing unit of a computer system in order to extend its instruction set or other capabilities.

COBOL COmmon Business-Oriented Language: a programming language used for business applications.

code (n.) Software, especially in machine-language form. Instructions. (v.) To write software. To program.

command A user input or programming-language statement intended to provoke some action. See *declaration*.

comparator A device which compares two voltages or numbers.

compiler A program which translates a *high-level language* into *assembly language* or *machine language*.

computer A machine which manipulates data under the control of a stored program.

conditional assembly The ability to omit or include a group of statements in an assembly-language program depending on the value of some expression at assembly time.

conditional compilation The ability to omit or include a group of statements in a high-level language program depending on the value of some expression at compilation time.

configuration control Keeping track of the components of some product, and their revision levels.

contact bounce The tendency of mechanical switches to produce noisy signals when switching.

control effort The magnitude of an input signal applied by a controller to a system being controlled.

control law The matrix relating the outputs of a controller to the states of the system being controlled.

controller A device which controls some ongoing process. In the context of this book, usually a computer.

convolution An operation combining two functions which corresponds to multiplying their Fourier or z-transforms.

core Magnetic core memory, an ancient form of RAM. Sometimes used generically for the main memory of a computer.

coroutine A subprogram whose entry point is different each time it is invoked.

correctness The property a program or algorithm has when it can be proved mathematically to perform (compute) some given function.

coupling The degree to which two or more computers or other devices are interconnected. See *loose coupling, tight coupling.*

CP/M Control Program/Microcomputers. A popular single-user operating system from Digital Research Inc.

CPU See Central Processing Unit.

CR Carriage Return control character (ASCII).

CRC See Cyclic Redundancy Check.

creeping features The tendency for features to be added to a product (especially a program) while it is still under development.

critical section A part of a program which references or modifies some data structure shared with another program executing in parallel, and within which the shared structure must not be modified by the other program while being referenced or modified. See *mutual exclusion.*

CRLF Carriage Return-Line Feed.

cross-reference A listing of program variables or electronic signals, showing where they originate and where they are used.

CRT Cathode Ray Tube (television), commonly used for display terminals.

CTSS Compatible Time-Sharing System. A timesharing system developed at MIT.

current loop A method of data transmission in which the quantity being modulated is the current in a circuit.

cursor An indicator on a CRT screen showing the point at which the next operation (usually inserting or modifying a character) will take place.

cut-off frequency The frequency at which the power output of a filter or other signal-processing device is one half of its maximum value.

Cyclic Redundancy Check (CRC) A *checksum* computed by the use of a shift register with exclusive-or feedback, or some computationally equivalent method.

DAC See Digital-to-Analog Converter.

daisy-chaining Connecting several devices by tying the input of one to the output of another. Usually in contrast to *busing* of signals.

Data Encryption Standard (DES) The ANSI standard method of encrypting data.

data rate The rate at which data are being sent or received. See *bit rate.*

data structure Several data items considered as a single entity or *object*. General term which includes *arrays, unions, records*, and so on.

data type An attribute of a data item, *object*, variable, or name, describing the structure and behavior of the object. Generally *class* is used in *object-oriented languages.*

DC Direct Current.

DCE Data Communication Equipment. A *modem*.

de-bouncing. Filtering out *contact bounce*.

deadlock A situation in which two or more tasks are waiting, each waiting for some other task in the group to do something.

deadly embrace Colorful term for *deadlock*.

debug To remove the *bugs* from a program or system.

debugger A program which helps to debug programs, usually by allowing the user to examine and modify data and instructions, to set *breakpoints*, and to *single-step* the program.

DEC Digital Equipment Corporation.

decentralized system A multi-processor computer system, especially one in which the computers are located at some distance from one another.

decibel A measure of the ratio of two quantities: $\log(a/b)/10$.

declaration A programming-language statement which provides information to the compiler about the data types and attributes of the names and objects being manipulated, rather than describing an action to be performed.

decompilation The process of converting *machine language* or *assembly language* into a *high-level language*, thus reversing the operation of a *compiler*.

decrement To decrease the value of a variable or register, especially by one.

default The value a variable takes on, or the action a program takes, if nothing else is specified.

delay An operation which causes a program to wait for a specified length of time. An signal-processing operation which causes its output to appear later in time than its input, but otherwise unchanged.

demand paging A *memory management* strategy in which blocks of memory are copied into main memory from disk or some other mass storage device when they are referenced (*i.e.* on demand). See *paging*.

dequeue (n.) A "double-ended" *queue*—a variable-length data structure from which either the last or the first item can be removed, and into which a data item can be inserted at either end. See *stack*, *queue*. (v.) To remove from a *queue*.

Design Objectives and Requirements Document (**DOR**) A document describing the intended characteristics of a product that has yet to be fully specified and designed. A formal statement of the intended goals for a project.

DES See *Data Encryption Standard*.

design (n.) A plan by which hardware and/or software can be constructed to meet a given set of specifications. (v.) To produce a design.

desk checking Checking the operation of a program by sitting at a desk with a listing of the program, simulating the operation of the computer.

device A piece of hardware, especially an *I/O device*.

device driver A program, task, or subroutine which transfers data to or from an I/O device. Usually the program which makes a *physical device* behave like an abstract, generalized *logical device*.

DFT See *Discrete Fourier Transform*.

digital filtering Filtering of signals represented as a sequence of digital samples taken at discrete time intervals.

digital Having to do with numbers (digits), especially when represented as electronic or other signals or devices which can be in one of a small number (usually two) of distinguishable states.

Digital-to-Analog Converter (DAC) A device which converts a digital signal (number) to a proportional voltage or other analog signal.

DIP Dual In-line Package. The most common form of package for IC's.

Direct Memory Access (DMA) I/O I/O transfers in which data are transferred directly between memory and a device without the intervention of the CPU. See *programmed I/O*.

directory A *file* which contains the names and locations of other files.

disassembly The process of converting *machine language* into *assembly language*, thus reversing the operation of an *assembler*.

Discrete Fourier Transform (DFT) The counterpart of the Fourier transform for a sampled signal. A mapping from the time domain (sequence of values) to the frequency domain (spectrum).

disk file A *file* stored on a disk or other mass-storage device.

distributed computing Computing with a decentralized system. See *multi-processor*.

distributed system A decentralized (*multi-processor*) system.

disturbance rejection A measure of the ability of a closed-loop system to cancel the effects of disturbances (unwanted inputs).

DLE Data Link Escape control character (ASCII).

DMA Direct Memory Access I/O.

DOD U.S. Department Of Defense.

DOR Design Objectives and Requirements document.

double buffering The use of two or more *buffers* for passing data between two processes, especially a *device driver* and some other program. Data can be written into one buffer while the other buffer is being emptied.

dribble file A *history file* containing a transcript of a user's terminal inputs. It can later be used as a *script* to reconstruct the session.

driver (1) A program which provides inputs to a program or system being tested or debugged. (2) A *device driver*.

DTE Data Terminal Equipment. A computer or terminal.

dynamic allocation Allocation of memory space or other resources while a program is running, as opposed to allocating during compilation or loading. See *static allocation*.

dynamic RAM RAM which needs to be periodically accessed or refreshed in order to keep its contents from deteriorating.

dynamic range The range of possible values of a signal, usually expressed as a ratio, in decibels.

EAROM Electrically Alterable Read-Only Memory (another term for *EEPROM*).

ECL Emitter-Coupled Logic, a fast form of bipolar transistor logic.

editor See *text editor*.

EDN An electronics trade magazine.

EEPROM Electrically Erasable Programmable Read-Only Memory. (Also called *EAROM*).

effective address The address at which the operand of a machine-language instruction is located, obtained by a computation based on the addressing mode and operands of the instruction.

EIA Electronic Industries Association. A standardizing association.

embedded (computer system) A computer system which is part of some non-computer product.

EMI Electro-Magnetic Interference.

emulator A piece of test equipment which simulates a microcomputer or other device, usually at the same speed as the device being simulated; as opposed to a *simulator*, which is usually software and running a much reduced speed. See *microprocessor emulator*.

ENIAC Electronic Numerical Integrator And Calculator: an early computer.

enqueue To put something on a *queue*.

EOT End Of Transmission control character (ASCII).

EPROM Erasable Programmable Read-Only Memory.

error The difference between the actual and expected outputs of a system. See *servomechanism*.

ERS See *External Reference Specification*.

ESC Escape control character (ASCII).

estimator The part of a controller which attempts to compute (estimate) the current state of the system based on its current outputs and past inputs.

ETX End TeXt control character (ASCII).

Eurocard A PC board conforming to the European standard for sizes and connectors.

event (1) Something occurring asynchronously to a task, usually external to the computer, although it may also be caused by another concurrently-executing task. (2) A synchronization method.

event-driven A system in which actions or tasks are scheduled based on the occurrence of external, asynchronous *events*.

exchange A *mailbox*.

exclusive-or A logical operation which returns a true (1) value if and only if an odd number of its inputs are true. See *inclusive-or*.

extent In a file, a set of contiguously-allocated blocks.

external reference A reference in one *module* to a name defined in another module. See *global definition, linker*.

External Reference Specification (ERS) The formal document describing the function and user interface of a product, as opposed to the details of its implementation.

extremal value A value at or just beyond the permissible range.

fan-out The number of gate inputs to which the output of a gate is be connected.

Fast Fourier Transform (FFT) The Cooley-Tukey algorithm for efficient computation of the *Discrete Fourier Transform (DFT)*.

FCC Federal Communications Commission.

FET Field Effect Transistor.

FFT See *Fast Fourier Transform*.

field A named component of a *record* data structure.

field-service testing Testing a defective device after it has been sold, for the purpose of fixing it. See *production testing*.

FIFO First-In, First-Out buffer (*queue*).

file server A task or (in a network) computer which implements a *file system*.

file system A collection of *files* and *directories*, and the implementation of the I/O operations on them.

file A data structure contained on an I/O device, usually a mass-storage device such as a disk. Files can be considered as externally-stored arrays of characters, records, or other data structures. Sometimes used as an alternative term to *logical device*. See *disk file*, *file system*, *logical device*.

filter A process, program, or device which transforms a single input into a single output. In electronics, a device which transforms a signal, usually by emphasizing or removing certain frequencies. In Unix and similar operating systems, a program which performs some operation on a character *stream*.

final test The last test performed on a product before it is shipped.

finite impulse response filter A digital filter which produces only a finite number of non-zero output samples in response to an impulse (unit pulse) input.

Finite-State Machine (FSM) A simple abstract machine having a finite number of internal states.

FIO FIFO buffer and parallel I/O (Zilog Z8038).

First-In, First-Out See *FIFO*.

fixed-point number An integer, or a number with a fixed precision after the decimal point. See *floating-point number*.

flag A single-bit variable.

flag register The *register* in a CPU which contains single-bit status indicators (*flags*) such as those that indicate "carry," "sign," and "zero."

flash ADC An *analog-to-digital converter* which generates an n-bit result by performing 2^n comparisons in parallel.

floating-point number A digital approximation to a real number, consisting of a fraction part and an exponent. The value represented is the fraction times a base (usually two) raised to the power of the exponent.

FM See *Frequency Modulation*.

FOO A nonsense name, commonly used in example programs. (From FOOBAR.)

FOOBAR Corruption of FUBAR (Fouled Up Beyond All Recognition).

foreground *Interrupt servers*, in a system with *interrupts*.

foreground/background system A uniprocessing system with interrupts. See *background*, *foreground*.

format (n.) A structuring or representation of data, especially as a sequence of characters. A description of a format. (v.) To translate data into a formatted representation, for example, especially, a conversion from binary to text.

Forth A programming language using threaded code and reverse Polish notation.

Fortran An early but still significant programming language. (From *For*mula *Trans*lation.)

Fourier series A mapping from a periodic function to a series of sine and cosine functions at multiples of the original function's fundamental frequency, which add to give the original function. A mapping from the time domain to the frequency domain (spectrum).

Fourier transform A mapping from a general function to an integral of sine and cosine terms. A mapping from the time domain to the frequency domain (spectrum).

Frequency Modulation (FM) *Modulation* of a signal by changing its frequency.

frequency response The characterization of a filter or other component in terms of its response to sine waves of various frequencies.

FSM See *Finite State Machine.*

functional language See *applicative language.*

functional testing (1) Testing a product to determine whether its implementation meets its specifications. See *production testing, field-service testing.* (2) Testing a product based only on its specifications (function), rather than on its implementation. See *structural testing.*

gain The ratio of output to input of a device whose output is equal to its input times a constant (the gain). If less than one, the gain is usually called a *loss.*

gate A hardware device whose output is a *logical function* of its inputs.

gate-level simulator A *simulator* in which the device being simulated is modeled as a collection of *gates.*

gateway A device which makes a connection between two or more networks by passing messages between them. See *internet.*

generic operation An operation, for example, addition, that may be applied to a variety of different data types. The implementation of the operation may be different for each set of operand types.

glitch A defect or *bug*, especially one in which a signal or variable takes on a spurious value for a brief period of time.

global Having a context greater than a single *module*. See *local.*

global definition A definition of a name or symbol in some *module* which may be referenced in other modules. See *global, local, external reference.*

GOTO A computer instruction that causes a transfer of control.

Gray code A binary code in which the representations of consecutive numbers differ in only a single bit position.

Hamming code An error-correcting code which relies on redundant parity-check bits to detect and correct errors in a word.

handle A number, sometimes but not always an address or an index in a table, which refers to an *object.*

handler A program, task, or subroutine which performs operations on a given *class* of *objects*. Often used to mean *device driver.*

handshake An exchange of signals between two devices, programs, or systems for the purpose of transferring data. Usually consists of an attention signal in one direction, followed by an acknowledgment signal in the other direction. Many variations are possible.

hardware Tangible, physical equipment (in the context of this book usually electronic). As opposed to *software.*

header A data structure which serves as a prefix to some other structure, such as a *buffer* or the code and data of a *task*, and which contains control information.

high-level language A programming language for which the statements do not have a simple, direct mapping into *machine language*, but are instead closer to the terms in which the user thinks of a problem.

high-pass filter A filter which passes only those frequencies above some cut-off frequency.

hooks Parts of a program or device which are provided for future extension or modification, especially by the user.

HP Hewlett-Packard Company.

HP-IB Hewlett-Packard Interface Bus. The IEEE 488 bus.

Huffman code A minimum-length encoding in which symbols are represented by a variable number of bits.

hysteresis The property of responding differently to rising and falling signals. (See *Schmitt trigger*.)

Hz Hertz, the unit of frequency (formerly CPS, for Cycles-Per-Second).

I/O Input/Output. (See *input, output*.)

I/O bus A *bus* which connects a computer with *I/O devices*.

I/O device A device which is used as an interface between a computer and something else. A device for performing *input* and/or *output*.

iAPX Intel logo for microcomputers.

IBM International Business Machines Corporation.

IC Integrated Circuit. (See *chip*.)

IEEE Institute of Electrical and Electronic Engineers, a professional organization which sets standards in the electronics field among other activities.

imager A program which generates a *memory image* of an *object module*, for subsequent *loading*.

implement (v.) To transform a *design* into actual hardware and/or software.

impulse A brief non-zero input which immediately returns to zero, ideally of zero, negligible, or minimum length. A unit pulse.

in-circuit emulator A *microprocessor emulator*.

include pre-processor A program which causes files, usually containing definitions common to several modules, to be inserted into (included in) source modules or other files.

inclusive-or A logical operation which produces a true (1) output if and only if one or more of its inputs are true.

increment To increase the value of a variable or register, especially by one.

incremental compiler A compiler which, when a source statement is changed, only needs to re-compile that statement and not the whole program.

incremental encoder A *shaft* or *position encoder* which produces a pulse for each resolvable change in position. See *absolute encoder*.

incremental linker A *linker* whose output is an *object module* in the same format as its input, so that modules combined by the linker may themselves be used as inputs to another run of the linker.

index The position of an element of an *array*.

index register A *register* used to hold the *offset* (*index*) portion of an *indexed addressing* calculation. See *indexed addressing*.

indexed addressing An addressing mode in which the *effective address* is the sum of an address contained in an instruction, and an offset contained in a register (*index register*). Sometimes used to mean *based addressing*.

indirect addressing An addressing mode in which the effective address is the value contained in the register or memory location specified in the instruction.

infinite impulse response filter A digital filter which produces an infinite number of non-zero output samples in response to an impulse (unit pulse) input. Implies the presence of feedback.

infix notation The usual notation for arithmetic operations, in which the operation symbol appears between its operands. (See *prefix, postfix*.)

input (n.) Information going into a computer or other system. (v.) Getting information into a computer. See *output*.

input/output (I/O) *Input* and/or *output*.

instance An *object* belonging to a particular class is said to be an *instance* of that class.

instruction set The collection of valid machine- language instructions for a computer.

instruction-level simulator A *simulator* which models the behavior of a computer by reproducing the action of its instructions, without regard to how the computer is actually implemented. A tool for software development.

insulation-displacement connector A device which makes a connection to an insulated wire by displacing (cutting through) the insulation. Generally there is a U-shaped slot into which the wire is forced.

integer A (possibly negative) number without a fractional part. In programming, usually represented by a computer *word*.

integrated circuit A circuit implemented on a single piece (*chip*) of silicon or other semiconductor.

integration (1) In "level of integration," a rough measure of the number of devices in an *integrated circuit*. (2) In a project, the phase in which separately implemented modules or components are combined. (3) A mathematical operation for finding the area under a curve. The inverse of differentiation.

interactive Engaging in a real-time dialogue with a human user.

interferometer A device for measuring small distances by means of the interference of light (or other) waves.

Internal Reference Specification (IRS) The formal document which describes the details of the implementation of a product. See *External Reference Specification*.

internet A connection of two or more *networks* to form a larger network. See *gateway*.

interpreter A program which implements a programming language by simulating the operation of each statement in turn.

interrupt A control transfer generated by an *asynchronous* event rather than by an instruction. (See *trap*.)

interrupt level (1) One of several *interrupts*, ranked by priority. (2) The *foreground* process. Code executed due to interrupts is said to be "running at interrupt level."

interrupt vectoring The process by which *interrupts* from different sources cause transfers of control to different addresses.

intra-line editing The process of correcting typing errors within a single line of input from a terminal. Usually includes the ability to delete the last character typed (often the backspace character), and the entire line (sometimes the delete or rubout character).

inverse The logical *not* operation.

invert To apply the logical *not* operation. To exchange one's for zero's and vice versa.

inverter (1) A *gate* which implements the logical *not* operation. (2) A device which converts direct current into alternating current.

iRMX Intel logo for real-time operating system.

IRS See *Internal Reference Specification*.

ISO International Standards Organization.

item-oriented Descriptive of a multitasking system in which tasks are associated with physical objects being processed. See *station-oriented*.

ITS Incompatible Timesharing System (see *CTSS*), a PDP-10 operating system developed at MIT.

jiffy A *tick*, especially when equal to $\frac{1}{60}$ second.

kernel The part of an operating system which implements multitasking and synchronization operations.

LAN Local Area Network.

Last-In, First-Out See *LIFO*.

latency time The time required for a system to begin responding to an event or request.

LCD Liquid Crystal Display. A low-power display technology.

LED Light-Emitting Diode.

LF Line Feed control character (ASCII).

life-cycle The progress of a product through various stages in its existence: *specification, design, implementation, integration, testing, production,* and *maintenance*.

LIFO Last-In, First-Out buffer (*stack*).

LINC Laboratory Instrumentation Computer. An experimental computer developed at MIT's Lincoln Labs.

linear A mathematical function having the property that $f(ax) = af(x)$ and $f(x+y) = f(x) + f(y)$. Often used in electronics as a synonym for *analog*.

linear difference equation A linear equation relating terms in a time series.

linear recurrence equation Linear difference equation.

linearity A measure of the deviation of a device's output from an ideal straight-line (linear) function of its input.

linker A program which combines *object modules*, replacing *external references* with the corresponding *global definitions*. Sometimes includes a *relocator* and *imager*. See *incremental linker*.

lint A Unix utility program which performs consistency checking of C programs.

LISP List Processor. A programming language, usually interpreted, specialized for symbol processing.

load module A *module* or linked set of modules in a form which can be loaded and executed.

load To transfer a program from an external mass storage device into the main memory of a computer.

loader A program for loading load modules. See *bootstrap loader*.

local (1) In close physical proximity to a CPU (as opposed to *remote*). (2) Accessible only within a single module or procedure (as opposed to *global*).

local area network A *network* confined to a small geographical area, such as a single building.

local definition The definition of a local variable.

local variable A variable which can be referenced only within the module or procedure in which it is declared. See *global*.

lock Any *mutual exclusion* method.

logic analyzer A device for displaying digital signals. A digital oscilloscope.

logical (1) *Boolean*. See *logical operation*. (2) As seen by the programmer or the computer, rather than as actually implemented. See *physical*.

logical address An address in a machine instruction or generated by the CPU. May be *mapped* into a *physical address*. See *memory management*.

logical device An I/O device with a *device driver* which makes it conform to a standardized interface, so that all devices may be treated alike. An interface between a program and a *logical I/O* system.

logical I/O I/O through logical devices. A system which maps logical devices into corresponding *physical devices* or *device drivers*.

logical operation An operation on the set of values {true, false} or {1, 0}. Also called a bitwise, or *Boolean* operation. See *and, exclusive or, inclusive or, not*.

loose coupling An interconnection between processors in a *multi-processor* system in which the processors do not share memory. See *tight coupling*.

loss A *gain* of less than one.

low-pass filter A filter which passes only those frequencies below some cut-off frequency.

LS Short for LSTTL.

LSB Least Significant Bit.

LSI Large-Scale Integration.

LSTTL Low-power Shottky TTL logic.

lvalue In the terminology of the C programming language, a value which may appear on the left-hand side of an assignment operator.

machine language The internal binary representation of a computer's instructions. The language in which programs are actually expressed while running.

macro A user-defined symbol in *assembly language* or a *high-level language* which is expanded into one or more symbols or statements at assembly or compilation time.

mailbox A system-maintained data structure or other construct which is the destination of a *message*. Also called an *exchange*, *port*, or *channel*.

mainframe A large computer. Now distinguished mainly by packaging (in several cabinets) and price (large) rather than by architecture or performance.

maintenance Making changes and improvements to a product after it reaches production. The phase in a product's *life-cycle* during which maintenance is done.

Manchester encoding An encoding for serial data in which a one bit is represented by a negative-going edge, and a zero is represented by a positive-going edge.

map In general, a mathematical function. More specifically, a function from *logical* *addresses* to *physical addresses*, or a device which implements such a function. See *memory management*.

marginal checking Testing a piece of electronic equipment by varying its power supply voltages or other parameters.

mark A "one" bit in a *serial* data stream. See *space*.

mask A bit pattern which is logically *anded* with some other value. So-called because bits in other value are copied into the result in bit positions corresponding to "one" bits in the mask, and "masked out" in positions corresponding to "zero" bits in the mask.

master-slave A *multi-processor* system in which one processor (the master) sends commands to the other (the slave). The slave may send data to the master, but not commands.

MDAC Multiplying DAC. A DAC whose output voltage is a digital fraction multiplied by an analog reference voltage.

memory bus A *bus* which connects a CPU with main memory.

memory image A *file* which contains a copy of the instructions and data of an executable program, exactly as they would appear in memory before the program is run.

memory management Any technique of *mapping logical addresses* into *physical addresses*, usually for the purpose of expanding the address space of a computer, or of improving memory utilization. A technique in which memory is allocated and associated with tasks at run time. See *bank switching*, *base-bound registers*, *demand paging*, *memory mapping*, *paging*, and *segmentation*.

memory mapping A *memory management* technique in which *logical addresses* are *mapped* onto *physical addresses*, usually in fixed-size pages. See *paging*.

memory-mapped I/O A method of *programmed I/O* in which the I/O devices are addressed as if they were main memory. In other words, I/O space is *mapped* into memory space.

menu A list of possible commands or programs, from which an interactive user is expected to select an action to be performed.

message Data passed from one task, process, or computer to another.

meta assembler An assembler in which all *opcodes* of the target machine are implemented as *macros*.

meta-language A language used for describing languages, especially a notation for syntax. For example, *BNF* and *regular-expression* notation.

method In *Smalltalk* and other *object-oriented* languages, a procedure associated with a *class* for performing some operation on *instances* of that class.

metric Measure, in the mathematical sense.

MFM Modified FM.

microcode The program in a bit-slice computer which interprets the user-level instruction set.

microcomputer (1) A computer implemented using a microprocessor (the sense used in this book). (2) A computer implemented using microcode (the term "microprogrammed computer" is preferred in this book, to avoid confusion).

microprocessor A computer's *central processing unit* (CPU) implemented as a single integrated circuit.

microprocessor analyzer A *logic analyzer* specialized for examining the signals on the pins of a microprocessor.

microprocessor emulator An *emulator* for a microprocessor, which replaces the microprocessor chip in a circuit. A sort of hardware *debugger*.

milestone A recognizable point in a product's *life-cycle* to which a target date is assigned.

MIMD Multiple Instruction Multiple Data multiprocessor system.

MITS Micro Instrumentation Telemetry Systems, a now-defunct company which produced the first successful microcomputer kit.

MMU Memory Management Unit.

mnemonic A symbol which represents an *opcode*.

modem (From modulator-demodulator.) A device which turns digital (or other) signals into an AC waveform (modulation) and vice versa (demodulation).

modified FM (MFM) An encoding for *serial* data in which a "one" bit is represented by a signal transition, and a "zero" by the absence of a transition (or vice versa).

module A section of a large program which can be compiled or assembled separately. A section of a program which has simple, well-defined interfaces with other such sections.

monitor (1) A *mutual exclusion* technique consisting of a data structure which can only be accessed by one process at a time. (2) A program which combines a *debugger*, some *device drivers*, and a *bootstrap loader*, usually implemented in PROM.

monotonic Giving increasing outputs for increasing inputs.

MOS Metal Oxide/Semiconductor: a kind of field- effect transistor

MP/M A multitasking version of CP/M.

MSB Most Significant Bit.

MSI Medium-Scale Integration.

MUFOM Microprocessor Universal Format for Object Modules. Proposed IEEE standard P695 for *object module* format.

multi-drop connection A serial *bus*.

multi-processor system A computer system containing two or more CPU's.

Multibus Intel's popular backplane bus.

MULTICS Multiple-access Computer System. A large timesharing system developed at MIT.

multiplexed Sending more than one signal over the same data-transmission medium.

multiplying DAC A DAC whose output is the product of a digital fraction and an analog reference signal.

multiprocessing *Multitasking*. Sometimes, multitasking in a multi-processor system.

multiprogramming Multitasking.

multitasking Running two or more *tasks* either simultaneously, or by sharing the processor's time among them.

mutual exclusion Preventing more than one task or process from simultaneously accessing or modifying a shared data structure or object.

NAK Negative Acknowledgement control character (ASCII).

name A symbol or number which represents a *variable*, *data structure*, *file*, or other *object*.

name server A process or task, especially on a network, which maps *names* into *objects* or *object handles*.

NAPLPS North American Presentation Level Protocol Syntax. A proposed ANSI standard for *teletext*.

nested interrupts A situation in which the program invoked by an interrupt can itself be interrupted.

network A system of interconnected computers.

NMOS N-channel MOS.

node (1) A computer on a network. (2) A signal in a circuit. A set of input and output terminals which are connected together. (3) A *record* or *structure*, usually linked to other nodes via *pointers*.

non-preemptive scheduling. Scheduling in which a *task* always runs until it explicitly reschedules itself, even if a task with higher priority is ready to be run. See *preemptive scheduling*.

Non-Return to Zero (NRZ) An encoding for *serial* data in which a "one" is represented by a high level, and a "zero" by a low level.

Non-Return to Zero Inverting (NRZI) An encoding for *serial* data in which a "one" is represented by a change in level, and a "zero" by no change.

non-terminal symbol A symbol in a meta-language which represents a syntactic entity, rather than a symbol in the language being described. See *terminal symbol*.

normal mode A mode of computer operation in which certain instructions, especially I/O instructions, are not permitted, and cause *traps*. Also called *user mode*. See *system mode*.

not The logical operation which produces a result of true (1) for an input of false (0), and a result of false (0) for an input of true (1). Also called *inverse* and *one's complement*.

NRZ Non-Return to Zero encoding.

null modem A direct connection between two terminals or computers which replaces a pair of *modems* and a transmission medium.

Nyquist frequency One-half the frequency at which a signal is being sampled.

object A *data structure*, especially when considered in combination with the set of operations permitted on it.

object file A *file* which contains an object module.

object module The result of processing a *source module* with a language processor (*assembler* or *compiler*). A *module* in *machine language* form, though possibly *relocatable*.

object-oriented language A programming language in which objects are the basic unit of information, and in which objects can only be manipulated by means of a specified set of operations.

OEM board A printed circuit board intended to be sold to OEM's.

OEM Original Equipment Manufacturer.

offset A number which is to be added to an address, especially as part of an *effective address* computation.

on-line Capable of supporting interactive users.

one's complement The logical *not* operation. Also see *two's complement*.

opcode The bit pattern in a machine language instruction which determines the arithmetic, logical, or control operation to be performed, as distinct from the parts of the instruction which select the operands. Sometimes also used to mean *mnemonic*.

open-loop control Control of a system in which the current state or output of the system is ignored.

operating system A program for managing computer resources, including processor time, memory, and I/O. See *file system*, *kernel*, *memory management*.

optimizer A program which attempts to improve the quality of the code generated by a *compiler*.

or See *inclusive or*.

original equipment manufacturer (OEM) Someone who buys electronic equipment to incorporate it into a product which is then sold to end users.

orthogonal (1) At right angles. Independent. (2) An *instruction set* is orthogonal if every operation can be combined with every addressing mode.

OS/360 Operating System/360. IBM's operating system for the System/360 mainframe computer.

oscilloscope A device for displaying analog waveforms on a CRT in real time.

output (n.) Information coming out of a computer or other system. (v.) Getting information out of a computer. See *input*.

package In the Ada programming language, a set of declarations for data structures and the operations that can be performed on them. An *object*.

packet A *message* in a *network*.

page A fixed-size, mappable block of memory. See *paging*.

page fault A *trap* generated when a *page* is referenced which is not resident in main memory. See *paging*.

page frame See *paging*.

paging A *memory management* technique in which *logical* memory is divided into fixed-size blocks (pages) each of which may be mapped to any equal-sized block of *physical* memory (called a page frame).

parallel Several bits, signals, or operations at one time.

parity checking A form of error detection in which a bit is added to each word of data so as to make the total number of "one's" in the word even or odd.

parser A program that recognizes a language.

parser-generator A program that turns a *meta-language* description of a language into a *parser* for that language.

Pascal A programming language, originally designed for teaching programming.

pathname A name which specifies an *object* (especially a *file* or a network *node*) by specifying a path (through a directory structure or network) that leads to that object.

PC 1) Printed Circuit (board). A method of constructing electronic equipment. 2) Personal Computer.

PDP Programmed Data Processor—DEC's trademarked name for a computer.

peripheral (adj.) Not central. I/O, as opposed to the central processing unit. (n.) An I/O device.

PET Personal Electronic Transactor: Commodore's name for an early personal computer.

phase plane A plot of position vs. velocity.

phase response A measure of the extent to which a filter delays signals of various frequencies. See *frequency response*.

physical An address or other value after being *mapped*. As implemented, rather than as seen by the programmer.

physical address An address in physical, as opposed to logical, memory. An address which has been mapped. See *logical address*.

physical device A specific piece of I/O hardware, as opposed to a *logical device*.

pipe A connection between two programs or tasks which appears to each task to be a logical I/O device.

PL/I A programming language developed by IBM, designed to be equally useful for scientific and business applications.

PL/M Programming Language/Microcomputers. Intel's subset of PL/I.

plant In control theory, the system being controlled.

PMOS P-channel MOS.

pointer The *address* of an *object* or *data structure*.

poles In the complex plane, the points at which the denominator of a rational function (the quotient of two polynomials) becomes zero.

polling Periodically interrogating the status of a device.

pop To remove from a *stack*.

port (1) The interface to a programmed I/O device, or the address of such an interface. An address in I/O space. (2) A *mailbox*.

position encoder A device for converting mechanical motion into a digital signal. See *absolute encoder, incremental encoder*.

postfix notation A notation in which the operator follows its operands. Also called "reverse Polish notation." See *Forth, infix notation, prefix notation*.

precision The number of bits or distinguishable values in the output of a device or computation, as opposed to its *accuracy*.

prediction estimator An *estimator* which attempts to compute the future state of a system, given the current outputs and past inputs.

preemptive scheduling Scheduling in which a *task* may be suspended in favor of a task with higher priority. See *non-preemptive scheduling*.

prefix notation The usual notation for mathematical functions and assembly-language instructions, in which the operator preceeds its operands. Also called "Polish notation." See *infix notation, postfix notation*.

primitive operations Operations out of which larger sequences of operations may be constructed, but which cannot themselves be (meaningfully) decomposed. Operations implemented by a computer, *virtual machine*, or *kernel*.

primitives See *primitive operations*.

priority encoder A device with numbered inputs whose output is the (binary) number of the highest-numbered input with a value of one.

process Any on-going sequence of events. Used more generally than *task*.

process control Control of a *process* (especially an industrial process) taking place outside the computer.

processor A computer. Sometimes, the *central processing unit* of a computer, as distinct from its I/O devices.

production testing Testing a product which has just been manufactured, to make sure that it works before being sold.

profile A listing of a program with a count of the number of times each statement has been executed.

program A sequence of instructions for controlling a computer.

program analysis system A program or set of programs for producing information about a program, including *cross-references*, *profiles*, and so on.

program counter The register in a computer which holds the address of the next instruction to be executed.

program status word The register in a computer which holds the flags, and sometimes other status information. Sometimes includes the *program counter*.

programmed I/O I/O in which instructions are used to transfer data between CPU and the I/O device. See *direct memory access*.

PROM Programmable Read-Only Memory.

protection Preventing unwanted accesses to data by a program or user.

protocol A set of conventions for communication, especially in a *network*.

pseudo-code Programs written in a formalized subset of English or other natural language not capable of direct computer execution.

pseudo-terminal An inter-task communication method in which one task simulates a user at a terminal interacting with the other task. See *pipe*.

push To put onto a stack.

Q-bus The backplane bus of DEC's LSI-11 microcomputer.

quality assurance Making sure that a product can be or is being manufactured in accordance with its specifications.

quantum See *time quantum*.

quasi-static RAM *Dynamic RAM* which refreshes itself, and so appears as *static RAM* to the user.

queue A variable-length data structure in which the first object inserted is the first to be removed (*First-In*, *First-Out* strategy).

queuing theory The theory of items waiting on queues, and processes waiting for service.

race condition A situation in which a small difference in the timing of two signals can make a large difference in a circuit's behavior.

railroad diagrams A way of representing the syntax of a language.

RAM Random Access Memory (Randomly-Alterable Memory).

RC Resistor-Capacitor. A circuit composed only of resistors and capacitors.

RCA Radio Corporation of America.

re-entrant program A program containing no data at fixed locations, so that the code can be shared by several concurrent tasks or processes.

Read-Only Memory (ROM) Memory which can be read, but not written (changed).

real world The world outside a computer system.

real-time Having to do with real-world time constraints.

real-time clock A device which provides interrupts, usually at regular intervals, but sometimes at programmable intervals, for performing timing operations in a computer.

receiver The task, process, or computer which receives a *message*.

record A *data structure* consisting of several sub-structures of possibly different types (called *fields*), accessible by name. Also called *structure*.

recovery time The interval between the time an event has been processed, and the time the system is ready to respond to the next event.

register (1) A byte or word of memory which is part of a CPU, as opposed to general-purpose memory. (2) Sometimes, a byte or word of general-purpose memory (memory register).

regression testing Running all previous tests every time a change is made, to ensure that the change has not introduced new bugs.

regular (architecture) See *orthogonal*.

regular expression A *meta-linguistic* description of a language recognizable by a *finite-state* machine.

regulator A *servomechanism* with a constant, zero input.

relay An electromagnetically-operated switch.

release A point in a product's *life-cycle* at which it is transferred from one organization to another.

reliability Freedom from defects. Ability to perform consistently in accordance with specifications.

relocatable Capable of being assigned to any location in memory. Said of *sections* of an *object module*.

relocator A program which assigns absolute locations in memory to *relocatable* memory *sections* in an *object module*. Often part of a *linker*.

remote Distant from a CPU. See *local*.

rendezvous In the Ada programming language, a method of inter-task communication involving synchronous message-passing with the syntax of a procedure call.

requirements A set of goals which the specification for a product is expected to fulfill.

reset A signal which puts a system into a known initial state.

resource manager A *task* which controls a resource. Other tasks may perform operations on the resource only by sending messages to the manager.

response time The interval between the time when an event occurs and the time a system begins to process (respond to) that event.

resume To make a *task* ready to run. See *suspend*.

ring buffer A *circular buffer*.

robot A programmable, general-purpose manipulator.

ROM *Read-Only Memory*.

round-robin scheduling. A scheduling technique in which *tasks* of equal priority are each run in turn for a pre-set length of time before another task is run.

routing Computing a path for getting a *packet* from one *node* of a *network* to another.

RS-232C A common standard for serial communication.

RS-422 A successor to RS-232C, using 5-volt differentially-driven signals.

RS-423 A successor to RS-232C, using voltages of $+5$ and -5 volts.

run time When a program or task is actually running, as opposed to when it is being assembled, compiled, or linked.

S100 Standard 100-pin bus, IEEE P696. MITS's backplane bus.

SASI Shugart Associates System Interface. Later standardized under the name *SCSI*.

saturate To use up the data-processing capacity or bandwidth of a system.

SCC Serial Communications Controller (Zilog Z8030).

scheduling Determining which of a set of potentially runnable *tasks* should be run next.

Schmitt trigger An interface device with *hysteresis* on its input, so that the voltage at which it will switch from zero to one is greater than the voltage at which it will switch from one to zero.

scientific notation The usual notation for very large or very small numbers, consisting of a number (usually between 0 and 10) multiplied by a power of ten. See *floating point number*.

SCR Silicon Controlled Rectifier. A form of *thyristor* switch.

script A *file* used as an input to a command processor or other program which usually takes its input from a terminal.

SCSI Small Computer System Interface.

SDLC Synchronous Data Link Control. A standard format for synchronous data transmission.

second source (n.) A company which manufactures a chip or other product designed by another company. (v.) To be a second source.

section An arbitrary *logical* division of a *module* which becomes a *segment* when loaded.

segment A block of contiguous memory locations with arbitrary boundaries.

segmented addressing A method of *memory management* in which memory is divided into *segments* of varying lengths. An address thus consists of a segment number and an *offset* from the base of the segment. See *base-bound registers*.

semantics Having to do with the meaning of statements in a language, rather than with their *syntax*.

semaphore A construct used for *signaling* and *mutual exclusion*.

sender The task, process, or computer which sends a *message*.

sensor A device which converts some physical quantity into an electrical signal which can be input to a computer (or other) system.

serial One bit at a time. See *parallel*.

server A *handler*.

servomechanism A control system in which the input to the controller is the *error*, or difference between the actual and expected outputs.

settling time The time required for a system to reach (or get within a predefined limit of) a steady state after a disturbance.

shaft encoder A device for converting mechanical rotation into a digital signal. See *absolute encoder*, *incremental encoder*.

shell In Unix and similar operating systems, the command processor. A command processor implemented as a user program.

side effects Effects which a subroutine has on variables which are not local to the subroutine.

signal (n.) (1) Any time-varying electrical quantity. (2) A *message* containing no data; all the information is contained in the fact that the message has been sent. (v.) To send a signal. An operation on *semaphores*.

signal generator A device for generating electrical signals, especially periodic waveforms.

signal processing Performing transformations on electrical signals, especially in real-time. See *filter*.

signature analysis A method for testing digital circuits by means of a cyclic redundancy checksum.

SIMD Single Instruction Multiple Data multiprocessor system.

simulator A program (or occasionally a piece of hardware) which models the behavior of a microcomputer or other device, usually at a much reduced speed. As opposed to an *emulator*, which is usually hardware and running at full speed. See *circuit simulator*, *gate-level simulator*, *instruction-level simulator*, *transistor-level simulator*.

single-chip microcomputer A *microcomputer* implemented as a single integrated circuit, complete with CPU, memory, and I/O.

single-step To execute a program a single instruction at a time under the control of a *debugger* or *emulator*.

SISD Single Instruction Single Data computer system.

Smalltalk An *object-oriented*, *interpreted* programming language.

SMC Standard Microsystems Corporation.

smooth To filter so as to remove high-frequency noise. Usually said of an operation on non-periodic signals.

snapshot A copy of the state of one or more variables or registers at some point in the execution of a program, usually displayed on a terminal by a *debugger*.

socket A *mailbox*, especially on a network.

software interrupt An instruction which generates a *trap*. A form of subroutine call. See *system call*.

software metric A measurement made on a program, usually on the text of the program rather than on its execution.

software Computer programs. See *hardware*.

SOH Start Of Header control character (ASCII).

source file A *file* containing a *module* in *source language*. A *source module*.

source language The language in which a program is written, either *assembly language* or some *high-level language*.

source module A *module* in *source language*.

source program A program in *source language*.

source-code control A method for tracking and controlling versions of source modules.

source-language debugger A *debugger* in which the program being debugged can be displayed and manipulated in *source language*.

space (1) A "zero" bit in a *serial* data stream. See *mark*. (2) A blank character. (3) Any set of entities which can be regarded as a mathematical space, especially, the set of objects which a computer can address. (See *address space*.)

SPDT Single-Pole, Double Throw switch.

specification A formal document describing what a product is supposed to do, or part of such a document.

spin wait See *busy wait*.

SSI Small-Scale Integration.

stability The ability of a system to avoid oscillations or "run-away" behavior in the presence of disturbances.

stack A variable-length data structure in which the last object inserted is the first to be removed *(Last-In, First-Out* strategy).

stack pointer A *register* or variable which contains the address of the top (last) element of a *stack*, especially the stack where subroutine return addresses are kept.

start bit A space bit which indicates the start of an asynchronously transmitted serial character.

state The set of variables which determine the behavior of a system. In a computer, the contents of the CPU's registers.

state space The mathematical space (vector space) generated by the *state* of a system.

state-transition diagram A graphical way of presenting the states of a finite-state machine, and the transitions between them.

static allocation Allocation of memory space or other resources when a program is compiled or loaded, as opposed to when it is run. See *dynamic allocation*.

static RAM A RAM whose data do not deteriorate when not being accessed or refreshed. See *dynamic RAM*.

static variable In C, a variable for which storage space is allocated at compile time. See *automatic variable*.

station-oriented Descriptive of a multitasking system in which tasks are associated with steps in a process. See *item-oriented*.

STD A backplane bus originated by Pro-Log and Mostek.

steady-state accuracy The *accuracy* of a system when its inputs are not changing, and after transients caused by a change in inputs have decayed.

stepping motor A motor which produces rotation in discrete steps in response to an input of digital pulses.

stop bit A mark bit at the end of a serially-transmitted character.

storage class In C, the attribute of a variable which is either *automatic* or *static*.

stream A sequence of data, especially of characters or bytes, going to or from an I/O device or a program.

stress testing Testing a system under extremal inputs.

string A sequence of characters in memory. An array of characters.

strongly-typed language A language in which variables have *data types*, and in which *type- checking* is strictly enforced.

structural testing Testing based on the structure (implementation details) of the device being tested. See *functional testing*.

structure See *record*.

structured assembler An *assembler* which uses *infix notation* for arithmetic and logical operations, rather than the more usual opcode *mnemonics*.

structured programming Any of several disciplined programming methods, usually based on *top-down programming*.

structured walkthrough A group *desk-checking* technique.

stub In *top-down programming*, a do-nothing routine which replaces a subroutine or program section which has not yet been written.

STX Start TeXt control character (ASCII).

successive-approximation ADC An ADC which derives its digital value a bit at a time starting with the high- order bit.

survival time The length of time during which an external event may be ignored. The length of time during which input data will remain valid. An upper bound on permissible *response time*.

suspend To put a *task* into a state in which it is not ready to run, and will not be run until *resumed*.

swapping A *memory management* method for multitasking, in which tasks which are not running are stored in external mass storage (swapped out).

symbol A *name*. A sequence of characters which represents some *object*.

symbolic debugger A *debugger* which knows about the *symbols* which were used in the source- language version of the program being debugged.

synchronize To make *synchronous*. To bring into a a fixed time relationship.

synchronous Occurring with a fixed time relationship to some clock or other periodic signal.

syntax The structure of statements in a language: the permissible order in which symbols may be combined. See *semantics*.

system Any collection of related parts.

system call A form of *trap* instruction or *software interrupt* used to perform an operating system function. An instruction which causes a control transfer from *normal mode* to *system mode*.

system mode A mode of computer operation in which all instructions are permitted. Usually restricted to the operating system. See *normal mode*.

system program A program which assists the development or execution of other programs.

task A *process* in a computer consisting of some code, some data, and a CPU state.

Task Control Block (TCB) The *data structure* used to describe and manage a *task*.

task descriptor block A task control block.

task level Processes which occur as part of a task, as opposed to *interrupt level*.

TCB See *Task Control Block*.

teletext Generic term for a home information utility based on digitally-encoded information, interaction via telephone, and television display.

terminal symbol In a meta-language description of a language, a symbol in the language being described.

test coverage A measure of the number of instructions or execution paths exercised by a set of test cases.

test-and-set An instruction which tests and modifies the value of a memory location in a single indivisible operation. A test-and-set may not be interrupted by another processor which may be sharing the memory.

text editor A program for creating and modifying files containing text.

thermal resistance A measure of the ability to transmit heat, usually expressed in degrees Celsius per Watt.

throughput Any measure of the number of events a system can process in a given period of time. See *bandwidth*.

thyristor A family of semiconductor switches based on a four-layer silicon structure similar to two merged transistors.

TI Texas Instruments Corporation.

tick One period of a *real-time clock*.

tight coupling An interconnection between processors in a *multi-processor* system in which the processors share common memory. See *loose coupling*.

time quantum The length of time a task in a *round-robin scheduling* system is run before being suspended in favor of another task.

time-slice A *time quantum*.

time-slicing See *round-robin scheduling*.

timeout A time limit set on the occurrence of some event.

timesharing Multitasking, especially in support of several interactive users.

tiny Basic A dialect of Basic with greatly reduced features. Usually there are only 26 variables, which may contain only 16-bit integers.

tolerance The permitted variation in a parameter.

token A symbol, especially in a language.

top-down parser A *parser* which operates by attempting to match a *non-terminal symbol* of its input language by setting as sub-goals the matching of the components of the corresponding phrase. See *bottom-up parser*.

top-down programming Programming by writing top-level routines before writing the routines they call.

topology The structure of the interconnections between things, as opposed to their physical locations.

TOPS-10 A timesharing system for the PDP-10.

trace A sequence of *snapshots* which provide a record of the execution of a program.

tracking ADC An ADC which operates by incrementing its digital output value whenever it is instantaneously less than the input value, and decrementing it when it is greater.

transactions Indivisible operations on a memory, file, or other object.

transfer function A function, usually a Laplace transform or *z-transform*, representing the behavior of a filter, defined as the ratio of the transform of the filter's output to the transform of its input.

transfer vector An array of jump instructions or subroutine addresses, to be used for transferring control to a routine by its index in the table, rather than by its actual address.

transient response The response of a system to a disturbance, or sudden change in its inputs, especially, its response to a step input.

transistor A semiconductor amplifier.

transistor-level simulator A *simulator* in which the device being simulated (usually an integrated circuit) is represented as a collection of transistors. Usually a greatly simplified model of the transistors is used.

trap A transfer of control similar to an *interrupt*, but occurring in response to the execution of an instruction. Includes both *system calls* and error conditions such as division by zero.

TTL Transistor-Transistor Logic, the main family of bipolar transistor logic.

TTY Teletype. Commonly used for any serial terminal.

Turing Machine An abstract machine consisting of a finite-state machine controlling an infinite tape which can be read, written on, and moved left and right.

two's complement The logical *negation* (*one's complement*) of a number, plus one. A representation for signed numbers in which a negative number is represented as its absolute value subtracted from a number one greater than the largest possible positive number. For example, on a 16-bit machine the two's complement of 1 is 65535.

type See *data type*.

type-ahead The ability to enter characters from a keyboard or terminal while a program is running. A service provided by an interrupt-driven terminal driver.

type-checking Checking to ensure that a variable declared as having a particular type is never assigned a value of a different type. Usually done at compile time, although some object-oriented languages do it at run time.

UART Universal Asynchronous Receiver-Transmitter. A serial interface IC.

UCSD University of California at San Diego. (UCSD Pascal is a dialect of the Pascal programming language.)

union A *data structure* consisting of one of a set of objects of different types. (So-called from the set union operation.)

uniprocessing system A computer system in which only one *task* is running.

Unix (from MULTICS), a popular small-computer timesharing system developed at Bell Labs.

user mode See *normal mode*.

utility program Any useful program provided with an operating system which runs as a user program rather than in *system mode* as part of the operating system.

variable (adj.) Changing, or capable of being changed. Different from one *instance* (of a *class* or *type*) to another. (n.) A location in memory capable of holding a value. A *name* for a *data structure* or *object* which can be modified.

variant record Pascal term for a *union*.

VAX A line of large minicomputers or small mainframes from DEC.

Versa-Bus Motorola's backplane bus for the 68000 microprocessor.

virtual Not real. Simulated. See *Logical*.

virtual machine A computer whose instruction set is augmented or replaced by operations implemented in software.

virtual memory A *memory management* technique in which a CPU is allowed to access more memory space than actually exists. When nonexistent memory is accessed, a *page fault* occurs and the data are *swapped* in from a mass storage device (possibly replacing some less recently used data).

VLSI Very Large-Scale Integration

VME Motorola's Eurocard version of the Versa-Bus.

volatile memory Memory in which the data disappears when power is removed.

VRTX A real-time kernel from Hunter and Ready.

wait line A signal to a CPU from memory or I/O devices which indicates that data being requested is not yet available.

wait (1) To suspend processing (of a task, process, or computer) until some event occurs or time has elapsed. (2) Specifically, an operation on a *semaphore*. See *signal*.

wall time Time of day in the *real world*.

watchdog timer A timer which generates an interrupt or reset signal to a computer if not periodically reset by the program.

wire-list A list of all the wires or signals in a circuit.

wire-wrapping Making electrical connections by wrapping thin wire around a sharp-edged square post. A prototyping technique.

word A basic unit of computer memory or data. In microcomputers, commonly 16 bits. In contrast to a *byte*, which corresponds to a *character*, a word usually holds an *address* or an *integer*.

word generator A device for generating digital signals, in either parallel or serial form. See *signal generator*.

word processing Text editing, especially when it includes formatting, and also especially when applied to documents rather than programs.

worst-case analysis Analysis of a design to determine its tolerance of component variation, assuming that all component values will take on the worst possible value.

z-transform A mapping from a function of a sampled data stream to a function of a complex variable, useful in the analysis of digital signal processing.

zero (of a complex function): A point in the complex plane at which the value of the function becomes zero. See *pole*.

ZRTS Zilog Real-Time Software, Zilog's real-time kernel for the Z8000.

B

Annotated Bibliography

This bibliography makes no pretence of being complete. It consists mainly of the works cited in the text, with a few suggestions for further reading.

REFERENCES

Aho, Alfred V. and Ullman, Jeffrey D. *Principles of Compiler Design*. Reading, MA: Addison-Wesley, 1977.

A good introduction to compiler design, including regular expressions, other grammars, and parsers.

Auslander, David M. and Sagues, Paul. *Microprocessors for Measurement and Control*. Berkeley, CA: Osborne/McGraw-Hill, 1981.

A few well-worked-out examples, including program listings in several different languages.

Bell, C. G. and Newell, A. *Computer Structures: Readings and Examples*. New York: McGraw-Hill, 1971.

Good introduction to computer architectures.

Brinch-Hansen, Per. *Operating System Principles*. Englewood Cliffs, NJ: Prentice-Hall, 1973.

Excellent introduction to operating systems, especially the operations needed in a multitasking kernel, with sample programs in Concurrent Pascal. Very readable.

Bromba, M. U. A. and Ziegler, Horst. Efficient Computation of Polynomial Smoothing Digital Filters. *Analytical Chemistry* 51(11):1760-2 (Sept. 1979).

An efficient recursive algorithm for least- squares filtering.

Brooks, Frederick P. *The Mythical Man-Month*. Reading, MA: Addison-Wesley, 1975.

How to manage (and how *not* to manage) a software project. Required reading for anyone attempting to do so.

Cooley, J. W. and Tukey, J. W., An Algorithm for the Machine Computation of Complex Fourier Series, *Mathematics of Computing*, 19: 297-301 (April, 1965).

The original reference on the FFT.

Foster, Caxton C. *Real Time Programming: Neglected Topics*. Reading, MA: Addison-Wesley, 1981.

A good introduction to many topics in real-time systems. Suitable as a textbook or self-study. Suggests experiments. Very readable.

Franklin, Gene F. and Powell, J. David. *Digital Control of Dynamic Systems*. Reading, MA: Addison-Wesley, 1980.

Digital filters and control systems. Dense but readable.

Gold, Bernard and Rader, Charles M. *Digital Processing of Signals*. New York: McGraw-Hill, 1969.

Includes a good treatment of FFT algorithms.

Goldberg, Adele and Robson, David. *Smalltalk-80: the Language and its Implementation*. Reading, MA: Addison-Wesley, 1983.

The reference manual for the Smalltalk language.

Horowitz, Paul and Hill, Winfield. *The Art of Electronics*. New York: Cambridge University Press, 1980.

It is difficult to praise this book too highly. An excellent introduction to electronics—a complete introductory course in 700 pages. Even includes chapters on minicomputers, microcomputers, and analog-digital interfacing.

Huenning, Goeffrey H. Designing Real-Time Software Systems. *Sigsmall Newsletter* 7(2): 34-39 (Oct. 1981).

Discusses the item-oriented/station-oriented distinction, among other topics.

IEEE P695 Working Group. The Microprocessor Universal Format for Object Modules. *IEEE Micro* 3(4) 48-66 (Aug. 1983).

Preliminary draft of the MUFOM object module standard.

Jensen, Kathleen and Wirth, Niklaus. *Pascal User Manual and Report*. Second Ed. New York: Springer-Verlag, 1975.

The reference manual for the Pascal language.

Kernighan, Brian W. and Plauger, P. J. *Software Tools*. Reading, MA: Addison-Wesley, 1976.

A book on programming, illustrated with complete examples of versions of some of the more useful Unix utilities, written in Ratfor, a C-like pre-processor for Fortran. The programs are very useful in their own right, and have been transported to many systems. A version is also available with the programs in Pascal.

Kernighan, Brian W. and Ritchie, Dennis M. *The C Programming Language*. Englewood Cliffs, NJ: Prentice-Hall, 1978.

The "White Book"—the original reference on C. Poorly organized but until recently the only reference available. Some introductory texts are now available.

Knuth, Donald E. *The Art of Computer Programming*. Vol. 1: *Fundamental Algorithms*. Reading, MA: Addison-Wesley, 1968.

Advanced programming. Definitive, and well- written. Vol. 1 contains many hints on how to make programs more efficient. Highly recommended.

Knuth, Donald E. *The Art of Computer Programming*. Vol. 2: *Semi-Numerical Algorithms*. Reading, MA: Addison-Wesley, 1969.

Arithmetic and random numbers.

Knuth, Donald E. *The Art of Computer Programming*. Vol. 3: *Sorting and Searching*. Reading, MA: Addison-Wesley, 1973.

How to sort and search data structures and files.

Martin, James. *Design of Real-Time Computer Systems*. Englewood Cliffs, NJ: Prentice-Hall, 1967.

Real-time systems in the sense of interactive transaction-processing. The sections of interest are those on on queuing theory and performance estimation.

McCarthy, John et. al. *LISP 1.5 Programmer's Manual*. Cambridge, MA: MIT Press, 1962.

Reference manual for the first version of LISP. Still widely applicable, but LISP now has many versions.

Meyer, T. H. and Southerland, I. E. On the Design of Display Processors. *Communications of the ACM* 11(6):410 (June 1968).

Introduces "the Wheel of Reincarnation."

Naur, Peter et. al. Report on the Algorithmic Language Algol 60. *Communications of the ACM* 3(5): 299-314 (May, 1960).

The famous "Algol 60 Report," one of the best-written pieces of software documentation ever.

Roberts, Steven K. *Industrial Design with Microcomputers*. Englewood Cliffs, NJ: Prentice- Hall, 1982.

Good anecdotes and advice on the rigors faced by real-time systems in the industrial environment. It would be a good idea to read this before sending your system out into the cold, cruel world.

Savitzky, Abraham and Golay, Marcel J. E. Smoothing and Differentiation of Data by Simplified Least Squares Procedures. *Analytical Chemistry* 36(8): 1627-39 (July 1964).

The paper that popularized least-squares filters. Includes tables of filter coefficients.

Steinier, Jean; Tremonia, Yves and Deltour, Jules. Comments on Smoothing and Differentiation of Data by Simplified Least Square Procedure. *Analytical Chemistry* 44(11): 1906-9 (Sept. 1972).

Corrections to the tables in the Savitzky-Golay paper.

Terrell, Trevor J. *Introduction to Digital Filters*. London: Macmillan, 1980.

One of the few books on digital filters that includes actual design methods. Rather tough reading, unfortunately.

Thomas, Rebecca and Yates, Jean. *A User Guide to the UNIX System*. Berkeley, CA: Osborne/McGraw-Hill, 1982.

A tutorial rather than a reference, with more about the utilities than the program development tools (such as *make* and *lint*). Not a substitute for the manuals, but a good way to get started.

United States Department of Defense. *Reference Manual for the Ada Programming Language*. Washington, DC: The United States Government, 1980.

Reference manual for Ada.

Winston, Patrick and Horn, Berthold. *LISP*. Reading, MA: Addison-Wesley, 1981.

One of the better introductions to the LISP language.

Wirth, Niklaus. *Programming in Modula-2*. Second Ed. New York: Springer-Verlag, 1982.

Reference manual for Modula-2.

Zarrella, John. *Microprocessor Operating Systems*. Suisun City, CA: Microcomputer Applications, 1981.

Chapters by manufacturers of various microprocessor operating systems. Mostly real-time systems. Good for seeing what systems are available.

Zarrella, John. *Operating Systems Concepts and Principles*. Suisun City, CA: Microcomputer Applications, 1979.

A simple introduction to operating systems.

SOURCES OF USEFUL INFORMATION

The Professional Press

Electronics Trade Magazines. Timely, but somewhat superficial in software-related fields. *Electronics Week* is probably the best, probably because you have to pay for it. *Electronic Design* and *EDN* are also good, and are free to people working in the electronics field. *Electronics Products* has all the latest product announcements, but little else.

Don't overlook the trade press in whatever field your product is in.

Association for Computing Machinery (ACM). Generally excellent, especially in software. *Communications of the ACM* has published many of the classic papers in computer science, and will no doubt continue to do so. *ACM Computing Surveys* publishes survey and tutorial papers. *Collected Algorithms* is a good source for programs (which are also available on magnetic tape).

IEEE Computer Society. Their Transactions are generally extremely technical. The magazines *Computer* and *Micro* are usually very readable. They occasionally publish draft standards.

Manufacturer's Literature. IC manufacturers publish application notes and specifications, and sometimes even collect them into books. These can often be extremely useful. Some of the application notes are fairly general, rather than applying strictly to one manufacturer's product.

Microprocessor and microcomputer manufacturers also publish reference manuals for their chips. The writing is often execrable, but they usually contain all the information you need. One gets good at reading manuals after a while.

The Hobbyist Press

A large number of books, mainly paperbacks from obscure new publishers, are available in computer stores (and other places). They appeal mainly to hobbyists, but are sometimes useful, especially if they concern the processor you have to use. The books with Interfacing in the title are likely to be of interest if you have to connect your computer to any kind of unique hardware, and are unfamiliar with electronics.

There are also many How to Program the . . . books (of varying quality) for almost any conceivable CPU, and numerous introductions to the popular programming languages.

Magazines.   Some of the hobbyist-oriented magazines are also good. They fall into two main groups: the general-audience magazines, of which *Byte* is probably the best (and the thickest!), and the ones oriented toward specific machines. If you are using one of the popular personal computers as either a software development system or the basis for your product, the latter are very worthwhile. Both types have helpful hints (things the manufacturer won't tell you) and reviews of new software and hardware products.

C

The C Programming Language

This Appendix is a programmer's guide to the C programming language. It is neither a tutorial nor a reference manual; both of these will be found in the book *The C Programming Language* by Kerhighan and Richie.[1] It is, instead, a quick-and-dirty introduction to the subset of the language used for the examples in this book, and is neither complete nor rigorous, although it attempts to come close. (The syntax descriptions are believed to be complete, but the verbal descriptions are sketchy in places.)

Throughout the discussion, comparisons are made with Pascal and Algol, two well-known languages which C resembles. A reader familiar with either of those languages, or with PL/I, should have no trouble learning C. C can also be learned by someone completely unfamiliar with high-level languages, although this may take somewhat longer. In any case, it is not necessary for the reader to be able to *write* C programs, only to read them.

Formal syntax descriptions are included here; the reader familiar with other programming languages will find them by far the easiest way to get a feeling for C's occasionally peculiar syntax. The text that accompanies the syntax descriptions is a brief and incomplete discussion of the corresponding semantics. It concentrates mainly on the differences between C and other languages.

C has been called a "write-only" language because it is possible to write very dense, incomprehensible programs in it. It is also possible to avoid this tendency and to write clearly; I have attempted to do so. In particular, I have avoided the use of assignment and conditional operators in expressions, and the uncontrolled use of pointers, both of which are open invitations to confusion.

BASIC SYNTAX

Identifiers

Identifiers (names and keywords) are made up of letters, digits, and underscores, and the first character must not be a digit. Upper and lower case letters are considered as different characters (in other words, **abc, Abc, ABC** are different names). All C keywords are lowercase.

Only the first eight characters of an identifier are significant, although more may be used.

Delimiters

White Space. Blanks, tabs, newlines, formfeeds, and comments, collectively called "white space," are required to separate identifiers, and are otherwise ignored.

Comments. Comments in C are enclosed between /* and */. Any characters can be so enclosed except a */ sequence (comments cannot be nested). It is usual to delimit large blocks of comment thus:

```
/*
 * body of comment goes here
 *     ...
 */
```

or thus:

```
/*****************************
** this way, you get a box   **
**    with blunt corners     **
*****************************/
```

In both cases, printing only the lines in a file that have an asterisk in column 2 will yield the major comments in a program.

Statements, Semicolons and Braces. A C program is a sequence of *statements*, each of which is simple, compound, or complex. A simple statement (such as an assignment) is *always* terminated by a semicolon. (Like PL/I, and unlike Algol and Pascal, in which semicolons *separate* statements rather than *terminate* them.) A compound statement (block) is a sequence of statements enclosed in braces { and } and is *not* terminated by a semicolon. A complex statement such as an **if** statement contains other statements, which are terminated as usual. The keywords (e.g. **if** and **else**) do *not* have semicolons after them (unlike PL/I).

C's use of semicolons can be slightly bizarre for a Pascal programmer, and misplacing them (either by insertion or omission) leads to cryptic and unrelated error messages from most compilers.

Objects and Identifiers

Properties of Identifiers. An identifier (other than a keyword, whose function is purely syntactic) has two properties: its *storage class*, and its *type*. The storage class describes how and when the storage associated with the identifier is allocated; the type determines the properties of the data stored there.

The possible storage classes are *static*, *automatic*, *register*, and *external*. Static storage is allocated when a module is compiled. Automatic storage is allocated when the block or procedure containing its declaration is entered, and is released when that block or procedure is exited. (Automatic storage is called "local" in Pascal and Algol.)

Register storage is a kind of automatic storage; the compiler attempts to allocate it in CPU registers if possible. External storage is allocated statically in some other module.

Objects and Pointers. An *object* is a piece of storage that can be manipulated. A *pointer* is an object's *address* in storage. In the C world, an expression that refers to an object is called an *lvalue*, from the left-hand side of an assignment statement. An lvalue is *not* a pointer! Instead, it is a pointer which has had the indirection operator * applied to it.

The distinguishing characteristic of an lvalue is that it can appear on the left-hand side of an assignment, where it represents the object to be replaced. On the right-hand side of an assignment, an lvalue represents the object to be *used*. The distinction is subtle and tricky. The simplest form of an lvalue is an identifier representing a simple variable or structure. To add to the confusion, an identifier representing an array or function is *not* an lvalue. (An array-name followed by an *index* (such as **a[0]**) *is* an lvalue.) Confusing? Yes.

The prefix operators * and **&** convert between lvalues and pointers. The operator * turns a pointer (an expression whose value is the address of an object) into an lvalue (a reference to the object itself); **&** turns an lvalue into a pointer to the object referred to (in other words, the address of the object).

Declarations and Programs

A C program is simply a sequence of variable and procedure declarations. Unless specifically declared as **static** or **external**, all such objects are accessible from other modules. (The declaration **static** is used ambivalently here: at the top level of a program module, it really means "non-global." *Everything* declared at the top level is either static or external.)

Somewhere in a collection of C modules is a procedure called **main** which is the top level of the program. (This is a Unix convention enforced by the standardized use of the linker. A small interface module is linked in front of every program, which in turn calls **main**.)

The Pre-Processor

The C compiler includes a *pre-processor*, a program which performs certain purely textual operations on C programs, including a simple form of macro expansion. Pre-processor statements are lines whose first character is a pound sign (**#**).

Notation

To describe the syntax of C, we will use the regular-expression notation of Chapter 10. Symbols and keywords in the language are quoted and set in boldface type, and syntactic categories are words set in roman type, possibly connected by dashes. Parentheses are used for grouping, and the following special symbols are used:

x?	*zero or one of x*
x*	*zero or more of x*
x+	*one or more of x*
a|b	*a or b*

A " | " is understood between lines; thus:

> constant:
> > integer-constant
> > floating-constant

defines a constant as either an integer-constant of a floating-constant.

Comments in the syntax are set in italics.

EXPRESSIONS

Order of Evaluation

Apart from ordering due to the precedence of operators, and except for the conditional operators **& &**, **| |**, and **?**, C does not define an ordering for evaluation of expressions. The parts of an expression may be rearranged in any order at the whim of the compiler, even in the presence of side-effects (such as embedded assignments and function calls). You are warned!

C has a large and bewildering set of operators for building expressions, and their precedences are often unexpected (for example, relational operators for equality and inequality have different precedence!). The liberal use of parentheses is advised.

Constants

(In the syntax descriptions below, note that there are no spaces inside of a constant, except for strings.)

> constant:
> > integer-constant
> > integer-constant "**L**"   *long*
> > character-constant
> > floating-constant
> > string

Integer Constants.   Integer constants are strings of digits. A leading zero is used to indicate octal notation, a leading **0x** indicates hexadecimal.

> integer-constant:
> > zero digit*   *octal*
> > non-zero digit*   *decimal*
> > "**0x**" hex-digit* *hexadecimal*

Hex digits are **0** through **9**, and the letters **a** through **f** in upper or lower case.

An **L** can be appended to an integer constant to make it a long value; a constant is also considered long if it represents a number too large or small to be represented as an ordinary integer.

Character Constants. A character constant represents the ASCII code of a single character.

character-constant:
 "'" character "'"   *normal char.*
 "'" "\" character "'" *special char.*

Special characters (such as linefeed) are represented using a backslash followed by one of the following characters:

 "**n**" *newline (linefeed)*
 "**r**" *return*
 "**t**" *tab*
 "**b**" *backspace*
 "****" *backslash*
 "**'**" *quote*
 ddd *arbitrary bit pattern*

(ddd are from one to three octal digits.)

Floating-Point Constants.

Floating-point constants are numbers in the usual computer form of scientific notation, with **En** standing in for 10^n, as in Fortran. A decimal point is required, but either the integer part or the fraction part (but not both) may be missing.

floating-constant:
 digit* "." digit+ exponent-part?
 digit+ "." digit* exponent-part?

Strings. A string is a sequence of characters enclosed in double quotes. The characters are stored in memory followed by a null (zero) character; the value of the constant is the *address* of this string. A string constant can be used anywhere the identifier of a static character array can appear. A double-quote character must be precedeed by a backslash; in addition, any of the escape sequences possible for character constants may be used.

exponent-part:
 "e" "−"? digit+

string:
 """" character* """"

Primary Expressions

> primary-expr:
>> identifier
>> constant
>> "(" expression ")"
>> primary-expr "[" expression "]"
>> primary-expr "." identifier
>> primary-expr "→" identifier
>> primary-expr "(" expression-list? ")"

> expression-list:
>> expression ("," expression)*

Arrays and Indexing.   An identifier that is the name of an array is automatically turned into a *pointer* to the first element of that array. A primary expression followed by an expression in square brackets denotes an element of an array in the usual way. Usually, the first primary expression is an array, but it could be a pointer to anything. C treats array indexing as *exactly equivalent* to addition of an integer and a pointer.

Structure Components.   The notations x.y and x—>y are used to select components of a structure or union, where y is the name of the component. The difference between the two notations is that in x.y the notation x refers to the structure itself (in other words, x is an lvalue), and in x—>y it is a *pointer* to the structure. In other words, x—>y and the clumsy expression (*x).y are equivalent. (In Pascal, this would be written x↑.y. The clumsiness in C comes from making * a prefix operator.)

As a rule of thumb, use . to select a component of an identifier declared as a structure, and —> to select a component of a structure that something is *pointing to*.

Function Calls.   A function call consists of a function followed by an argument list in parentheses. The parentheses are required even when the function has no arguments. Notice that the function part of the function call might be an expression whose value is a pointer to a function, rather than a simple identifier.

The ability to treat pointers to functions as ordinary values which can be passed as parameters or even stored in arrays is one of the most valuable features of C. It is not used often, but can often simplify programs immensely. In real-time programs it can be used to write schedulers, and dispatchers for interrupt routines, system calls, commands, and logical I/O drivers.

In C, the number and type of the operands of a function or procedure can vary, and so is determined entirely by what you put in the parameter-list. (This, by the way, is why you can tack L onto a constant to make it long.) Many C programs are written on the assumption that an integer and a pointer are the same size; this is often true, but not always. Lint can be used to find inconsistencies in the use of functions.

Unary Operators

The unary operators fall into two classes: those that simply operate on values, and those that operate on objects in memory (and consequently require lvalues as their operands).

> unary-expr:
> > primary-expr
> > prefix-op primary-expr
> > unary-expr postfix-op

Simple Unary Operators.   The simple unary operators simply return values, without side-effects on memory.

> prefix-op:
> > "—"   *arithmetic negation*
> > "~"   *bitwise complement*
> >   *logical negation*
> >
> > "*"   *pointer → lvalue*
> > "&"   *lvalue → pointer*
> >
> > "(" type-name ")"*type conversion*
> > "**sizeof**" expression
> > "**sizeof**" "(" type-name ")"

The most unusual operation is !, which returns zero if its operand is equal to zero, and one otherwise. We have already met * and &.

The (type-name) operator is used to convert the value of its operand to an object of the named type. It is called a *type-cast*.

The **sizeof** operator produces the size of its operand, in bytes.

Assignment Unary Operators.   The next group of unary operators require an lvalue as their operand, and actually modify the object referred to by incrementing or decrementing it. The prefix and postfix forms differ in that the prefix forms return the *new* value, and the postfix forms return the *old* value. (This notation can also be found in some assembly languages. It is used on the PDP-11, for which the first C compiler was written.)

> prefix-op:
> > "++"   *increment*
> > "——"   *decrement*
> >
> postfix-op:
> > "++"   *increment*
> > "——"   *decrement*

Infix Operators

Like unary operators, infix operators are divided into two main groups: *simple* and *assignment*, with the assignment operators having lower precedence. Within the simple operators, however, it is useful to distinguish two subgroups which we might call *arithmetic* and *logical*. Unlike the arithmetic operations, for which the order of evaluation of their operands is not specified, the logical operators imply a specific order of evaluation.

Arithmetic Infix Operators. In general, the arithmetic infix operators associate to the left. In other words, $a - b - c$ is equivalent to $(a - b) - c$. However, associative operations such as addition may be re-ordered, and the operands may be evaluated in any order.

> expr1:
> (primitive-expr mult-op)* primitive-expr
> mult-op:
>   "*"   *multiplication*
>   "/"   *division*
>   "%"   *remainder*

> expr2:
> (expr1 add-op)* expr1
> add-op:
>   "+"   *addition*
>   "−"   *subtraction*

The + and − operations can be applied between a pointer and an integer. The integer is multiplied by the size of the object the pointer points to. Thus, addition can be used to index the elements of an array. These operations are, in fact, exactly equivalent by definition. (As is usual in C, no bounds checking is done, or possible for that matter.)

> expr3:
> (expr2 shift-op)* expr2
> shift-op:
>   "<<"   *left shift*
>   ">>"   *right shift*

The shift operations shift the bit pattern of the left-hand operand by the number of positions specified by the right-hand operand.

> expr4:
> (expr3 relational-op)* expr3
> relational-op:
>   "<"   *less than*
>   ">"   *greater than*

> "< ="   *less than or equal*
> "> ="   *greater than or equal*

expr5:
> (expr4 equality-op)* expr4

equality-op:
> "= ="   *equal*
> "! ="   *not equal*

Relational and equality operators yield zero if the relation specified is false, and one otherwise.

expr6:
> (expr5 " & ")* expr5   *bitwise and*

expr7:
> (expr6 " ∧ ")* expr6   *exclusive or*

expr8:
> (expr7 " | ")* expr7   *inclusive or*

The above operators operate on the *bit-patterns* of their operands. Thus, applying them to the results of a relational expression does *not* do the right thing! Both operands are evaluated, and they may be evaluated in any order.

Logical Infix Operators. The logical operators are the solution to the problems mentioned for the bitwise operators above. They operate on the *truth-value* of their operands, with zero being false, and anything else being true. They are evaluated strictly from left to right.

expr9:
> (expr8 " & & ")* expr8   *logical and*

expr10:
> (expr9 " ‖ ")* expr9   *logical or*

expr11:
> expr10 ("?" expr10 ":" expr10)?

In the **& &** and **| |** operations, the second operand is not evaluated if the truth-value can be determined from the first. In the conditional operation **? . . . :** (the only three- operand operation in C), the result is the value of the second operand if the first operand is true, otherwise the result is the third operand. The operand whose value is not used is not evaluated.

Assignment Infix Operators. The assignment infix operators group from right to left, and all require an lvalue as their left-hand operand. The assignment operators are = (plain assignment), and = precedeed by any of the arithmetic or bitwise operators (not the relationals).

The compound operators **x op= y** are equivalent to **x = x op y**. The difference is that the left-hand expression is evaluated only once, which matters if **+ +**, **= =**, or a function with side-effects is involved.

exper12:
    expr11 (assign-op expr11)*
assign-op:
    " = "
    " + = "
    " − = "
    " * = "
    " / = "
    " % = "
    " < < = "
    " > > = "

    " & = "
    " ∧ = "
    " | = "

WARNING! The = (assignment) operator is often mistakenly used (and blithely accepted by the compiler) when = = (equality) is intended. The result is a bug which is *very* difficult to find. It's practically invisible.

Finally, we get to the last operator, with the lowest precedence.

expression:
    (expr12 ",")* expr12

The value of the comma operator is the value of its right-hand operand. The left-hand operand is evaluated only for its side-effects. Since the comma is also used to separate the parameters of a procedure, expressions containing the comma *operator* must be enclosed in parentheses in this case.

TYPES

Types In C

Like most modern languages, C permits the user to use and define data structures, including the familiar *arrays*, *strings*, and *structures* (which Pascal calls *records*), and the slightly less familiar *unions* (which Pascal calls *variant records*). Again, as in most languages, this description of an object's structure is called its *type*, and of course the basic elements of which these compound structures are composed also have their types (e.g. integer).

Unlike Pascal and other "strongly-typed" languages, however, C is extremely permissive (some have even said "promiscuous") about data types. C permits any object to be treated as a member of any type. Some of the more flagrant abuses, such as treating a simple object as if it were a structure, result in warnings from the compiler, but they are still permitted. This gives C an immense flexibility, permitting very efficient code. It also permits very strange and obscure bugs. Most C addicts feel that the exchange is worth while.

Some of the disadvantages of C's permissiveness are alleviated by a program called *lint*, which performs type-checking and other kinds of consistency checking on C programs. It also checks for consistency among a set of separate modules, and is able to recognize certain kinds of portability problems (it knows the limitations of various C compilers, and can also recognize some machine-dependent operations). It is *much* more difficult to program in C without *lint*.

Declarations

A C program is simply a sequence of declarations. A declaration is used to associate a type and a storage class with an identifier. (Note that if an identifier has not been previously declared, it will be declared when it is first encountered. This is a bad feature C has inherited from Fortran, and can lead to obscure errors. Fortunately, if the identifier is later declared, the compiler will give you an error message.)

> declaration:
> > decl-specifier declarator-list? ";"
> decl-specifier:
> > storage-class
> > type-specifier
> > storage-class type-specifier
> storage-class:
> > **"auto"**
> > **"static"**
> > **"extern"**
> > **"register"**
> > **"typedef"**

The **typedef** storage class associates an identifier with a type, and does not actually reserve storage. The meanings of the storage classes have already been discussed. The default for the type- specifier, if not given, is integer.

At the outer level of a module, the default for the storage class is static but accessible as an **extern** from other modules. Objects declared **static** are local to the module. Inside a procedure body, the default storage class is **auto**.

Elementary Types

The basic data types of C are character, called **char**, integer, called **int**, and floating-point, called **float**. Other types derived from these include **short, long,** and **unsigned** variants, and the structured types: structures (**struct**), unions, and arrays.

> type-specifier:
> > modifier + simple-type?
> > modifier* simple-type
> > typedef-identifier
> > structured-type

simple-type:
 "**char**"   *character*
 "**int**"   *integer*
 "**float**"   *floating-point*
 "**double**"   *double-precision f. p.*
modifier:
 "**short**"
 "**long**"
 "**unsigned**"

A modifier such as **long** or **unsigned** can be used by itself; **int** is understood as the type being modified. (The type **int** is the default for *everything* in C.)

Declarators

The declarator list in a C declaration is the oddest part of the language. Essentially, the identifier being declared is *used in an expression* that evaluates to one of the elementary types. This expression thus defines the way the value of the object can be accessed.

declarator-list:
 (init-declarator ",")* init-declarator
init-declarator:
 declarator initializer?
declarator:
 identifier
 "(" declarator ")"   *grouping*
 "*" declarator   *pointer*
 declarator "()"   *procedure*
 declarator "[" constant-expr? "]" *array*

Note that the types of a procedure's arguments are *not* declared. The *constant-expr* which declares the size of an array is optional. If the array is initialized, its size can be determined from the size of the initializer. Multi-dimensional arrays are declared as arrays of arrays. All arrays start with element **array[0]**.

Initializers. Objects that are not external can be initialized. Static objects are initialized when the program is loaded; automatic ones when the procedure or block containing them is entered. Unions cannot be initialized.

initializer:
 " = " expression
 " = " "{" init-list ","? "}"
init-list:
 expression
 "{" init-list "}"
 (init-list ",")* init-list

The initializers in braces correspond to structures or arrays in the object. All but the outermost layer of braces are optional, as is a comma at the end of the list.

Structures and Unions

A structure or union is an object consisting of named *members* or fields; it corresponds to a *record* in Pascal. The difference between a structure and a union is that the members of a structure are stored sequentially in memory, and so are all present simultaneously. The members of a union, on the other hand, are stored at the same location, and so are alternative structures for the object, only one of which can be present at any one time.

Unions correspond to the Pascal notion of variant records.

> structured-type:
> > struct-prefix struct-body
> > struct-prefix identifier struct-body?

The identifier in the second form of structured- type is a *tag* by which the structure or union may be referred to. They permit the body of the structure to be defined once, and also permit self- referential structures to be defined.

> struct-prefix:
> > **"struct"**
> > **"union"**
> struct-body:
> > "{" struct-declaration* "}"
> struct-declaration:
> > type-specifier struct-decl-list ";"
> struct-decl-list:
> > (struct-declarator ",")* struct-declarator
> struct-declarator:
> > declarator (":" constant-expr)?
> > ":" constant-expr

The : construct in a structure declarator specifies the size of a bit field within a word.

Procedures

A procedure internal to a module (as opposed to an identifier that names an external procedure) is declared somewhat differently from other identifiers.

> procedure-declaration:
> > decl-specifier? proc-declarator proc-body
> proc-declarator:
> > declarator "(" parameter-list? ")"

```
parameter-list:
        (identifier ","* identifier
proc-body:
        declaration* block
```

The declarations preceding the procedure body declare the identifiers in the parameter list (in any order). It is worth mentioning that a semicolon after the proc-declarator, or after the proc-body, will produce a marvelous string of syntax errors. Note that a procedure cannot contain declarations for procedures local to itself, which greatly simplifies scope rules and stack frames.

STATEMENTS

The statements of C, with three exception, are a fairly tame lot, and much like the statements of languages like Pascal. The exceptions are the **for** statement, the **switch** statement, and the expression statement. These are very much like Pascal's **FOR**, **CASE**, and assignment statements, but have some odd quirks.

```
statement:
        ";"                             null statement
        expression ";"                  value discarded
        block
        conditional-statement
        loop-statement
        switch-statement
        control-statement
```

Expression Statements

An expression statement is an expression followed by a semicolon. The value of the expression is discarded, so the expression ought to have side-effects. This kind of statement includes assignments (remember that = is an expression operator) and procedure calls (all procedures in C are assumed to return a value). The + + and − − operators are also used in expression statements.

Blocks

Blocks, or compound expressions, are used for three purposes (just as they are in Algol and Pascal): as the bodies of procedures, as used for grouping statements for conditional and looping statements, and to group statements with the declarations of some identifiers local to the block.

```
block:
    "{" declaration* statement* "}"
```

Unlike Algol and Pascal, however, a block may not contain function declarations unless they are **extern**.

Conditional Statements

The conditional (**if**) statement in C is straightforward, except that its syntax is more like that of Basic or Fortran rather than Pascal. Conditions in C statements are always enclosed in parentheses. A condition can be any C expression, with any non-zero value being taken as true.

> conditional-statement:
>   "**if**" condition statement ("**else**" statement)?
> condition:
>   "(" expression ")"

Looping Statements

C has three kinds of looping statements: the **while** loop, which is ordinary; the **do ... while** loop, which corresponds to the Pascal **repeat ... until** loop (but with the opposite sense of the termination condition); and the **for** loop, which is wild and wonderful.

> looping-statement
>   "**while**" condition statement
>   "**do**" statement "**while**" condition ";"
>   "**for**" "(" for-init ";" for-cond ";" for-next ")" statement
> for-init:
>   expression?
> for-cond:
>   expression?
> for-next:
>   expression?

The **for** statement is equivalent to:

```
for-init;
while (for-cond) {
    statement
    for-next;
}
```

with a missing for-cond meaning **while (1)** ....

The **for** statement is immensely powerful. It can, however, be tamed, and used to simulate the ordinary Pascal/Algol/Fortran iteration statement. For example,

```
for ( i = 1; i <= 10; i++) statement
```

is the equivalent of the Pascal

```
for i = 1 to 10 do statement
```

Switch Statements

The **switch** statement, derived from the Algol switch statement, is similar to the Pascal **CASE** statement. The main oddity is the ability to "fall through" from one case to another, unless a **break** statement is included. This can lead to strange bugs and tricky coding.

> switch-statement:
>   **"switch"** "(" expression ")" switch-body
> switch-body:
>   "{" (statement | case)* "}"
> case:
>   **"case"** constant-expr ":"
>   **"default"** ":"

There may be at most one **default** label, and no two **case** labels may have the same value.

The effect of this statement is to evaluate the expression, and then start execution in the switch-body at the label whose constant-expr matches the value of the expression. If there is no match, execution starts at the **default** label if there is one, otherwise the entire body is skipped.

WARNING. Each **case** group should be terminated with a **break**; statement; otherwise execution will simply continue. This "feature" is used to allow the labeling of a single group of statements with more than one case label. Otherwise, it is confusing.

Control Statements

The next group of statements are all simple, and are used for controlling the execution sequence in various ways.

> control-statement:
>   **"break"** ";"   *exit loop*
>   **"continue"** ";"   *re-start loop*
>   **"return"** expression? ";"   *exit subroutine*
>   **"goto"** identifier ";"
>   identifier ":"   *label for goto*
>   ";"   *null statement*

The **break** statement is used to exit from the body of a loop or a switch statement. The **continue** statement skips to the loop- continuation part of a loop: after the "statement" of the loop but before the test in the **while** and **do** loops, and before the for-next part of a **for** loop.

The **return** statement returns a value from a function. If the expression is missing, the value returned is undefined.

THE PRE-PROCESSOR

The following statements are interpreted by the C pre-processor. All start with a **#** character as the first character of a line. They do purely textual substitutions or deletions, before the rest of the compilation process is done.

> pre-processor-stmt:
> "**#define**" identifier token-string
> "**#define**" identifier "(" identifier+ ")" token-string
> "**#include**" '"' filename '"'
> "**#include**" '<' filename '>'
> "**#if**" constant-expression
> "**#ifdef**" identifier
> "**else**"
> "**#endif**"

The **#define** statement is used to define macros; its most common use is to define names for constants, as in

$$\text{\#define pi 3.14159265}$$

Note that there is *no semicolon*! If there were, it would be included in the definition of the identifier, which is usually not what is wanted.

The **#include** statement copies the contents of another file into the compiler's input. If the filename is enclosed in quotes, it is looked for on the user's current directory; if enclosed in brackets, ⟨ ... ⟩ , it is looked for in the system's library directory.

The **#if** and **#ifdef** statements, along with **#else** and **#endif**, are used for conditional compilation. The **#ifdef** statement tests the given identifier to see whether it is defined (with **#define**); **#if** can be used to "comment out" large blocks of program.

I/O

There are no I/O statements built into the C language. Almost all C systems include a library of standard I/O procedures, based on the ones in Unix. Their discussion is beyond the scope of this appendix; none of the standard library routines are used in this book. Many real-time applications do not have an I/O system, which makes C's lack of any I/O facilities a definite advantage.

Similarly, there are no other interfaces to the operating system in C. The operating system runs a program by calling it as a procedure, passing it an array containing the tokens on its command line, and the program exits by simply returning. All other interaction with the operating system occurs by means of library procedures, which can execute system calls or do anything else that may be required.

It is worth mentioning one of the usual I/O routines, because the C programmer is almost certain to use it. The most common and useful output routine in C is called **printf**, for print formatted data. It takes a variable number of arguments, the first of which is a string which tells how to format the other arguments. Naturally, **printf** requires at least a logical I/O system for its use. This routine is often used as a debugging tool, to print out the values of variables while executing a program.

REFERENCES

1. Kernighan, Brian W. and Ritchie, Dennis M. *The C Programming Language*. Englewood Cliffs, NJ: Prentice-Hall, Inc., 1978.

Index

Index